MENTOR'S GUIDE  Cap

Module 2

Theology and Ethics

The Kingdom of God

God's Reign Challenged

God's Reign Inaugurated

God's Reign Invading

God's Reign Consummated

Capstone Module 2: The Kingdom of God Mentor's Guide

ISBN: 978-1-62932-022-9

First edition 2005, Second edition 2011, Third edition 2013, Fourth edition 2015.

The Urban Ministry Institute is a ministry of World Impact, Inc.

Contents

1
2
3
4

About the Instructor

Rev. Dr. Don L. Davis is the Executive Director of The Urban Ministry Institute and a Senior Vice President of World Impact. He attended Wheaton College and Wheaton Graduate School, and graduated summa cum laude in both his B.A. (1988) and M.A. (1989) degrees, in Biblical Studies and Systematic Theology, respectively. He earned his Ph.D. in Religion (Theology and Ethics) from the University of Iowa School of Religion.

As the Institute's Executive Director and World Impact's Senior Vice President, he oversees the training of urban missionaries, church planters, and city pastors, and facilitates training opportunities for urban Christian workers in evangelism, church growth, and pioneer missions. He also leads the Institute's extensive distance learning programs and facilitates leadership development efforts for organizations and denominations like Prison Fellowship, the Evangelical Free Church of America, and the Church of God in Christ.

A recipient of numerous teaching and academic awards, Dr. Davis has served as professor and faculty at a number of fine academic institutions, having lectured and taught courses in religion, theology, philosophy, and biblical studies at schools such as Wheaton College, St. Ambrose University, the Houston Graduate School of Theology, the University of Iowa School of Religion, the Robert E. Webber Institute of Worship Studies. He has authored a number of books, curricula, and study materials to equip urban leaders, including *The Capstone Curriculum*, TUMI's premiere sixteen-module distance education seminary instruction, *Sacred Roots: A Primer on Retrieving the Great Tradition*, which focuses on how urban churches can be renewed through a rediscovery of the historic orthodox faith, and *Black and Human: Rediscovering King as a Resource for Black Theology and Ethics*. Dr. Davis has participated in academic lectureships such as the Staley Lecture series, renewal conferences like the Promise Keepers rallies, and theological consortiums like the University of Virginia Lived Theology Project Series. He received the Distinguished Alumni Fellow Award from the University of Iowa College of Liberal Arts and Sciences in 2009. Dr. Davis is also a member of the Society of Biblical Literature, and the American Academy of Religion.

Introduction to the Module

Greetings in the strong name of Jesus Christ!

Of all the subjects preached and taught by Jesus of Nazareth, none are as significant and controversial as the subject of the Kingdom of God. Both conservative and liberal scholars agree that Jesus' favorite subject, the one he preached and taught upon most often, is the Kingdom of God. It was his salvation message, master plan, and heart theology. Sadly, the modern Church seems to pay little attention to what Jesus considered to be most important in his prophetic and Messianic ministry. Our hope is that your heart will be gripped by the kingdom story - the King and his Kingdom - and see its importance in the life of personal discipleship and ministry.

The first lesson, ***God's Reign Challenged***, focuses upon God as the sovereign majesty. It discusses how the absolute sovereignty and lordship of God was defied, both by the devil and his angels, and the first human pair, Adam and Eve, through their willful disobedience in the garden. This rebellion produced tragic results in the world, in human nature, and the release of the demonic into the world. In spite of our rebellion, however, God intends to restore all heaven and earth back under his reign, and constitute again a universe where his name is glorified, and his justice and peace rule forever.

In our second lesson, ***God's Reign Inaugurated***, we will explore God's intent to eradicate all disobedience and rebellion as a result of the Fall - God becomes a Warrior in this fallen realm. God made a covenant with Abraham as his solemn promise to bring a Seed through whom the *shalom* and justice kingdom reign would be brought back to earth. This covenant promise was renewed with Isaac and Jacob, to the Israelite nation, to the tribe of Judah, and finally to the family of David. Here we trace in bold line the origins of the Messiah, so the reign of God would be brought back into this fallen and sin-cursed world. Jesus of Nazareth is the Kingdom's presence realized, with God's reign demonstrated in his incarnation, death, resurrection, and ascension.

Lessons three and four deal with ***God's Reign Invading*** and ***God's Reign Consummated*** respectively. Now that our Lord Jesus has died, risen, and ascended into heaven, the Kingdom of God is being proclaimed throughout the world by his Church. The Church of Jesus Christ is the locus–the place or context--of God's salvation, of the empowering presence of the Holy Spirit, and of authentic kingdom *shalom*, the place where God's presence and power are freely being displayed. The Kingdom of God will be consummated at the Second Coming of Jesus, where death, disease, and all evil will be put down, all heaven and earth shall be renewed, and God will become All-in-all.

The Story of the Kingdom is the story of Jesus, and God's intent is to bring the world back under his rule in him. Our prayer is that your love and service to him will abound as you study the Word of God on the forever rule of God!

We praise God for his kingdom story, and your interest as a student of his Holy Word!

- Rev. Dr. Don L. Davis

Course Requirements

Required Books and Materials

- Bible and Concordance. (For the purposes of this course, your Bible should be a translation [ex. NIV, NASB, RSV, KJV, NKJV, etc.], and not a paraphrase [ex. The Living Bible, The Message]).
- Each Capstone module has assigned textbooks which are read and discussed throughout the course. We encourage you to read, reflect upon, and respond to these with your professors, mentors, and fellow learners. Because of the fluid availability of the texts (e.g., books going out of print), we maintain our *official* Capstone Required Textbook list on our website. Please visit *www.tumi.org/books* to obtain the current listing of this module's texts.
- Paper and pen for taking notes and completing in-class assignments.

Suggested Readings

- Beasley-Murray, G. R. *Jesus and the Kingdom of God.* Grand Rapids: Eerdmans, 1986.
- Ladd, George Eldon. *Crucial Questions about the Kingdom of God.* Grand Rapids: Eerdmans, 1952.
- ------. *The Presence of the Future.* Grand Rapids: Eerdmans, 1974.
- Snyder, Howard A. *The Community of the King.* Downers Grove: InterVarsity Press, 1977.

Course Requirements

Summary of Grade Categories and Weights

Category	Weight	Points
Attendance & Class Participation	30%	90 pts
Quizzes	10%	30 pts
Memory Verses	15%	45 pts
Exegetical Project	15%	45 pts
Ministry Project	10%	30 pts
Readings and Homework Assignments	10%	30 pts
Final Exam	10%	30 pts
Total:	100%	300 pts

Grade Requirements

Attendance and Class Participation

Attendance at each class session is a course requirement. Absences will affect your grade. If an absence cannot be avoided, please let the Mentor know in advance. If you miss a class it is your responsibility to find out the assignments you missed, and to talk with the Mentor about turning in late work. Much of the learning associated with this course takes place through discussion. Therefore, your active involvement will be sought and expected in every class session.

Quizzes

Every class will begin with a short quiz over the basic ideas from the last lesson. The best way to prepare for the quiz is to review the Student Workbook material and class notes taken during the last lesson.

Memory Verses

The memorized Word is a central priority for your life and ministry as a believer and leader in the Church of Jesus Christ. There are relatively few verses, but they are significant in their content. Each class session you will be expected to recite (orally or in writing) the assigned verses to your Mentor.

Exegetical Project

The Scriptures are God's potent instrument to equip the man or woman of God for every work of ministry he calls them to (2 Tim. 3.16-17). In order to complete the requirements for this course you must select a passage and do an inductive Bible study (i.e., an exegetical study) upon it. The study will have to be five pages in length (double-spaced, typed or neatly hand written) and deal with one of the aspects of the Kingdom of God which are highlighted in this course. Our desire and hope is that you will be deeply convinced of Scripture's ability to change and practically affect your life, and the lives of those to whom you minister. As you go through the course, be open to finding an extended passage (roughly 4-9 verses) on a subject you would like to study more intensely.The details of the project are covered on pages 10-11, and will be discussed in the introductory session of this course.

Ministry Project

Our expectation is that all students will apply their learning practically in their lives and in their ministry responsibilities. The student will be responsible for developing a ministry project that combines principles learned with practical ministry. The details of this project are covered on page 12, and will be discussed in the introductory session of the course.

Class and Homework Assignments

Classwork and homework of various types may be given during class by your Mentor or be written in your Student Workbook. If you have any question about what is required by these or when they are due, please ask your Mentor.

Readings

It is important that the student read the assigned readings from the text and from the Scriptures in order to be prepared for class discussion. Please turn in the "Reading Completion Sheet" from your Student Workbook on a weekly basis. There will be an option to receive extra credit for extended readings.

Take-Home Final Exam

At the end of the course, your Mentor will give you a final exam (closed book) to be completed at home. You will be asked a question that helps you reflect on what you have learned in the course and how it affects the way you think about or practice ministry. Your Mentor will give you due dates and other information when the Final Exam is handed out.

Grading

The following grades will be given in this class at the end of the session, and placed on each student's record:

A - Superior work

B - Excellent work

C - Satisfactory work

D - Passing work

F - Unsatisfactory work

I - Incomplete

Letter grades with appropriate pluses and minuses will be given for each final grade, and grade points for your grade will be factored into your overall grade point average. Unexcused late work or failure to turn in assignments will affect your grade, so please plan ahead, and communicate conflicts with your instructor.

Exegetical Project

Purpose

As a part of your participation in the Capstone *Kingdom of God* module of study, you will be required to do an exegesis (inductive study) on one of the following Scripture passages:

- ❐ Matthew 12.22-30
- ❐ Mark 10.17-27
- ❐ Luke 4.16-21
- ❐ Luke 11.15-23
- ❐ Luke 18.15-17
- ❐ Isaiah 11.1-9

The purpose of this project is to give you an opportunity to do a detailed study of a major passage on the Kingdom of God. The hope is that, as you study the passage, you will be able to show how it illumines or makes plain the significance of the Kingdom for the Church. Hopefully, too, you will be able to relate its meaning directly to your own personal walk of discipleship, your leadership in your church, and your urban ministry.

Outline and Composition

This is a Bible study project, and, in order to do *exegesis*, you must be committed to understand the meaning of the passage in its own setting. Once you know what it meant, you can then draw out principles that apply to all of us, and then relate those principles to life. A simple three step process can guide you in your personal study of the Bible passage:

1. What was *God saying to the people in the text's original situation*?
2. What principle(s) does *the text teach that is true for all people everywhere*, including today?
3. What is *the Holy Spirit asking me to do with this principle here, today*, in my life and ministry?

Once you have answered these questions in your personal study, you are then ready to write out your insights for your *paper assignment*.

Here is a *sample outline* for your paper:

1. List out what you believe is *the main theme or idea* of the text you selected.
2. *Summarize the meaning* of the passage (you may do this in two or three paragraphs, or, if you prefer, by writing a short verse-by verse commentary on the passage).

3. *Outline one to three key principles or insights* this text provides on the Kingdom of God.

4. Tell how one, some, or all of the principles may relate to *one or more* of the following:

   a. Your personal spirituality and walk with Christ

   b. Your life and ministry in your local church

   c. Situations or challenges in your community and general society

As an aid or guide, please feel free to read the course texts and/or commentaries, and integrate insights from them into your work. Make sure that you give credit to whom credit is due if you borrow or build upon someone else's insights. Use in-the-text references, footnotes, or endnotes. Any way you choose to cite your references will be acceptable, as long as you 1) use only one way consistently throughout your paper, and 2) indicate where you are using someone else's ideas, and are giving them credit for it. (For more information, see *Documenting Your Work: A Guide to Help You Give Credit Where Credit Is Due* in the Appendix.)

Make certain that your exegetical project, when turned in meets the following standards:

- It is legibly written or typed.
- It is a study of one of the passages above.
- It is turned in on time (not late).
- It is 5 pages in length.
- It follows the outline given above, clearly laid out for the reader to follow.
- It shows how the passage relates to life and ministry today.

Do not let these instructions intimidate you; this is a Bible study project! All you need to show in this paper is that you *studied* the passage, *summarized* its meaning, *drew out* a few key principles from it, and *related* them to your own life and ministry.

Grading

The exegetical project is worth 45 points, and represents 15% of your overall grade, so make certain that you make your project an excellent and informative study of the Word.

Ministry Project

Purpose

The Word of God is living and active, and penetrates to the very heart of our lives and innermost thoughts (Heb. 4.12). James the Apostle emphasizes the need to be doers of the Word of God, not hearers only, deceiving ourselves. We are exhorted to apply the Word, to obey it. Neglecting this discipline, he suggests, is analogous to a person viewing our natural face in a mirror and then forgetting who we are, and are meant to be. In every case, the doer of the Word of God will be blessed in what he or she does (James 1.22-25).

Our sincere desire is that you will apply your learning practically, correlating your learning with real experiences and needs in your personal life, and in your ministry in and through your church. Therefore, a key part of completing this module will be for you to design a ministry project to help you share some of the insights you have learned from this course with others.

Planning and Summary

There are many ways that you can fulfill this requirement of your study. You may choose to conduct a brief study of your insights with an individual, or a Sunday School class, youth or adult group or Bible study, or even at some ministry opportunity. What you must do is discuss some of the insights you have learned from class with your audience. (Of course, you may choose to share insights from your Exegetical Project in this module with them.)

Feel free to be flexible in your project. Make it creative and open-ended. At the beginning of the course, you should decide on a context in which you will share your insights, and share that with your instructor. Plan ahead and avoid the last minute rush in selecting and carrying out your project.

After you have carried out your plan, write and turn in to your Mentor a one-page summary or evaluation of your time of sharing. A sample outline of your Ministry Project summary is as follows:

1. Your name
2. The place where you shared, and the audience with whom you shared
3. A brief summary of how your time went, how you felt, and how they responded
4. What you learned from the time

Grading

The Ministry Project is worth 30 points and represents 10% of your overall grade, so make certain to share your insights with confidence and make your summary clear.

God's Reign Challenged

page 305 1

Lesson Objectives

Welcome in the strong name of Jesus Christ! After your reading, study, discussion, and application of the materials in this lesson, you will be able to:

page 305 2

- Describe how God as Lord, reigns over all, but that his reign was challenged through satanic rebellion in the heavenlies, and through the voluntary rebellion and disobedience of the first human pair on earth.
- Demonstrate how this challenge resulted in the curse upon creation, leading to death, and the greatest of all human tragedies, called by the Church, "the Fall."
- How this disobedience by Satan and the first human pair has produced tragic and corrupting results in three spheres of personage and existence: *kosmos* (the world), *sarx* (fleshliness of human nature), and *kakos* (ongoing influence and chaos of the evil one).
- Recite from memory a passage relating to the challenge of God's reign.

Devotion

The Reign of the LORD's Anointed

page 305 3

Read Psalm 2.1-12. Does God laugh? In one of the most amazing texts in Holy Scripture, we read here of the nation's desire to oppose the reign of the Lord and his Anointed One. In response to this futile attempt of the nations to break away from God's kingdom rule, the psalmist suggests that the Lord will laugh at their puny, little efforts to resist his rule. As a matter of fact, the Lord affirms that he has set his King upon Zion, his holy mountain, and that his Son will reign unopposed as Lord of all. The Lord's Anointed will possess the nations to the ends of the earth, and shall shatter those resistant nations like jars of clay. The psalmist ends this grand vision with a plea to the kings of the earth to be discerning and take warning. They ought to worship the LORD, as King over all, and do right homage to the Son by kissing his feet, lest his wrath and anger are unleashed as they are consumed in his fierce wrath. Let's agree wholeheartedly with the psalmist in verse 12: "Blessed are all who take refuge in him" (Ps. 2.12).

Nicene Creed and Prayer

page 305 4

After reciting and/or singing the Nicene Creed (located in the Appendix), pray the following prayer:

> *Eternal God, our Father, we thank you that you alone are God, reigning high above the heavens and earth as the Sovereign Lord God. Even though your righteous reign was opposed by angels and humankind, you have restored your reign in your Son, and will soon make all things here on earth as they are in heaven - consistent with your holy and good will. Be glorified through us as we live out your righteous reign in the midst of your people, the Church, as a witness to our communities and our world. In Jesus' name, Amen.*

1

Quiz

No quiz this lesson

Scripture Memorization Review

No Scripture memorization this lesson

Assignments Due

No assignments due this lesson

CONTACT

A World Out of Control

1

page 306 5

Imagine yourself talking with one of your neighbors about the current condition of society and the world. How would you answer your neighbor if they made the following statement: "From everything that I see in society, and from all appearances in the world, I think that God, if he is real, either is not in control, or is unable to deal with the level of evil within it. Everything is falling apart. God cannot possibly be in control - the world is simply too messed up!" Does this statement jive with your thinking? Why or why not? How might you answer someone who made this suggestion about our world today?

Evidence of God's Rule on Earth

While the Bible teaches that God is Almighty, the world appears to be completely unaware of his power and glory. Come up with five reasons why it makes good sense to say that even though the world is reeling from injustice, oppression, and violence, God is still an Almighty God, possessing all power and authority, and in full control of all things.

If God Really Loved Us . . .

3 Imagine yourself called to the home of a dear family whose son was recently killed in a needless gang shootout. As you are there helping to comfort the family, one of the members says before all present, "The fact that this happened shows that God doesn't really love us. If God really loved us, these kinds of things would never have happened. How could a good God allow this kind of stuff to happen to someone so young and so innocent?" What would your answer be to him and the others who heard this comment in the wake of such a tragedy?

1

CONTENT

God's Reign Challenged

Segment 1

Rev. Dr. Don L. Davis

Summary of Segment 1

page 306 6

God as Lord, reigns over all, but his reign was challenged through satanic rebellion in the heavenlies, and through the voluntary rebellion and disobedience of the first human pair on earth. This challenge resulted in the curse upon creation, leading to death, and the greatest of all human tragedies, called by the Church "the Fall."

Our objective for this first segment of *God's Reign Challenged* is to enable you to see that:

- God is the Sovereign majesty of the universe.
- His lordship was defied, both by the devil and his angels, and the first human pair, Adam and Eve, through their willful disobedience in the garden.
- Sin in the world occurs through this defiance of God's majesty and his personal kingdom reign.
- God's intent is to restore all heaven and earth back under his reign, and constitute again a universe where his name alone is glorified, and his justice and peace will rule forever.

Video Segment 1 Outline

I. God Almighty, the Triune God, Whose Name Is YHWH (the Father, Son, and Holy Spirit), Is Lord of All.

page 307 📖 *7*

A. God is self-existent, containing life in and of himself, deriving life from his own person and being.

1. Exod. 3.14
2. John 5.26
3. Acts 17.25

B. The Lord God is Creator and Owner of all things.

page 307 📖 *8*

1. *Ex nihilo*
2. Gen. 1.1
3. Jer. 10.10-13
4. Indeed, the triune God is the Lord; Father, Son, and Holy Spirit, who reigns as King, and created all things for his glory.

C. God's sovereignty is rooted in his person, and demonstrated in all his works.

page 307 📖 *9*

Dr. Lewis Chafer, founder of Dallas Seminary, and Dr. Walvoord, in speaking of God's sovereignty suggest:

> *. . . the attributes of God make clear that God is supreme over all. He yields to no other power, authority or glory, and is not subject to any absolute greater than himself. He represents perfection to an infinite degree in every aspect of his being. He can never be surprised, defeated, or uncertain. However, without sacrificing his authority or jeopardizing the final realization of his perfect will, it has pleased God to give to [humankind] {men} a measure of freedom of choice, and for the exercise of this choice God holds [humankind] {men} responsible.*
>
> Lewis Sperry Chafer and John Walvoord. **Major Bible Themes.** Grand Rapids: Zondervan, 1975. p. 42.

1. Dan. 4.34-35

2. The Lord is God, the infinitely perfect God, who is worthy of our worship and obedience.

3. The reign of God has been challenged.

   a. By the mortal enemy of humankind, the devil

   b. By the first human pair

page 308 📖 10

II. The Devil's (Satan's) Rebellion in the Heavenlies Represents the First and Most Serious Challenge to God's Sovereignty in the Universe.

A. The Old Testament description of Satan as Lucifer, Son of the Morning

1. A created being, cf. Col. 1.16

2. A personal being (note his personality in the temptation of Jesus, cf. Luke 4.1-13)

B. The overarching principle of Satan's rebellion and biblical demonism: resistance to the will of God through pride, self-exaltation, and chaos, Isa. 14.12-17

1. I will ascend into heaven.

2. I will exalt my throne above the stars of God.

3. I will sit on the mount of the congregation on the farthest sides of the north.

4. I will ascend above to the heights of the clouds.

5. I will be like the Most High.

6. The devil's fate: vv. 15-17

7. The supreme motive of satanic activity: "I will be like the Most High."

   a. Genesis 3: enticement to adopt this philosophy

b. Characteristics of rebellion

(1) Self-sufficiency

(2) Independence from God

(3) Self-centeredness

(4) Selfishness

c. Satan's pride is the beginning of rebellion in the universe, and the ultimate cause of all sin and injustice.

C. War in the heavenlies: Satan's sin and the chain of rebellion

1. The fall of a significant number of angels (i.e. demons), Rev. 12

2. The temptation of the first human pair in the garden

III. The Reign of God Was Challenged in the Disobedience of Adam and Eve: the Fall, Gen. 3.

A. The Fall of humankind is unexplainable.

1. They were perfectly and wonderfully made innocent, and therefore able to be deceived.

2. The state of humankind before the Fall

a. They lived for an undetermined amount of time in fellowship with God.

b. They lived under God's blessing and care.

c. They were granted dominion over creation, naming the creatures.

d. They walked in communion with God in a perfect environment free from the effects of sin.

e. Made in innocence, they were made in the image of God, possessing a complete personality, able to make moral decisions and follow God's directions.

B. The Garden scene of Genesis 3

1. Note the devil: how is he described?

2. The serpent's conversation with Eve, the mother of all living, regarding the tree of life

a. The serpent's passion to resist God's rule, Gen. 3.4-5

b. The tragic response of the woman and man, Genesis 3.6-7

3. The essence of the serpent's deception: note the parallel with 1 John 2.16

a. Saw it was good for food - lust of the flesh

b. Pleasant to the eyes - lust of the eyes

c. Power to make wise - the pride of life

d. Note the same parallel in Jesus' temptation, Matt. 4; Mark 1; Luke 4

C. The tragic result of Adam and Eve's sinfulness: subordination, struggle and shame, selfishness, estrangement, and finally, death

1

page 308 🕮 11

Conclusion

» The triune God is supreme Lord, reigning over all.

» His reign was challenged through satanic rebellion in the heavenlies, and through the voluntary rebellion and disobedience of the first human pair on earth.

Segue 1

Student Questions and Response

page 309 🕮 12

Please take as much time as you have available to answer these and other questions that the video brought out. Be clear and concise in your answers, and where possible, support with Scripture!

1. How does the Bible describe the reign and rule of Almighty God in the universe? What is the meaning of the term "sovereignty?"
2. When theologians say that the God of the Bible is "self-existent," what do they mean?
3. Why is it important for us to teach, consistent with the Bible's own claims, that God created the world *ex nihilo*?
4. According to Scripture, how far does the sovereignty and rule of God extend throughout the world, and the universe? Explain your answer.
5. How would you describe the "overarching principle of Satan's rebellion" in the universe?

6. How did the video characterize "the supreme motive of satanic activity?" Do you agree with this statement? Why or why not?

7. Satan's rebellion affected two other spheres of life in the universe. What are they, and what happened as a result?

8. How can we explain the fall of humankind - what reasons can we give for their decision to rebel against the rule and reign of Almighty God?

9. How does Satan's temptation of Eve parallel with how John the Apostle described the evil that is in the world (e.g. 1 John 2.16)?

10. What was the tragic result of Satan's rebellion in the heavenlies, and Adam and Eve's disobedience in the Garden? What term have theologians given for this terrible event?

God's Reign Challenged

Segment 2

Rev. Dr. Don L. Davis

Summary of Segment 2

page 309 13

The disobedience of Satan and the first human pair has produced tragic and corrupting results in three spheres of personage and existence: *kosmos* (i.e. the world), *sarx* (i.e. fleshliness of human nature), and *kakos* (i.e. the ongoing influence and chaos of the Evil One).

Our objective for this second segment of *God's Reign Challenged* is to enable you to see that:

- The disobedience of Satan and the first human pair has produced tragic and corrupting results in three spheres.
- *Kosmos* represents the present world structure and system of rebellion and sin.
- *Sarx* represents the fleshliness and sinfulness of human nature, with its imputed guilt and result of physical and spiritual death.
- *Kakos* represents the release of Satan and the demonic into the sphere of the universe and world, with his subsequent control and manipulation of human life and structures through the power of evil.

Video Segment 2 Outline

I. The Fall's First Result, the Emergence of the *Kosmos*: the Greek Word Meaning "This Present World Structure and System of Rebellion and Sin."

page 310 📖 14

A. The Fall has produced the *kosmos*, the current godless world system that operates according to the principles of rebellion that founded it.

1. It operates under the direct authority of the devil, under his direct control, Matt. 4.8-10.

2. The entire world lies under the sway of the Evil One, 1 John 5.19.

3. The Holy Spirit indwelling believers is greater than the one (Satan) who is in the world, 1 John 4.1-4.

B. Satan, as God's arch enemy, controls this present world system through its greed, lust, and pride.

1. A domain filled with rebellion, temptation, and injustice

2. A system in deep, ongoing conflict with God

3. A structure which God himself will one day judge and destroy

4. God's hatred of the present world system, James 4.4

page 310 📖 15

C. Principalities and powers: structures and hierarchies of resistance and sin

1. The present world system is subject to the participation and interference of various principalities and powers.

2. Spiritual forces of darkness influence and animate the affairs of human beings.

3. Note the opposition to Daniel's prayer by spiritual forces in Daniel 9-10.

D. The underlying spiritual impulse of the *kosmos*: lust, greed, and pride, 1 John 2. 15-17

1. The command to disciples: do not love the world or the things in it.

    a. Note the conflict between God and the world.

    b. Those loving the world do not possess God's love within themselves.

2. The world summarized: all that is in the world (the lust of the flesh, the lust of the eyes, and the pride of life) is not of the Father but of the world's own system.

3. The world system is passing away, as well as its lusts.

4. The first major effect of rebellion in the universe has been the emergence of this world system of lust, pride, and greed.

page 311 16

II. The Fall's Second Result, the *Sarx*: the Twisting and Turning of Human Nature (as Result of Adam's Transgression). Four Aspects of Sin Are Important to Note.

A. Personal sin: all that is done, thought, and said in our lives which is against or fails to correspond to God's character.

1. Rom. 3.23

2. Lack of conformity to God's character and will by deeds we've done or failed to do

3. Sin as the offshoot of the disobedience of the first human pair who rejected God's rule

B. Sin nature: the "flesh," i.e. sinful nature of human beings

1. Rom. 5.19

2. Eph. 2.3

3. Adam's resistance to God's reign provided him with a depraved and degenerate nature.

    a. Adam's children share his guilt and nature.

    b. Adam's disobedience reflected now in our will, conscience, and intellect.

1

c. The Holy Spirit in the disciple: the power to overcome the flesh, Rom. 8.1-4

C. Imputed sin and guilt: guilty as charged in light of Adam's sin. How? (See Romans 5.12-18).

1. Rom. 5.12. Sin enters into the world through one man, and death through sin.

1

2. Rom. 5.15. Many die through the trespass of one, Adam.

3. Rom. 5.17. Due to the trespass of one, Adam, death has reigned over all humankind through his sin.

4. Rom. 5.18. Condemnation is reckoned on all human beings through the trespass of one, Adam.

5. By God's reckoning, the entire world, both Jew and Gentile, are said to be under sin, e.g. Rom. 3.9 and Gal. 3.22.

D. Death, the fourth and final aspect of sin's effect

1. Rom. 6.23

2. Physical death AND spiritual death

a. No union with God

b. Severed and separated from the source of life

3. The need for redemption: the shed blood of Jesus Christ, John 14.6

page 311 📖 17

III. The Fall's Third and Most Devastating Result, *Kakos*: the Release of the Devil and His Demons in the Midst of the World

A. Introductory truths about the Evil One

1. The devil's personal strength cannot be estimated.

a. He possesses the power of death, Heb. 2.14.

b. He possesses the power of sickness, as illustrated in Job's case, Job 2.7.

c. His ability to withstand God's people, such as sift Peter as wheat, Luke 22.31

2. The devil is aided by demons who do his will and serve him.

a. He is neither omnipresent, omnipotent, nor omniscient.

b. Through his emissaries he can touch every part of the world.

B. *Kakos* is "blasphemer against God": Satan works as a perpetrator of idolatry and profanity.

1. Sick passion to make himself like the Most High

2. Isa. 14.12-14

3. Satanic longings: the desire for glory and honor only appropriate to God

4. The devil's work is essentially blasphemy.

   a. Seeks God's glory for himself

   b. Seeks the honor due to God alone

5. How does this passion for supremacy over God work?

C. *Kakos* is "deceiver of the world": Satan works as a deceiving spirit among the nations.

1. Paul's words in 2 Corinthians 4.3-4

2. Jesus' words in John 8.44

3. The effect of the devil's ability to lie

1

a. The devil is the father (source) of all lies.

b. Deception is the core of satanic activity.

c. All false religion and philosophy originate in demonic and satanic activity.

D. *Kakos* is "accuser of the brethren": the work of Satan as the enemy of the people of God.

1

1. He seeks to influence Christians directly, but can be effectively resisted.

a. By the blood of the Lamb, Rev. 12.9-11

b. By the armor of God, Eph. 6.10-18

c. By faith in the Word of God (i.e. the shield of faith), Eph. 6.16-17

2. Contrasting the devil's power and influence over the lost and the saved

a. Oppression and discouragement of the saved

b. Never the indwelling and overcoming of the saved, 1 John 4.4

3. The devil's work of accusation, Rev. 12.9-11

4. The antidote to the devil's accusation: Jesus is our advocate, 1 John 2.1-2.

Conclusion

» God Almighty is Lord and reigns over all.

» God's reign was challenged through satanic rebellion in the heavenlies, and through the voluntary rebellion and disobedience of the first human pair on earth.

» This challenge has produced tragic and corrupting results in three spheres: *kosmos* (i.e. the world), *sarx* (i.e. fleshliness of human nature), and *kakos* (i.e. the ongoing influence and chaos of the Evil One).

1

Segue 2

Student Questions and Response

page 312 📖 18

Please take as much time as you have available to answer these and other questions that the video brought out. Be clear and concise in your answers, and where possible, support with Scripture!

1. The Fall's first result was the production of the *kosmos*. To what does this Greek term refer?
2. Under whose direct authority and control does the *kosmos* operate? What is the relationship of the Holy Spirit (who indwells believers) to the *kosmos*?
3. According to John the Apostle, through what three elements does the current godless world system operate and function? Explain.
4. What is the relationship that one who loves the *kosmos* has with the Father of our Lord Jesus Christ? Why?
5. *Sarx* represents the Fall's second result. To what does this term refer?
6. What are the four aspects of sin associated with *sarx* that now are produced on all people everywhere because of the Fall?
7. According to the video, what is the Fall's "most devastating result?" What does the *kakos* possess over humankind in terms of death, sickness, and interference with God's people?

8. What are the three senses in which *kakos*, according to the Bible, challenges God's reign? How do these understandings of *kakos* help us better comprehend the problems of the city and spiritual warfare today?

Summary of Key Concepts

This lesson highlights certain key truths regarding the reign of God, and its challenge in Satan's rebellion and the disobedience of Adam and Eve.

page 312 19

- The triune God, *YHWH* (Father, Son, and Holy Spirit), is the Sovereign Majesty of the universe, self-existent, who created the world *ex nihilo* for his glory.
- As Creator and Owner of all things, God's sovereignty is rooted in his person, and demonstrated in all his works in creation and his actions in history.
- God's reign and right to rule was challenged, initially and most significantly by the devil in his rebellion in heavenlies.
- The overarching principle of satanic rebellion is pride; his twisted desire to receive the honor and glory that is due to God alone.
- Satan's rebellion resulted in the fall of many angels who followed his path, as well as the temptation, disobedience, and voluntary rebellion of Adam and Eve in the Garden of Eden. This rebellion in heaven and earth is referred to as "the Fall."
- The Fall's first result was the production of the *kosmos*, the current godless world system which operates on the power of greed, lust, and pride.
- The Fall's second result was the emergence of the *sarx*, the twisting and turning of human nature, resulting in acts of personal sin, the introduction of a sin nature in human beings (i.e. the "flesh"), imputed sin and guilt through Adam's trespass, and physical and spiritual death.
- The Fall's third and most devastating result was the release of the *kakos*, the devil who now operates in the world as blasphemer against God, deceiver of the world, and accuser of the brethren. Through Jesus Christ, we can overcome him by the Holy Spirit through the Blood and the word of our testimony, (cf. 1 John 4.4; Rev. 12.9-11).

1

Student Application and Implications

page 312 20

Now is the time for you to address your own questions in discussion with your colleagues in class. In thinking about this material and the concepts you just reviewed, what particular questions come to mind about it? Maybe the following might spur your own specific and critical questions.

* How should you come to understand the meaning of God's sovereignty in a world so unjust and ungodly?
* Is it fair to you that the Bible teaches that our current condition is the direct result of satanic and human rebellion committed centuries ago?
* What doesn't make sense yet to you concerning the results of the Fall? Are there any gaps in your understanding of *kosmos*, *sarx*, and *kakos*?
* Do you struggle at all with the concept of God's rule being challenged in the first place? In other words, if God was almighty, why did he allow anyone, even Satan, to challenge his reign?
* Can God hold others responsible, since it appears that their sin and disobedience is the result of what Satan and Adam did, not what they did? How does this work itself out?
* To what degree do we who believe now differ from others who do not know Christ? Are we still subject to the devil's control, to sin's power, and to the world's temptations? What tools, promises, blessings, and provisions has God given us to live under his reign today?

CASE STUDIES

Gangs in the Inner City

1

page 313 21

Today, tens of thousands of young people participate in gangs which wreak havoc on hundreds of inner city neighborhoods around the country. Many innocent men, women, boys, and girls live in fear of their lives because of the activity and efforts of these gangs, most of whom identify themselves with violence, cruelty, and crime. Yet, for many of those who participate in them, these groups are the only family that they have ever known. Much love, respect, and commitment flow between its members and their families, even though they experience together much pain. In looking at the gang situation in the inner city, how does the theology you studied this week make sense of it. Even further, are there ways that this gang reality is not explained by the themes covered in "God's Reign Challenged." What insights help us to understand this city reality better?

Mass Murder of Jews in WWII

2 During the Second World War, over six million Jews were killed during the conflict of the war in Europe. Hundreds of thousands of innocent children and babies were slaughtered due to Hitler's insane campaign to rid the world of all Jewish people–old men, women, boys, girls, teens, middle aged folk–anyone of Jewish heritage. How can we say that God is in control when so many millions of innocent people have been needlessly tortured and murdered, as in this terrible example of the Jews?

Resistance to Daniel's Prayer in Daniel 9-10

3 In the book of Daniel, we see this godly saint praying to God on behalf of the children of Israel. As you recall, the people of Israel were in captivity due to the injustice and idolatry they practiced before, and, as a result of God's discipline, he allowed his people to be sent into captivity. In deep intercessory prayer (see Daniel 10), Daniel seeks God after three weeks of mourning. He is visited by an angel who tells him that he ought not to fear, because from the first day that he had set his heart on understanding this and on humbling himself before God his words were heard, and that he, the angel, had come because of Daniel's prayers. However, "the prince of the kingdom of Persia withstood me 21 days, but Michael, one of the chief princes, came to help me, for I was left there with the kings of Persia" (see Daniel 10.12-14). Most believe this is a citation about the kind of spiritual warfare that is taking place all around us, invisible yet potent and real. What is your opinion of this important but controversial case study? How does such a text help or hinder our understanding of God's reign being challenged today?

1

Restatement of the Lesson's Thesis

God as Lord, reigns over all, but his reign was challenged through satanic rebellion in the heavenlies, and through the voluntary rebellion and disobedience of the first human pair on earth. This challenge, known theologically as "the Fall," has resulted in the curse upon creation, leading to corruption and death. It has produced tragic results in three distinct spheres: *kosmos* (the production of a godless world system), *sarx* (the imputed and imparted sin upon human nature), and *kakos* (ongoing influence and chaos of the Evil One).

Resources and Bibliographies

page 313 📖 22

If you are interested in pursuing some of the ideas of *God's Reign Challenged*, you might want to give these books a try:

Chapters 1-4 in Beasley-Murray, G. R. *Jesus and the Kingdom of God*. Grand Rapids: Eerdmans, 1986.

"The Ultimate Goal in the Universe" in Billheimer, Paul. *Destined for the Throne*. Minneapolis: Bethany House, 1975.

Chapter 2 in Ladd, George Eldon. *The Presence of the Future*. Grand Rapids: Eerdmans, 1974.

1

Ministry Connections

Now is the time to try to nail down this high theology to a real practical ministry connection, one which you will think about and pray for throughout this next week. What in particular is the Holy Spirit suggesting to you in regards to the reign of God, and its challenge today? What situations come to mind when you think about how the truth of God's reign is being challenged, and your own life and ministry today? Give yourself time to meditate in the presence of the Lord on these matters, and he will reveal to you what it is, and what you ought to do as a result of what he reveals.

Counseling and Prayer

page 313 📖 23

Make a commitment to pray and ask God to provide insight and wisdom into how his reign has been contested in the place where you live and minister. Pray that God the Holy Spirit will provide power to you to give clear testimony where you live and work as to Christ's kingdom reign, and the offer for new life in Christ as Lord. Pray that God will give you opportunities to communicate clearly and effectively to those whom you are called to minister the truth regarding God's reign, its challenge, and the effects of that challenge on their lives.

Scripture Memory

Isaiah 14.12-17

Reading Assignment

To prepare for class, please visit *www.tumi.org/books* to find next week's reading assignment, or ask your mentor.

Other Assignments

page 314 24

You will be quizzed on the content (the video content) of this lesson next week. Make sure that you spend time covering your notes, especially focusing on the main ideas of the lesson. Read the assigned reading, and summarize each reading with no more than a paragraph or two for each. In this summary please give your best understanding of what you think was the main point in each of the readings. Do not be overly concerned about giving detail; simply write out what you consider to be the main point discussed in that section of the book. Please bring these summaries to class next week (Please see the "Reading Completion Sheet" at the end of this lesson.)

Looking Forward to the Next Lesson

page 314 25

Our next study will discover how God inaugurated his kingdom reign through the covenant with Abraham and his dealings with his people in the Old Testament. Even though we disobeyed God in rejecting his reign, he did not leave us but has committed himself to reestablish his reign in us through the promise of his Son, whom we know to be Jesus of Nazareth, the Son of God.

1

Name ______________________________

Date ______________________________

For each assigned reading, write a brief summary (one or two paragraphs) of the author's main point. (For additional readings, use the back of this sheet.)

Reading 1

Title and Author: ____ Pages __________

Reading 2

Title and Author: ____ Pages __________

LESSON 2

God's Reign Inaugurated

page 315 📖 1

Lesson Objectives

Welcome in the strong name of Jesus Christ! After your reading, study, discussion, and application of the materials in this lesson, you will be able to:

- Show from Scripture that since the Fall, the reign of God has been inaugurated in this present world.
- Describe how God is bringing his reign concretely into the world in an intentional way, firstly, in his own predisposition as a Warrior over his enemies.
- Show how through the covenant promise of deliverance given to Abraham God worked out his Kingdom's inauguration, and through the history of God's dealings and workings with Israel, his covenant people.
- Articulate how Jesus of Nazareth in the world represents the Kingdom's presence realized in his incarnation, death, resurrection, and ascension.
- Recite from memory a passage relating to the inauguration of God's reign.

2

Devotion

Have You Heard the Announcement?

page 315 📖 2

Read Mark 1.14-15. We all like to hear things announced. We like to hear good news, especially when it involves getting a gift, receiving a blessing, obtaining something you have longed for. When Jesus spoke these words in Mark, he had just recently started to proclaim the Good News. Having been baptized by John the Baptist and endured the temptation of the devil in the wilderness, Jesus comes to Galilee. Mark gives us a time frame to gauge the date by: it is the time after John was put in prison. So, it was early in the ministry of Jesus, late in the announcement that John the Baptist had made regarding Jesus as the coming Anointed One. Jesus, at this critical moment in salvation history comes announcing, literally inaugurating (commencing), his kingdom preaching and ministry. Jesus recognized the importance of that time, suggesting that "the time is fulfilled," that is, that time spoken of by the prophets that God's reign had arrived. Without fanfare, without trumpets, fireworks, or great gatherings and official dignitaries, the Messiah announces that the Kingdom has come, i.e. that it was "at hand." God's rule, which had been promised and longed for, had now arrived with the coming of Jesus of Nazareth into the world. As spectacular and great as this announcement, very few heard it for what it was–the inauguration of the reign of God, the end of the devil's rebellion, the end of the curse, and the promise of new life in God's Kingdom. Only a handful got the message that day. What about today? Do you hear the Son of God proclaim in our time today that "the Kingdom of God is at hand?" His advice is as life-giving and wonderful today as it was that most ordinary-looking day back in Galilee; if we hear him speak now, today, we can return to God, turn from sin, and embrace the truth of the Good News in Christ. We can come under God's reign only if we respond to the announcement, to the voice of the Savior today.

Nicene Creed and Prayer

After reciting and/or singing the Nicene Creed (located in the Appendix), pray the following prayer:

> *Almighty God, through the death of Thy Son Thou hast destroyed sin and death, and by his resurrection hast brought innocence and eternal life, in order that we, being redeemed from the power of the devil, may abide in Thy Kingdom. Grant that we may believe this with a whole heart and, steadfast in faith, praise and thank Thee; through Thy Son Jesus Christ our Lord, Amen.*
>
> ~ Martin Luther in Andrew Kosten. **Devotions and Prayers of Martin Luther.** Grand Rapids: Baker Book House, 1965. p. 49.

2

Quiz

Put away your notes, gather up your thoughts and reflections, and take the quiz for Lesson 1, *God's Reign Challenged.*

Scripture Memorization Review

Review with a partner, write out and/or recite the text for last class session's assigned memory verses: Isaiah 14.12-17.

Assignments Due

Turn in your summary of the reading assignment for last week, that is, your brief response and explanation of the main points that the authors were seeking to make in the assigned reading (Reading Completion Sheet).

How Would You Answer the Following Question?

page 316 3

"God began to inaugurate (i.e. start out, commence) his kingdom reign in my life when . . . ." Can you pinpoint the time that God began his kingdom work in your life? Did he begin it the day you repented and believed? The day that you became a member of your local church fellowship? On the day when you were physically born, or before that? If you had to suggest a date when God's kingdom work began in your life, what would you say?

True or False?

"It is best to suggest that the Kingdom of God has never had any beginning or inauguration, since God has always been God, and as God, he has always been in charge." What is right about this statement? Is there anything here that could be misleading? Does the reign of God in a person's, a family's, or a nation's life have a beginning, or has God always been Lord of our lives, whether we acknowledge it or not?

2

Free Will

Throughout the history of philosophy and theology, godly, sincere people have debated over the question of free will, that is, do we actually have any such thing as free will? Think about it for a moment. If you were asked, "Are we free?", what would you say? What are we as human beings, free to do? Are we slaves to sin, to God, or do we have a choice in everything that we consider, do, and encounter? If we do not have free will, how can God hold us accountable for what we say and do?

CONTENT

God's Reign Inaugurated

Segment 1

Rev. Dr. Don L. Davis

Summary of Segment 1

page 316 📖 4

Since the Fall, the reign of God has been inaugurated in this present world, first, as God's own predisposition as a Warrior over his enemies, through the covenant promise of deliverance given to Abraham, and through the history of God's dealings and workings with Israel, his covenant people.

Our objective for this first segment of *God's Reign Inaugurated* is to enable you to see that:

- From the beginning, God has intended to eradicate all disobedience and rebellion as a result of the Fall.
- God acts in the world as Warrior against those who oppose his Kingdom in this present fallen realm.
- Through his covenant with Abraham, God has given his solemn promise to bring a Seed through whom the shalom and justice kingdom reign would be brought back to earth.
- Through the people of Israel, i.e. those covenant descendants of Abraham, Isaac, and Jacob, God has worked to bring forth the Messiah, and through this One to inaugurate the reign of God into this fallen and sin-cursed world.

2

Video Segment 1 Outline

page 317 📖 5

I. The Reign of God Has Been Inaugurated Because God Almighty Has Become a Warrior for Peace and Justice in this Present Fallen Realm.

A. *Proto-evangelium*: enmity between the serpent and the Seed

1. The Bible's two unequal parts:

   a. From Genesis 1.1 through Genesis 3.15

   b. From Genesis 3.16 to the end of the book, Revelation 22.21

2. In God's condemnation and judgment of the serpent in Genesis 3.15, the Lord gives the basic structure of spiritual power in the universe, the Kingdom's drama in miniature.

3. Identity of the characters of God's kingdom drama

   a. Permanent, unyielding conflict between the serpent and the woman

   b. Seed of the woman - the Messiah to come

   c. Seed of the serpent - offspring of the serpent

   d. The serpent's head would be crushed, and the Seed's heel would be bruised.

B. Tremper Longman and Daniel Reid: the picture of God as Divine Warrior begins in Genesis and sustains to Revelation.

C. God as Divine Warrior in the *proto-evangelium*: Genesis 3.15 as God's announcement of his predisposition in the world

1. He is opposed to the serpent.

2. He will work to produce the Seed.

3. In the end, the Seed will crush the serpent entirely.

D. God as Divine Warrior in Scripture

2

1. Before the great victory at the Red Sea, Moses spoke of God's fighting for Israel, Exod. 14.13-14.

2. Moses' song after the Exodus and destruction of Pharaoh's armies, Exod. 15.1-3

3. On the Ark's movement, Moses asks the Lord to rise up as a Mighty Warrior, Num. 10.35-36.

4. David before Goliath, 1 Sam. 17.45-47

E. Five stages of God as Divine Warrior (Longman and Reid)

1. **Phase I** - God as Divine Warrior fighting Israel's flesh and blood enemies

2. **Phase II** - God as Divine Warrior fighting Israel itself

3. **Phase III** - God as Divine Warrior as Israel's prophets see into the future and tell of the coming of Jehovah's Servant, the One through whom God would restore all things under his reign and dominion

4. **Phase IV** - God as Divine Warrior in Jesus of Nazareth as the Conquering Lord

5. **Phase V** - God as Divine Warrior is anticipated by the Church who represents the Risen Lord as his agent of the Kingdom, and Jesus returns to earth and restores all things for his glory

2

page 318 📖 6

II. The Reign of God Has Been Inaugurated through God's Abrahamic Covenant and God's Promise.

A. God made a covenant with Abraham, from whose lineage God would manifest the Seed who would crush the serpent, Gen. 12.1-3.

1. God, the Divine Warrior, covenants with Abram to make him a great nation.

a. He would be blessed.

b. His name would be great.

c. Those blessing Abram would be blessed.

d. Those cursing Abram would be cursed.

e. All of the families of the earth would bless themselves in his person.

2. Jesus of Nazareth is the Seed of Abraham.

a. Gal. 3.13-14

b. The promise of Abraham renewed, Gen. 15.5

B. The covenant promise of Abraham is renewed in the patriarchs: Isaac and Jacob.

1. Promise of the righteous Seed to restore the reign of God

2. Renewed in Abraham's sons, Isaac and Jacob, as heirs of the Promise

C. The Promise identified and specified: the tribe of Judah

1. Jacob's prophetic attestation of the coming Warrior with Judah's tribe, Gen. 49.8-10

2. The Scepter will not depart out of Judah until the Kingdom is made real for all humankind.

page 318 📖 7

III. God's Reign Has Been Inaugurated through His People Israel, Whom God Chose as the Head of the Nations out of Whom Messiah Would Come.

A. Israel is chosen to be a kingdom of royal priests to display God's glory.

1. Exod. 19.3-6

2. Israel is chosen to be a vessel through whom God would make himself known to the nations.

B. Of the families of Judah in Israel, God extends the covenant promise to King David which becomes the family through which God's Messianic Seed would come, 2 Sam. 7.12-16.

1. Now we can trace the history.

   a. The *proto-evangelium*, Gen. 3.15

   b. The covenant of Abraham, Gen. 12.3

   c. The identification of Judah as the tribe from which Messiah would eventually come, Gen. 49.8-10

   d. The covenant with David's clan, 2 Sam. 7.12-17

2. Confirmation to David as the family through which Messiah himself would come

C. The Lord became Divine Warrior fighting against his people as enemy (in exile and captivity), still with the richness of the prophet's vision of Messiah.

1. Israel's disobedience: the breaking of his covenant through idolatry, immorality, and rebellion

2. The Lord's judgment on his own covenant people: sending them into captivity and exile, actually fighting against his own people

a. The Northern Kingdom of Israel was exiled to Assyria in 722 B.C.

2

b. The Southern Kingdom was exiled to Babylon in 586 B.C.

D. The Lord as Warrior, Lam. 2.3-5

1. He has withdrawn from them his right hand.

2. He has burned like a flaming fire in Jacob.

3. "The Lord has become like an enemy; he has swallowed up Israel."

E. The promise of restoration (the prophetic books of Scripture)

1. God is aware of his judgment upon his people.

2. He will restore his people from captivity, and fulfill his covenant with Abraham.

Conclusion

» From the beginning, God has intended to eradicate all disobedience and rebellion as a result of the Fall.

» God has made a covenant with Abraham as his solemn promise to bring a Seed through whom the shalom and justice kingdom reign would be brought back to earth.

» Israel is God's covenant people through whom the Messiah would finally come (through Abraham, the Patriarchs, Judah, and David).

2

Segue 1

Student Questions and Response

page 319 📖 *8*

Please take as much time as you have available to answer these and other questions that the video brought out. Be clear and concise in your answers, and where possible, support with Scripture!

1. How does the Bible describe God's desire in freeing humankind from the slavery and the selfishness of the "serpent?" When did God determine to eradicate all signs of the curse and Fall?

2. What is the *proto-evangelium*, and why is it important for our understanding of the Kingdom of God?

3. Why is it significant that God makes the promise regarding the Seed and the serpent immediately after the Fall? What does it suggest about God's intent to overcome the effects of the Fall?

4. How are the themes of God as Divine Warrior and the *proto-evangelium* related? What are some of the ways that God revealed himself in the Old Testament as Divine Warrior?

5. According to Longman and Reid, what are the five phases of God as Divine Warrior mentioned in Scripture? How does God's role as Divine Warrior work itself out in the exile and captivity of Israel and Judah?

6. What are the specific promises included in God's covenant with Abraham? How is the Abrahamic covenant related to God's promise in the *proto-evangelium*?

7. Through what tribe in Israel does God renew the covenant of Abraham? Of that tribe, what is the family through whom we later learn the Messiah will come?

8. What was God's original purpose for his people Israel, according to Exodus 19? How did Israel do in being a light to the nations on behalf of Almighty God?

9. What is the relationship of Jesus of Nazareth to the seed of Abraham? What is the relationship of Jesus of Nazareth to the seed of the woman mentioned in the *proto-evangelium*?

2

God's Reign Inaugurated

Segment 2

Rev. Dr. Don L. Davis

Summary of Segment 2

page 319 9

God has been working since the beginning to eradicate all disobedience and rebellion as a result of the Fall, through the unfolding of his covenant promise to Abraham to bring a Seed. This promise can be traced through God's covenant people, through Judah, David. In spite of God's people's moral failure and idolatry, through them emerged the Anointed One, Jesus of Nazareth, who represents the Kingdom's presence realized. With final power and authority, God's reign has been demonstrated in Jesus' incarnation, death, resurrection, and ascension.

Our objective for this second segment of *God's Reign Inaugurated* is to enable you to see that:

- In the person and works of Jesus of Nazareth, God's kingdom Reign has been gloriously inaugurated (in a final sense), and realized in the world.
- Jesus gave witness and life to God's reign as the *Christus Victum* in his suffering, death, and burial.
- Jesus provided indisputable proof of the Kingdom's inauguration and realization as *Christus Victor* in his glorious resurrection and ascension.

Video Segment 2 Outline

page 320 📖 10

I. The Kingdom Reign of God Has Been Inaugurated and Realized (in a Final Sense) in the Person and Works of Jesus Christ.

"The distinctiveness of the Kingdom of God, in the person and work of Jesus of Nazareth, is that the reign of God has come and is now present, in some degree on earth."

A. Jesus of Nazareth declared himself to be the fulfillment of Messianic promise.

1. Luke 4.18-19

2. Fulfillment of the Year of Jubilee prophecy of Isaiah 61

B. Jesus of Nazareth is the Word made flesh: Jesus is himself the Incarnation of the Kingdom.

1. John 1.14-18

2. Jesus' coming into the world represents the fulfillment of the promise of Abraham, the beginning of the end of Satan's rule and authority, and the inauguration of the age to come in this present age.

C. Signs of the Kingdom's presence realized in Jesus' coming

1. Luke 17.20-21

2. Luke 10.16-20

3. Luke 11.17-20

D. In Jesus' entrance of the world we experience the "presence of the future," G.E. Ladd, "the already/not yet" Kingdom.

page 321 11

1. In Jesus the Kingdom has already come, Luke 17.20.

   a. Kingdom power and beauty displayed

   b. The reign of God is inaugurated.

   c. The rebellious prince, Satan, the great deceiver and blasphemer was wounded, crippled, bound, through Jesus' death and resurrection.

2. The final consummation of the Kingdom is not yet.

   a. The final destruction of the devil comes later, Rev. 20.

   b. The Church engages in warfare with the enemy in this present time, Eph. 6.10-18.

   c. The Second Coming or *parousia* (Greek for "Second Arrival")

      (1) Satan will be destroyed, his rule finally put down.

      (2) The full manifestation of God's kingly power will be revealed in the glorification of the saints, and in a restored heaven and earth.

E. Display of the Kingdom as "already" (inaugurated and realized)

1. His *mission*, 1 John 3.8

2. His *birth* represents the invasion of God's reign into Satan's dominion, Luke 1.31-33.

3. His *message* was that the Kingdom of God was at hand, Mark 1.14-15.

4. His *teaching* represents the ethics of the Kingdom, Matt. 22.37-38.

5. His *miracles* reveal for all to see his kingly authority and power, Mark 2.8-12.

6. His *exorcisms* represent the "binding of the strong man," Luke 11.14-20.

7. His *life and deeds* reveal the glory of the Kingdom, John 1.14-18.

8. His *death* represents the defeat of Satan, and the penalty of sin, Col. 2.15.

II. Second, God's Reign Is Inaugurated and Realized through Jesus as *Christus Victum*, the Warrior Whose Death Defeats the Powers of Evil, and Pays the Penalty of Sin.

A. Jesus Christ as Paschal Lamb of the Covenant

1. As the spotless lamb was the sign of God's covenant mercy, so Jesus now has become the Paschal Lamb of the new covenant, 1 Cor. 5.7-8.

2. In Jesus of Nazareth, the Passover of God, the fulfillment of God's penalty on sin and forgiveness to his people is done.

B. As Ultimate Sacrifice and Great High Priest: the body and blood of Jesus

1. Jesus is the completion of the Levitical priesthood and sacrificial system of the old covenant.

2. Furthermore, Jesus stands as our one and final High Priest who sacrifices his own blood in the Tabernacle in the heavens before the Father.

3. Heb. 9.11-12.

C. Twice strong: Jesus' suffering and death (penalty for sin, power over evil)

1. Jesus as God's Divine Warrior, through his suffering and death, defeats Satan, the curse, hell, and our punishment by bearing it in his own body.

2. Jesus bears further on the cross the penalty of our sin, and the power of evil to plague and destroy our lives.

3. The destruction of death and the message of freedom, Heb. 2.14-15

4. Jesus as Warrior of God in the cross

III. Finally, the Kingdom Is Inaugurated in Jesus as the *Christus Victor*, the One Who Overcomes through His Resurrection and Ascension.

A. The cardinal revelation of Christianity, according to the Apostle Paul, is the teaching of the resurrection of Christ. If Christ has not been raised, says Paul:

1. The preaching of the Apostles was worthless.

2. Our faith in their testimony is in vain.

3. The Apostles are charlatans, liars, since they are found to have misrepresented God.

4. Our faith is futile.

5. We are still in our sins.

6. Those Christians who have fallen asleep have completely perished, having hope only in this life.

7. Finally, we are the most pitiful people on the planet.

8. But thank God! 1 Cor. 15.20.

B. The resurrection of Jesus is the sign of God's propitiation, the proof of our justification, and the sign of Jesus' exaltation.

C. The certainty of the resurrection: testimony and appearances

1. Jesus predicted his death and resurrection, Matt. 16.21.

2. Appearances

a. Mary Magdalene, John 20.11-17

2

b. The women at the tomb, Matt. 28.9-10

c. Peter, Luke 24.34

d. The disciples on the road to Emmaus, Mark 16.12-13

e. The ten with Thomas absent, John 20.19-24

f. The eleven disciples a week after the resurrection, John 20.26-29

g. Seven disciples by the Sea of Galilee, John 21.1-23

h. The five hundred, 1 Cor. 15.6

i. James, the Lord's brother, 1 Cor. 15.7

j. The eleven disciples on the mountain of Galilee, Matt. 28.16-20

k. The disciples at his ascension, Luke 24.44-53

l. Stephen prior to his martyrdom, Acts 7.55-56

m. Paul on the road to Damascus, Acts 9.3-6

n. Paul in Arabia, Acts 20.24

o. Paul in the temple, Acts 22.17-21

p. Paul in prison at Caesarea, Acts 23.11

q. The Apostle John at the Apocalyptic vision of Revelation, Rev. 1.12-20

D. What his resurrection signifies

1. His resurrection is a sign of his divine Sonship, Rom. 1.4.

2. His resurrection is a fulfillment of the Davidic covenant as Peter suggests in his sermon at Pentecost, Acts 2.25-31.

3. His resurrection also reveals that Christ is now the source of new life for all who believe in him, 1 John 5.11-12.

4. His resurrection is to a place of headship and exaltation as Head of the Church, Eph. 1.20-23.

5. His resurrection proves that our justification before God has been accomplished through him alone, Rom. 4.25.

6. And Jesus, as Lord of life, was resurrected as the first fruits of the great company of believers who will share in his resurrection glory, 1 Cor. 15.20-23.

E. The ascension is a visible sign of Jesus' authority and headship, his exaltation as God's triumphant Warrior, and Commander of the armies of God.

In conjunction with the inauguration of the Kingdom of God through Jesus of Nazareth, Jesus has ascended into heaven. Why?

1. As a visible sign of his authority and headship, worshiped above by God's holy angels, Heb. 1.3-4

2. As Head of the armies of God and Lord of the harvest, Matt. 28.18-20

3. As Head of the Church, Eph. 1.20-23

4. As a sign of his absolute preeminence and lordship over all, Phil. 2.9-11

page 322 📖 12

Conclusion

» Jesus of Nazareth is supreme, the Anointed One of God through whom the promises of Abraham have been fulfilled.

» In him, the Lord of all, the Kingdom's presence realized, demonstrated in his incarnation, death, resurrection, and ascension.

Segue 2

Student Questions and Response

page 323 📖 13

The following questions were designed to help you review the material in the second video segment related to Jesus' inauguration and realization of the Kingdom of God. Answer the questions, concentrating on the "big ideas" and principles associated with the inauguration idea, as well as Jesus' role in bringing the Kingdom into reality. Be clear and concise in your answers, and where possible, support with Scripture!

1. In what ways can it be claimed that Jesus of Nazareth declared himself to be the fulfillment of the Old Testament witness to the Messiah?
2. What are some of the signs in Jesus' life that testify that in him the Kingdom has been inaugurated and realized to some degree?
3. Explain the relationship embodied in the phrase, "the already/not yet" Kingdom. In what ways can the Kingdom be said to be already present? In what ways can we also know that the Kingdom is still yet future?
4. What is the meaning of the word *parousia*, and how does it relate to the whole idea of the Kingdom yet to come?
5. How does Jesus compare with the Passover Lamb of the Old Testament celebration? In what ways could Jesus be said to be the Paschal Lamb of the new covenant?
6. In what two ways does the death of Christ reveal the power of the Kingdom of God present today?
7. According to Paul, why is the resurrection the cardinal teaching of Christianity? How do we know that the resurrection of Jesus is a certainty–what evidence is there for it?
8. What are some of the things that the resurrection signifies about the Kingdom?

2

9. As a sign of Jesus' authority and Headship, how does the ascension contribute to our understanding that in Jesus, the Kingdom has been inaugurated?

CONNECTION

Summary of Key Concepts

This lesson focuses upon the critical ways that the Old and New Testaments give witness that the Kingdom of God has been inaugurated, through God's covenant promise to Abraham and the Patriarchs, through the tribe of Judah and family of David, and finally in the person of Jesus Christ, who as *Christus Victum* (i.e. through his death on the cross) and *Christus Victor* (i.e. through his resurrection and ascension) has ushered in this present age the Kingdom of God.

- God from the beginning committed himself to overturn the affects of the Fall by becoming a Warrior against his enemies, opposing the serpent while providing grace for the Seed of the woman who would come and conquer his enemies.
- The *proto-evangelium* (cf. Gen. 3.15) represents the first and most decisive declaration of the triune God's commitment to defeat his enemy, the serpent, through the Seed of the woman, whom we now know to be Jesus of Nazareth, the Lord of all.
- God as Divine Warrior made a covenant with Abraham to bless all the families of the earth through his Seed, which we know to be Jesus of Nazareth.
- God renewed his covenant promise from Abraham, to Isaac and Jacob, to the people of Israel, to the tribe of Judah, to the family of David, and finally through Jesus Christ, who has realized the Kingdom in a final sense through his person and work.
- In Jesus of Nazareth, the covenant promises of Abraham and the prophetic promises of the Old Testament witness to Messiah have been fulfilled. Jesus is the fulfillment of the Messianic promise.
- In Jesus's life and ministry, the authority and power of God's reign has been inaugurated and manifested. Although much of the Kingdom's fulfillment is future, the Kingdom already has been demonstrated in the incarnation of Jesus on earth.

- Jesus' death broke the power of the devil and his minions, as well as paid the penalty for our sins. As ultimate sacrifice and Great High Priest, Jesus has paid it all for humankind, as the *Christus Victum*.

- Jesus' resurrection occurred: a sign of his divine Sonship, a fulfillment of the Davidic covenant, a confirmation that God has forgiven us for our sins, and a token of the first fruits of all those who one day will rise again to eternal life through faith in him.

- The ascension of Jesus to the Father's right hand is a visible sign of Jesus' authority and headship, as Head of the Church and the armies of God, as Lord of the harvest work of mission, and as Conquering Lord of all, who soon will come and consummate the Kingdom.

Student Application and Implications

Now is the time for you to discuss with your fellow students your questions about the Kingdom of God inaugurated and realized today. The implications of Jesus having brought the Kingdom into view are numberless and important, and undoubtedly you will have questions regarding the significance of his work on your life and ministry. What particular questions do you have in light of the material you have just studied? Maybe some of the questions below might help you form your own, more specific and critical questions.

* Can we actually pinpoint a time when the Father determined to overturn and overthrow the events of Satan's rebellion and Adam and Eve's disobedience?

* If the Kingdom is already present in some degree today, why is the world still so incredibly unjust and oppressed? More specifically, why are the poor still mistreated, abused, and overlooked if the Year of Jubilee has come into focus already?

* Will the specific promises about a literal, physical Kingdom be fulfilled, or are they to be understood only in a spiritual way?

* Why does it appear as if the devil is still so powerful and strong if Jesus defeated him decisively on Calvary at the cross? How much can we as believers appropriate of this great power, and how do we do it?

* What role does the city play in terms of the Kingdom of God today? If the Kingdom is already present in some fashion, what does this mean for us in urban ministry?

* To what extent can we ask God to do the same works in and through us that he did in Jesus, if the kingdom authority is present in our midst today?

* Why are so few Christians and churches experiencing the explosive authority and power of God's rule if Jesus in some real sense ushered in God's reign?

* Christians disagree much regarding end time prophecy and doctrine. How does this teaching of the Kingdom help resolve or make even more difficult to understand the Bible's teaching on the end times?

CASE STUDIES

A Triumphant Discovery

1

2

page 323 14

A sincere Christian brother, after hearing the teaching that the Kingdom of God is already present, took it to mean that all of the kingdom power and blessing is available for us today. He immediately began to teach in his Sunday school class that Jesus has ushered in the Kingdom, and therefore we no longer need to experience any of the devil's interference or jabs. Specifically, he began to teach the teens that they no longer had to get sick, or be without money, or sin, or even be emotionally discouraged. As a result of his teaching, factions broke out among the teens and their parents. Some sided with the Christian brother, while others affirmed that "in the world we will have tribulation." Both sides have gone to the Bible and have emphasized those Scriptures which support their respective points; that we have victory in Christ, or, that we struggle and fight in this world, with the flesh, the devil, and this wicked system of temptation. With both sides mildly bruised and a little confused, they ask you to come and clarify the meaning of the "already" in the "already/not yet" Kingdom. How would you help this struggling fellowship come to understand the true meaning of the "already" and the "not yet" in regards to the Kingdom of God?

Everything Is for Later

2

In sharing the teaching of this lesson with some friends in church, a visiting graduate student of a well-known seminary begins to say how this view is heretical. Believing strongly in the view that all kingdom life and power has been postponed to a future age, the graduate student begins to share how Israel was given a kingdom offer but refused it, killing the Messiah who invited them. Having rejected Jesus' kingdom offer, he says we are now in the Church-age which comes in between the time of Jesus' kingdom offer, and the time of the Second Coming, when Israel will eventually accept God's kingdom offer, and the Davidic Kingdom will be set up in the future. Now, no manifestation of the Kingdom is present, everything dealing with the Kingdom is for later. What would you say to this student? Does his view sound credible? How would you answer such an interpretation in light of what you learned in today's sessions?

Restatement of the Lesson's Thesis

Since the Fall, God has sought to eradicate and overturn its effect by bringing his reign into this present world. He began to demonstrate his rule concretely by taking the predisposition as a Warrior over his enemies. Through his covenant promise to Abraham, God determined to bring a Seed into the world which would crush the serpent's head and bless the families of the earth. The promise was renewed in the patriarchs, in Israel, to the tribe of Judah and the family of David. Finally, in the person and works of Jesus of Nazareth, the kingdom rule of God has been inaugurated in a final sense in this world. As *Christus Victum*, he delivered us from the power of the devil, sin, and death, and as *Christus Victor*, he has risen from the grave and ascended into heaven as Lord of all. Although not fully realized, the Kingdom has come in the person of Jesus Christ.

2

Resources and Bibliographies

If you are interested in pursuing some of the ideas of God as a Divine Warrior, you might want to give these books a try:

Dawson, John. *Taking Our Cities for God*. 2nd. ed. Altamonte Springs: Charisma House, 2001.

Lind, Millard. *Yahweh is a Warrior: The Theology of Warfare in Ancient Israel*. Scottsdale: Herald Press, 1980.

Ministry Connections

The interconnections of Jesus' victory have great relevance for every part of our ministry. Now is the time to try to nail down this high theology to a real practical ministry connection, one which you will think about and pray for throughout this next week. What in particular is the Holy Spirit suggesting to you in regards to the reign of God, and its challenge today? What situation comes to mind when you think about how the truth of God's reign being inaugurated, and your own life and ministry today? Give yourself time to meditate in the presence of the Lord on these matters, and he will reveal to you what it is, and what you ought to do as a result of what he reveals.

Counseling and Prayer

page 324 15

The appropriate kind of prayer in light of the teaching of this lesson is worship, praise, and thanksgiving. To see the resolve of the triune God to come to our aid, to fight our foes, to overturn the effects of the Fall, to send his Son who took on the devil and death for us - this mighty love ought to produce in us a dramatic outpouring of thankful praise. God did not abandon us in our weakened state, but gave his best for us. We ought to find ways to show what it means to appropriate the victory of Jesus over our enemies and watch God work through our humble faith. Perhaps there are those in your family or church, at work or in the neighborhood whom we can lift up to God on behalf of Jesus.

ASSIGNMENTS

2

Scripture Memory

Luke 11.15-20

Reading Assignment

To prepare for class, please visit *www.tumi.org/books* to find next week's reading assignment, or ask your mentor.

Other Assignments

Please read carefully the reading assignments above, and as last week, write a brief summary for them. Also, now is the time to begin to think about the character of your ministry project, as well as decide what passage of Scripture you will select for your exegetical project. Do not delay in determining either your ministry or exegetical project. The sooner you select, the more time you will have to prepare!

Looking Forward to the Next Lesson

So far in this Kingdom module we have focused on the Fall and its effects, and in this lesson, on God's resolve to eradicate the effects of the Fall by returning his reign into the universe through his Son. How exciting it is to know that God the Father loves us so much that he sent his finest Warrior, his own Son, down to earth to do battle against those forces and powers which held us captive and made our lives miserable and difficult! In our next lesson we look at how Jesus has transferred his kingdom authority to his people, the Church, and how we are called now to exhibit his glory in the world, and act as his deputies, affirming his kingdom rule to the very ends of the earth.

Name ______________________________

Date ______________________________

For each assigned reading, write a brief summary (one or two paragraphs) of the author's main point. (For additional readings, use the back of this sheet.)

Reading 1

Title and Author: ______________________________ Pages __________

Reading 2

Title and Author: ______________________________ Pages __________

God's Reign Invading

page 325 1

Lesson Objectives

Welcome in the strong name of Jesus Christ! After your reading, study, discussion, and application of the materials in this lesson, you will be able to:

- Show that the Church of Jesus Christ, as his body and agent, is itself the locus (the place and/or context) of God's salvation, of the empowering presence of the Holy Spirit, and of the authentic expression of the Kingdom's life and witness.
- See that the Church of Jesus Christ is not only a context, but an agent, a willing and available servant to God in order to advance kingdom purposes in the world.
- Recite from memory a passage relating to the invasion of God's reign.

Devotion

page 325 2

The Violence of the Kingdom

3

Read Luke 14.26-33. No one would expect Jesus to be a person associated with conflict and violence. One so gentle and humble hardly seems the right candidate to have his name and reputation associated with such rugged and grisly realities. Yet, throughout his life and ministry Jesus affirmed that he did not come to bring peace but a sword, resulting even in the separation and alienation of so-called intimate family members (Matt. 10.34). He taught that allegiance with him and his Kingdom demanded all of the life of the disciple (Matt. 13.44 ff.), and that one would necessarily have to rid oneself of all one possessed in order to surrender fully to him (Mark 10.21). As G. E. Ladd has suggested, "The presence of the Kingdom demands radical, violent conduct. Men cannot passively await the coming of the eschatological Kingdom as the Apocalyptists taught. On the contrary, the Kingdom has come to them, and they are to actively, aggressively, and forcefully seize it" (*The Presence of the Future*. New York: Harper and Row, 1974, p. 164). To be a disciple is to carry one's cross, to hate one's own life, and to forsake everything one has for the treasures in heaven. A kingdom lifestyle that demands no change, no violence is hardly one which is associated with the Son of God, who is the Warrior of God to restore the reign of God in the earth. Let us, therefore, stand and fight as soldiers fully armored for battle (Eph. 6.10-18), fully understanding that Jesus was manifested in order to destroy the works of the devil (1 John 3.8). To love Jesus is to hate the world and set one's affections on the things above where Christ sits, at God's right hand (Col. 3.1-3). As a disciple of Jesus, arm yourself with a mind to do battle, for the fight is on!

Nicene Creed and Prayer

After reciting and/or singing the Nicene Creed (located in the Appendix), pray the following prayer:

> *Our Father in heaven, we praise Thy Name. We glorify Thy Name and ask Thee that Thy will may be done and that Thy light may break into Thy Church. We ask Thee to guide our ship. We long to be a little part of Thy true, great Church and ask Thee to guide this ship through wild oceans and through all dangers and clefts. Amen.*
>
> ~ Henri Arnold. **May Thy Light Shine.**
> Rifton, NY: Plough Publishing House, 1985. p. 170.

Quiz

Put away your notes, gather up your thoughts and reflections, and take the quiz for Lesson 2, *God's Reign Inaugurated.*

3

Scripture Memorization Review

Review with a partner, write out and/or recite the text for last class session's assigned memory verse: Luke 11.15-20.

Assignments Due

Turn in your summary of the reading assignment for last week, that is, your brief response and explanation of the main points that the authors were seeking to make in the assigned reading (Reading Completion Sheet).

CONTACT

Commitment to Christ, Church, or What?

1

page 326 📖 *3*

How would you respond to the statement: "No one can claim to be intimate with Jesus Christ while ignoring or rejecting his people, the Church." In this day of televangelists, individualized Christianity, and church-hopping, does this statement make sense to you? Many believe that while every Christian ought to belong to a church of some kind, it is not absolutely necessary to be intimately involved in a church in order to be spiritual. As long as one's heart is open, they are committed to

Christ and the Scriptures, and are maintaining a "close walk" with God, then everything is fine. Or is it?

Taking Things a Little Too Far

What do you make of the current teaching of the "health-wealth" gospel? This teaching, to be overly simplistic, emphasizes that because a Christian has come under the government and authority of Almighty God, that there now exists no need for the believer to be sick, to lack, or to be broke. The heart of this, according to this doctrine, is rooted in the authority of the Christian. When Jesus ascended into heaven, the claim is made that because Jesus possessed all authority, and because he turned that authority over to his people, the Church, then the Church can exercise dominion directly over the devil, and thwart his intentions to harm or hurt the Church. As a matter of fact, some who hold to this doctrine believe that if you are sick or broke or experiencing defeat, it is your fault alone. God has given the grace, and all you need do is affirm it. Is this right on the money or is it taking things a little too far?

What Model Works Best?

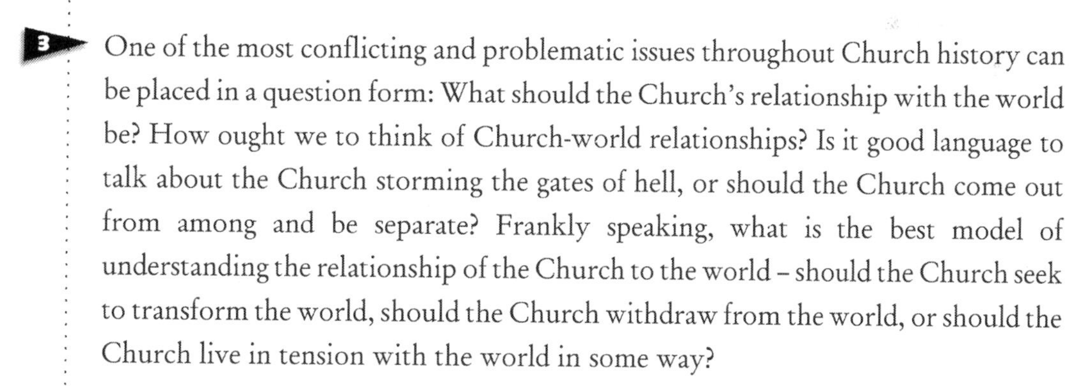
One of the most conflicting and problematic issues throughout Church history can be placed in a question form: What should the Church's relationship with the world be? How ought we to think of Church-world relationships? Is it good language to talk about the Church storming the gates of hell, or should the Church come out from among and be separate? Frankly speaking, what is the best model of understanding the relationship of the Church to the world – should the Church seek to transform the world, should the Church withdraw from the world, or should the Church live in tension with the world in some way?

CONTENT

God's Reign Invading

Segment 1

Rev. Dr. Don L. Davis

Summary of Segment 1

page 327 📖 4

The objective of this segment is to show how the Church of Jesus Christ, as his body and agent, is itself the locus (the place and/or context) of God's salvation, of the empowering presence of the Holy Spirit, and of the authentic expression of the Kingdom's life and witness.

Our objective for this first segment of *God's Reign Invading* is to enable you to see that:

- The Church of Jesus Christ is the *locus* (place or context) of God's salvation.
- The Church is the locus of the empowering presence of the Holy Spirit.
- The Church is the locus of God's authentic kingdom *shalom*.
- Yes, the Kingdom of God is invading this realm in the presence and practice of the Church of Jesus Christ!

Video Segment 1 Outline

page 327 📖 5

I. The Church Is the Locus and Arena of God's Salvation.

General comments about the Church:

- God's Kingdom (his reign and rule) is invading the world through the Church of Jesus Christ.
- The community of the triune God: the people of God (2 Cor. 6.16), the body of Christ, with Jesus as its head (Eph. 1.22-23), and the temple of the Holy Spirit (1 Cor. 3.16-17).
- *Ekklesia's* two meanings:
    1) The union of all true believers in Christ, living and dead. Sometimes this concept is referred to as "The Church Universal."

2) Also, the New Testament speaks of the Church as a gathering or company of believers in any locality, or a group of assemblies like these, as in 1 Corinthians 1.2, Galatians 1.2, or Philippians 1.1. We refer to these individual assemblies as "local churches."

- The fourfold Nicene Creed theology of the Church (ecclesiology).

1) The Church is *one* united by faith to Jesus Christ.

2) The Church is *holy* (the Church is set apart as God's people for his possession and use).

3) The Church is *catholic* (universal, including those from every nation, tribe, people, and kindred).

4) The Church is *apostolic* (founded on eye-witness testimony of the prophets and the apostles).

A. The Church is the custodian of the Gospel and the Word of God.

3

1. The steward of the mysteries of God, the pillar and ground of the truth, 1 Tim. 3.15-16

2. Possesses the authoritative revelation regarding the person of Christ, and the working of his Kingdom, Matt. 16.18-19

B. The Church is the place where God's forgiveness and healing are experienced by the blood of Jesus Christ.

1. Believers in Christ have received by faith the forgiveness of God, 1 John 2.12.

2. Those who believe have been delivered from Satan's domain and have received redemption, the forgiveness of sins, Col. 1.13.

3. In the company of the saints of God there is forgiveness given and experienced.

C. The Church is the location of the physical ingathering of the members of the body of Christ.

page 328 📖 6

1. Believers are members of Christ's body, and individually, members of one another, Rom. 12.3-8.

2. The body metaphor: the Church is the extension of Jesus in the world.

a. As those giving testimony and bearing witness

b. As those giving evidence to the reality of the Kingdom's presence in contemporary space and time

c. The life of the age to come right in our neighborhoods today

II. The Church Is the Locus or Context of the Empowering Presence of the Holy Spirit.

page 329 📖 7

The Church, both as individuals and as members, is indwelt by God's empowering Holy Spirit, 1 Cor. 3.16-17.

Believers together make up a dwelling place where God, the Holy Spirit dwells, Eph. 2.21-22.

A. The Holy Spirit in the Church is the supreme sign of Kingdom present.

1. Jesus' pre-ascension promise to the believers: the Holy Spirit will come upon you, Acts 1.8.

2. The Day of Pentecost: the outpouring of the Holy Spirit (in fulfillment of the Joel prophecy), Acts 2.8

B. The Holy Spirit in the Church is the guarantee and down payment looking to the full blessing of the Kingdom to come.

1. The Spirit as "the guarantee of our inheritance," Eph. 1.13-14

2. God's seal and the Holy Spirit in our hearts as the guarantee of his covenant promise for redemption, 2 Cor. 1.21-22

3. Mighty kingdom works and fruits of the Spirit on us now serve as the down payment of the full installment to come.

4. *Arrabon*: down payment, pledge, first installment ("guarantee")

C. Also, the Holy Spirit is the living Lord, empowering, leading, and directing the Church.

1. The Holy Spirit is God: God in the midst of the people of God today.

2. Every local church has access by faith in Jesus Christ to the promised Holy Spirit.

3. What is the ministry of the Holy Spirit in the midst of the body, the Church?

    a. He will guide us into all truth, John 15.26.

    b. He will glorify Christ in the midst of the body, John 16.14.

    c. He will reveal Christ to the lost, Matt. 16.17.

    d. He will unify believers in the body, Eph. 4.3.

    e. He will call out faithful men and women to ministry, Acts 13.2.

    f. He will provide gifts to the members of the body as he wills for its edification, 1 Cor. 12.7.

    g. *The Holy Spirit is nothing less than the Lord, the Spirit, providing us with signs and wonders of the Kingdom's power right in the midst of our local church.*

III. The Church Is Also the Locus of Authentic Kingdom Life.

G.E. Ladd's points about the Kingdom:

- The Church is not the Kingdom, but a *manifestation* of it.
- The Kingdom *creates* the Church.
- The Church *witnesses* to the Kingdom in the world.
- The Church is the *instrument* of the Kingdom.
- The Church is the *custodian* of the Kingdom.

A. The Kingdom of God is seen in the life and witness of the Church.

1. The *Shekinah* glory of God appears now in the Church in the person of the Holy Spirit, Eph. 2.21-22.

2. The called-out *ekklesia* of God is here, 1 Pet. 2.8-9.

3. God's Sabbath rest is now being enjoyed by faith in the midst of the Church, Heb. 4.3-10.

4. The blessings of the Year of Jubilee are practiced and enjoyed in the body, Col. 1.13.

5. The Holy Spirit indwells the Church, 2 Cor. 1.20.

6. The powers of the age to come and Satan is crippled in the Church's midst, Gal. 3.10-14.

7. The *shalom* of God (wholeness) is experienced in the Church, Rom. 5.1.

8. We possess the saving power of the Gospel of Christ, Rom. 10.9-10.

The Church is the place where we can come and experience the power and presence of God's Spirit, and enjoy the benefits of God's rule over our lives!

B. The Kingdom of God is expressed in her life, witness, and testimony.

1. For the Church, the Kingdom is both gift and task.

3

a. The Kingdom is gift: God's rule is available to all who believe in his Son.

b. The Kingdom is task: the Church is salt (preserving) and light (enlightening and exposing) in the life of the Kingdom.

2. The Church in the world, Matt. 5.13-16

Conclusion

» The Church of Jesus Christ is the locus, the place or context, of God's salvation.

» The Church of Jesus Christ is the locus of the empowering presence of the Holy Spirit.

» The Church of Jesus Christ is the locus of authentic kingdom life.

3

Segue 1

Student Questions and Response

The questions below are designed to help you identify the key points in our last video segment on the Church as the locus of the Kingdom. Please answer the following questions carefully, be clear and concise in your answers, and where possible, support with Scripture!

page 330 📖 *8*

1. In what sense can the Church be called "the community of the triune God?" What are the two meanings of *ekklesia* (the called-out ones) in Scripture?
2. What is the meaning and interpretation of the fourfold definition of Church in the Nicene Creed? Why are these definitions important for an understanding of the Church?
3. As the locus of the empowering presence of the Holy Spirit, in what way is the Spirit the down payment (*arrabon*) of the kingdom blessings to come? How does this relate to the Old Testament understandings of the Church (cf. Peter's statement at Pentecost)?
4. In what sense can it be said that the Church is the "custodian" or "steward" of the revelation of God in Christ?

5. What is the relationship between the body of Christ and the forgiveness of sin? Can one experience God's forgiveness and not be a part of the body of Christ? Why or why not?

6. Give several examples from the Scriptures which support the idea "the Holy Spirit of God is the Lord of the Church, empowering, directing, and guiding her in the world."

7. In what ways is the Kingdom of God seen and expressed in the Church's life? Why is it important to affirm the truth that the Church is where the Kingdom's power (God's sovereign rule) is experienced?

8. In what way is it right to speak of the Kingdom as both gift and task for the Church?

God's Reign Invading

Segment 2

Rev. Dr. Don L. Davis

3

Summary of Segment 2

The Church of Jesus Christ is an *agent*, a willing and available servant of God to advance his kingdom purposes in the world.

page 331 📖 9

Our objective for this second segment of *God's Reign Invading* is to enable you to see that:

- The Church of Jesus Christ is an agent, a willing and available servant to God to advance his kingdom purposes in the world.
- The Church is the agent of the Kingdom of God through its worship of God as King and Lord.
- The Church is the agent of the Kingdom of God through its apostolic witness.
- The Church is the agent of the Kingdom of God through its zeal for good works.
- The Church is the agent of the Kingdom of God by being God's vessel for prophetic signs and wonders.

Video Segment 2 Outline

I. The Church Is the Agent of the Kingdom through its Worship of God as King and Lord.

page 331 📖 10

The Father's desire: those who will worship him in spirit and in truth, John 4.24.

A. The Church's most fundamental identity: to declare God's wonderful deeds in worship to the world, 1 Pet. 2.9-10.

B. The nature of eternal life is knowing God the Father, and Jesus Christ, the One sent by him, John 17.3.

C. The worship of Almighty God in the Church is one of the most distinctive characteristics of the historical Church.

1. It was the habit and practice of the earliest Christian fellowships.

2. Paul's directions to the Corinthians to meet and set aside their offerings on the first day of the week, 1 Cor. 16.2.

3. Heb. 10.23-25

D. Paul's instruction regarding worship in the Church makes it a central priority of the believers gathered, Eph. 5.18-20.

E. Old Testament people of God and New Testament Church: connected in their worship of Almighty God

1. The book of Psalms

2. The worship of the temple

The Church's first work as the agent of God is to glorify his name in worship.

F. The place of worship for the redeemed community: the visions of the saints of God in the Apocalypse of John the Apostle.

page 332 📖 11

II. The Church Is the Agent of the Kingdom of God through its Apostolic Witness.

A. We are called to **give witness of the good news of the Kingdom in Jesus Christ.**

1. The members of Christ's body are called to be ambassadors of Jesus Christ, 2 Cor. 5.18-21.

2. The Great Commission, the command to make disciples of Jesus worldwide, is given to the Church, Matt. 28.18-20.

3. The call to witness to the ends of the earth, in the power of the Holy Spirit, Acts 1.8

4. Individual believers are called to give compelling testimony in life and word to those in their sphere of influence, 1 Pet. 3.15-16.

a. A historically demonstrated fact: where Church exists, mission exists.

b. Every congregation and Christian is called to minister.

B. We are also called to **safeguard and protect the supremacy and necessity of the apostolic witness to Jesus Christ.**

1. Christian faith - what the Apostles believed and taught about Christ and his Kingdom

2. God has entrusted the mysteries of the Christian faith to the Church - to defend, articulate, and announce, 2 Tim. 2.15.

3. Called to defend the faith "once delivered to the saints" by the Apostles, Jude 3

4. The certainty of false teachers and loose listeners in the Church, Acts 20.28-38; 1 Tim. 4.2-4

5. The Church stewards God's truth, and entrusts them to faithful witnesses who can equip others, 1 Cor. 4.2; 2 Tim. 2.2.

C. Evangelization is directly related to contextualization: sharing and defending the good news of the Kingdom go hand in hand, Millard Erickson.

III. The Church Is the Agent of the Kingdom of God through its Zeal for Good Works.

A. The Church was recreated in Christ to do good works, and be zealous for good deeds.

1. We will do greater deeds than Christ, John 14.12-13.

2. As our lights shine in doing justice and compassion, others will glorify God, Matt. 5.16.

3. We are God's workmanship created in Christ for good works, Eph. 2.10; Titus 2.11-14.

4. Called to be an agent of good in a fallen and sick world

5. While the Church does not through its good works bring in the Kingdom, we do give undeniable testimony as to its presence through our actions and advocacies, Phil. 1.27-28.

B. This agency for good works is especially in deeds of freedom, wholeness, and justice in ministry to the poor.

1. Jesus inaugurated his ministry with the Year of Jubilee quote of Isaiah 61 about his anointing to preach to the poor, Luke 4.18ff.

2. The story of the Good Samaritan as an example of fulfilling the second commandment, Luke 10

3. Pure and undefiled religion before God the Father: visiting orphans and widows in their affliction, and an unspotted testimony in the world, James 1.27.

4. The poor as rich in faith and heirs of the Kingdom to come, James 2.5

5. Ministry to the poor serves as a litmus test of the authentic faith of those who profess to be in the Kingdom, 1 John 3.17-18.

page 333 12

IV. The Church Is the Agent of the Kingdom of God by Being God's Vessel for Prophetic Signs and Wonders.

A. The Church can expect continuing signs of the presence and lordship of Christ in the Church's ministry and mission.

1. The book of Acts details what Jesus began to do and teach, and continued to do through his Church, cf. Acts 1.1.

2. The Church is granted authority to represent Christ in the world, and therefore do violence to the demonic forces which now enslave it, Matt. 16.18.

3. New Testament vision of the Church: the Warrior of God doing battle against the forces of this present darkness, Eph. 6.10-18

B. The Holy Spirit confirms the Word of Christ with signs following its proclamation.

1. The Church, in carrying out its mandate, confronts the power of the Evil One, 1 Pet. 5.8.

2. The Church as the champion of God, is called to engage the enemy directly, doing battle by the Word and faith against the rulers of this present darkness, Eph. 6.10ff.

3. Though the Church is in the world, the weapons of its warfare are not of the world but effective to do violence to the kingdom of Satan, 2 Cor. 10.3-5.

4. The nature of satanic opposition - what is it?

   a. Persecuting the leaders of the Church

   b. Menacing the members of the Church

   c. Resisting the message of the Gospel

5. Persecution is the norm for those living godly in the present world in Christ, 2 Tim. 3.12.

6. As representatives of Jesus in such a violent and resisting world, the Holy Spirit will confirm the Word of the Kingdom with kingdom signs and power, Mark 16.19-20.

C. The power of the Holy Spirit will be displayed as the Church advances the Kingdom of God to the ends of the earth.

1. The Church in the world as "the Church Militant"

   a. The Church Militant exists in between the times, in the already/not yet Kingdom.

   b. The Church Militant represents Christ's interests as soldiers represent their foreign land, 2 Tim. 2.3-4.

2. The Church has been given authority to represent Jesus in power, for the Kingdom of God is not in word alone, 1 Cor. 4.20.

3. Because the Kingdom is present, so is Christ's resurrection power to demonstrate the Kingdom's reality in the world!

Conclusion

» The Church of Jesus Christ is the locus and arena of God's salvation, for the empowering presence of the Holy Spirit, and of the authentic expression of the Kingdom's life and witness.

» The Church of Jesus Christ is the agent of worship, witness, works, and wonders in the world, advancing the Kingdom in the power of the Holy Spirit.

Segue 2

Student Questions and Response

page 334 13

These questions are designed to help you review and discuss the truths of the Church as the agent of the Kingdom's life and presence in the world today. Please take as much time as you have available to answer these and other questions that the video brought out. Be clear and concise in your answers, and where possible, support with Scripture!

1. What is the meaning of the term "agent?" How does the Church function as an agent of the Kingdom of God in its worship of Almighty God?

2. Why is worship so integral to the Church's identity and responsibility in the world? Can the Church accomplish its task in the world if it fails as a worshiper of God? Why or why not?

3. What are the two ways in which the Church is called to be an agent of God through its "apostolic witness?" Why is it so important that the Church in the world safeguard the doctrine and teachings of the Apostles about Christ?

4. What is the relationship between the Church serving as the protector of the apostolic witness, and sharing that witness with the lost? Can the Church fulfill its call as a witness without doing both? Why or why not?

5. According to the Scriptures, why is it necessary for the Church to maintain and be zealous for good works? What precisely do good works have to do with giving expression to the Kingdom in the world?

6. Ministry to the poor and the oppressed have a special place in the life of the Church - why? If a congregation fails to do justice and compassion among the poor, what does that neglect say of its ability to give witness to the Kingdom in its location?
7. In what sense does the Bible assure us that the works which Jesus did in demonstrating the Kingdom of God will continue in the life and deeds of the Church?
8. How does the Holy Spirit work in confirming the legitimacy and power of the Word of God through the Church's ministry today? What should our assurance be that the Holy Spirit will work in Christ's resurrection power as we go forth into the world with the Gospel?

CONNECTION

Summary of Key Concepts

This lesson focuses on the ways that the Church of Jesus Christ serves as the locus (place or context) where the Kingdom of God is expressed and revealed, as well as its agent, the means by which the Kingdom of God is given witness and advanced in the world. Although the Church is not the Kingdom of God per se, it is the primary means by which the Kingdom is manifested. The Kingdom creates the Church, as God has worked sovereignly in the person of Jesus to defeat the powers of the Evil One, but the Church gives witness to the Kingdom in its community and through its ministry.

- The Church of Jesus Christ is the locus of God's salvation. Through the Church, the Kingdom's forgiveness and reconciliation is made known to the world, and offered through its gospel ministry. As custodian of the Word of God, the Church shares the mysteries of God's love with the lost.
- The Church is the locus of the empowering presence of the Holy Spirit. The Holy Spirit is the *arrabon*, the down payment and guarantee of the inheritance which shall be revealed at the Second Coming of Jesus Christ. The Church, as the Holy Spirit's dwelling place, experiences all the blessings, fruit, and joy associated with the Spirit's active ministry through the members of the Church.
- The Church is the locus of the Kingdom's life and power. In the midst of the community of believers is experienced the power of answered prayer,

3

regeneration and new life, the wholeness of God in righteousness and peace, and the powers of the age to come, all in a community of love.

- This theme of the Church as locus of the Kingdom is the Church's gift and task. As gift, it is made manifest through the grace of God in the Spirit. As task, the Church is called to give witness to God's rule through its life together and its interactions with the lost in the world.

- The Church is not only the locus of the Kingdom; it is also the agent of the Kingdom, firstly and primarily, in its worship of Almighty God. This is the fundamental identity of the Church, a Kingdom of royal priests called to show forth God's excellencies and deeds through its life and worship.

- The Church is the agent of the Kingdom in its apostolic witness. The Church is called to defend and safeguard the apostolic testimony about Christ, as well as give faithful witness to the Gospel of the Kingdom among the lost throughout the world.

- The Church is the agent of the Kingdom in its zeal and continuance of good works, especially in works of justice and compassion on behalf of the poor. As Jesus inaugurated and gave validity to his kingdom call through his ministry to the poor, so the Church continues this kingdom witness through its works on behalf of the poor, who are rich in faith and called to be heirs of the Kingdom.

- The Church is the agent of God in being God's vessel for prophetic signs and wonders which confirm its kingdom ministry in the world. The Church in the present age is the Church Militant, engaging the powers of darkness with the weapons of God's warfare. As she gives witness to God's rule in the world, the Church can expect the Holy Spirit to confirm his Word with signs of transformation, justice, healing, deliverance, and salvation.

3

Student Application and Implications

Now is the time for you to discuss with your fellow students your questions about how the Church is both the locus and agent of the Kingdom. Your questions are of the utmost importance. The ideas, questions, and concerns that you have now must be discussed and debated. The truth regarding the Church in this lesson is full of important implications, and undoubtedly you now have questions regarding the significance of these truths for your work in the Church, and for your life and ministry. The following questions may help you form your own, more specific and critical questions.

* Is it possible to claim salvation in Christ while disdaining or rejecting the Church? Is it a package deal - in other words, if you get Jesus, must you also take the Church as well?

* What do you do if you minister among people who have never experienced the Church as it is described in Scripture? How do you help people come to experience the Church as God describes it?

* Is it right to tie the Kingdom so closely to the life and health of the Church? In what ways is the Kingdom demonstrated separate from the Church?

* To what extent can we expect the Holy Spirit to show signs and wonders in the ministries represented here, among our student's churches and ministries? What conditions, if any, are necessary to fulfill in order to see the power of God connected to our ministry of the Word?

* How do we overcome the violence, pain, and difficulty of the city as the agent of the Kingdom? It seems as if the city is so big and we are so small - how do we change our attitude about ourselves and what we do?

* What is the relationship between the invasion of God's rule into the city and the powers of darkness that hold it in bondage? What must we do to be aware of the specific ways that the devil holds city people in bondage?

* Is it possible to be in the Church and yet not be under God's rule? If so, how?

* What are the steps to see revival come to a church or Christian community which does not appear to be giving powerful witness to God's rule in its life and witness?

* What role do leaders play in seeing the Church become a locus and agent of the Kingdom?

* Churches can become so ingrown and fragmented - how do you take a biblical vision and share it among churches so as to challenge them to give witness to the Kingdom of God *together*?

CASE STUDIES

Is this the Real Thing?

1

page 335 14

Recently in a small church, the young people experienced a remarkable turn to the Lord. After months of prolonged prayer and open sharing among one another, this group of about 100 or so high schoolers began to see God do remarkable things in their midst. In addition to a large number of students sharing their faith with their friends and seeing them come to the Lord, a number of students confessed their sins before the Lord and the people, admitting abuse of alcohol, drugs and illicit sexual activity. The worship of the group was phenomenal - hours seemed to pass without any sense of loss in the intensity, freshness, and genuineness of worship. While the effect of these changes seemed only to be affecting the youth, the entire church became interested and started looking at the impact of this fresh outpouring and wondered if it would spread to the whole church. In light of the teaching we discussed today in class, what ought the youth group leader teach these young people about their experience? What are they to do as young Christians in a larger, less animated and alive church? How can they be used to be a better witness of the Kingdom, both inside and outside their church?

On the Verge of Giving Up

2

A young pastor of a small urban church worked tirelessly to see God move in the church for years, to no avail. It is a small denominational church, which functions as a step child in the larger denomination. Many of the members are locked in conflict with each other, and a strong number have expressed disappointment in his leadership of the church. He has sought out the latest materials on church growth and revitalization, but nothing has seemed to work. Frankly, he is deeply discouraged right now. He is aware of your understanding of the relationship between the Church and Kingdom. What would you say to this young urban pastor to encourage him in his ministry? Should he resign and look for another church, hang in there with the seemingly few, disgruntled members? How can he so change his own view as to get the necessary encouragement to go on?

Who's Really Showing the Kingdom?

3

One deacon, Mr. Jones, has become excited over the last 12 months about a prison ministry that has recently begun in his church. About 3-4 workers each week go to the local precinct jail and form friendships with the inmates, meeting physical needs and sharing Christ with them. The results have been wonderful! Over 20 men and women have made decisions for Christ, and most will be eligible to leave for work release if not outright exit from the prison system soon. Mr. Jones has gone to the pastor suggesting that the church should create a program to bring these new believers into their church, discipling them and working with them to get them solidly established back in the community. The pastor has received some calls from worried members that a great influx of prisoners might cause upset in the church, "and besides, many of these people have done horrible things. Should we expose the children of the church to such types of people?" Mr. Jones has asked you for advice. In light of what you know about the Church, the Kingdom, and urban ministry, what would you propose that he, the pastor, and the church do to meet this opportunity and need?

Restatement of the Lesson's Thesis

The Church of Jesus Christ, as his body and agent, is itself the locus (the place and/or context) of God's salvation, of the empowering presence of the Holy Spirit, and of the authentic expression of the Kingdom's life and witness. The Church of Jesus Christ is not only a locus, it is also God's agent, a willing and available servant to God in order to advance kingdom purposes in the world as the Church Militant in this present age.

Resources and Bibliographies

If you are interested in reading more regarding the Church of Jesus Christ as locus and agent of the Kingdom of God in the present world, you might want to give these books a try:

Perkins, John. *With Justice for All.* Ventura: Regal Books, 1984.

Sider, Ron. *Rich Christians in an Age of Hunger.* Downers Grove: InterVarsity Press, 1977.

Snyder, Howard A. *The Community of the King.* Downers Grove: InterVarsity Press, 1977.

Stott, John W. *Involvement: Being a Responsible Christian in a Non-Christian Society.* Vol. 1. Old Tappan: Fleming H. Revell Co., 1985.

Ministry Connections

Seeking to relate these truths to your own ministry through your church represents the core of this teaching. How God might want you to change or alter your ministry approach based on these truths is largely dependent on your ability to hear what the Holy Spirit is saying to you about where you are, where your pastoral leadership is, where the members of your church are, and what specifically God is calling you to do right now, if anything, about these truths. Plan to spend good time this week meditating on the Church's call to be locus and agent of the Kingdom, and how your ministry and that of your church reflects that call. As you consider your ministry project for this module, you can possibly use it to connect to these truths in a practical way. Seek the face of God for insight, and come back next week ready to share your insights with the other learners in your class.

Counseling and Prayer

Perhaps there are some specific needs which the Holy Spirit has surfaced through your study and discussion of this material on the Church. Do not hesitate to find a partner in prayer who can share the burden and lift up your requests to God. Of course, your instructor is extremely open to walking with you on this, and your church leaders, especially your pastor, may be specially equipped to help you answer any difficult questions arising from your reflection on this study. Be open to God and allow him to lead you as he determines.

3

ASSIGNMENTS

Scripture Memory

1 Peter 2.9-10

Reading Assignment

To prepare for class, please visit *www.tumi.org/books* to find next week's reading assignment, or ask your mentor.

Other Assignments

page 335 📖 15

As usual you ought to come with your reading assignment sheet containing your summary of the reading material for the week. Also, you must have selected the text for your exegetical project, and turn in your proposal for your ministry project.

Looking Forward to the Next Lesson

Next session we complete our Kingdom module by focusing on the consummation of the Kingdom, and all of the difficult but glorious issues associated with the coming of Jesus back to earth to establish his Kingdom in the world. Praise God that God's promise will one day be literally fulfilled, when our Lord returns to destroy the devil and his minions forever and bring God's kingdom *shalom* forever back into this world. Is it little wonder that it is called "the Blessed Hope?" (cf. Titus 2.11-15).

Module 2: The Kingdom of God
Reading Completion Sheet

Name ______________________________

Date ______________________________

For each assigned reading, write a brief summary (one or two paragraphs) of the author's main point. (For additional readings, use the back of this sheet.)

Reading 1

Title and Author: ______________________________ Pages __________

Reading 2

Title and Author: ______________________________ Pages __________

God's Reign Consummated

page 337 1

Lesson Objectives

Welcome in the strong name of Jesus Christ! After your reading, study, discussion, and application of the materials in this lesson, you will be able to:

- Define eschatology and its significance for Christian discipleship.
- Outline briefly the biblical conception of death, and then discuss together the Bible's teachings on the intermediate state.
- Focus on the Second Coming of Jesus Christ, the resurrection from the dead and the final judgment, and the Kingdom consummated with God as All-in-all.
- Recite from memory a passage related to the consummation of God's reign.

Devotion

Who Is Worthy to Consummate God's Reign?

page 338 2

Read Revelation 5.1-14. In one of the loftiest visions regarding the end of time in John's apocalyptic vision of the book of Revelation, we are transported to the very throne of Almighty God. In his right hand, the Mighty One held a scroll, which if opened, would begin the "beginning of the end" of God's cosmic program to restore his reign to the universe. In a scene filled with anguish and angst, John saw that there was no one in heaven or in earth found worthy to open the scroll, or even to look at it. In response to this predicament, John said that he wept bitterly and much - in all of the universe no one was found to be worthy. Just at the climactic moment, one of the elders said to the weeping Apostle, "Weep no more; behold, the Lion of the tribe of Judah, the Root of David, has conquered, so that he can open the scroll and its seven seals." John, turning again to the fateful scene, sees a Lamb standing in the midst of the throne and the four living creatures. This Lamb appeared to have been freshly slain, had seven horns (speaking of his authority) and seven eyes (speaking to the Spirit of God sent into the earth). It is at that moment that the twenty-four elders and the four living creatures sang a song of the worthiness of the Lamb because he was slain and redeemed to God a people from every tribe, kindred, nation, and tongue.

In a real sense this great prophetic scene underscores one of the fundamental convictions of saints and sages since the beginning of time. Only God in Christ is worthy to be glorified, to receive honor, praise, wisdom, and strength; for only Jesus of Nazareth, the risen and reigning Lord of all, has proven himself worthy to bring the rule of God into the earth. No amount of warfare, programming, human effort, technology, philanthropy or human good will usher us into the reign of God. The Kingdom's consummation has always been dependent on the power and will of the Lamb who was slain. Because of this, it cannot be defeated or thwarted. Praise God, since the Kingdom is dependent on the Son, it will be consummated, for he does all things well. All praises be to God, the Lamb alone is worthy to bring God's reign to consummation on the earth!

Nicene Creed and Prayer

After reciting and/or singing the Nicene Creed (located in the Appendix), pray the following prayer:

> *Eternal God, our Father, and the Father of our Lord Jesus Christ, we exalt your name for you alone are the true God of heaven and earth. Your Son, our Lord Jesus Christ, among all other so-called lords and gods, is the only one worthy to bring your kingdom rule to earth in full splendor. We exalt your name in him, and pray that you will give us the wisdom and strength to honor and glorify you as that day draws near when your Son will make the kingdoms of the world his own. In Jesus' name we pray. Amen.*

4

Quiz

Put away your notes, gather up your thoughts and reflections, and take the quiz for Lesson 3, *God's Reign Invading.*

Scripture Memorization Review

Review with a partner, write out and/or recite the text for last class session's assigned memory verse: 1 Peter 2.9-10.

Assignments Due

Turn in your summary of the reading assignment for last week, that is, your brief response and explanation of the main points that the authors were seeking to make in the assigned reading (Reading Completion Sheet). Also, if you have not already done so, please turn in to your instructor your proposal for your Ministry Project, as well as your passage selection for your Exegetical Project.

Much Ado about Nothing

page 339 3

In discussing the latest series of sermons that their pastor had been giving on the topic of the end times, one couple debated whether or not such preaching was really helpful for the church, and the growth of the Christians in it. It appeared as if the pastor was concentrating on a lot of the details of the prophetic word, and many of the those in the audience were getting lost with the various theories he was covering about the rapture, the great tribulation, the lake of fire, and other subjects, all of which seemed far away from their struggles as teachers at the local high school. After much conversation, they agreed that such subjects, while good for the seminarian or church leader, are not of much importance for the living of the Christian life for "ordinary Christians." Do you agree with their analysis? Why or why not?

A Good God Wouldn't Demand It

What do you think of the idea that has become popular about God's final judgment on sin, especially among cults like the Jehovah's Witnesses, which say that a good and loving God could not possibly demand eternal punishment for those who transgressed his law? Does it seem reasonable or unreasonable to you to expect that God would require eternal retribution from those who fail to repent and believe in Jesus Christ? Doesn't this appear extreme - is there anyone on earth who has actually been bad enough to merit eternal punishment from God? How would you begin to resolve these questions, if confronted with them?

Get to the Important Stuff First

In discussing the next batch of lessons they would be teaching their teens in their discipleship class, two urban youth workers disagreed over the need to instruct their students on the "last things." Since in the five years they have led the teens they had not said one word about these things, one of the leaders thought that they should. This leader believed it was critical for Christians to understand these things, for they represent the most important things in the Christian life. His teaching partner disagreed, saying that while the biblical teaching on the last things has a place, it is more important to speak about love and faith, the really important stuff first, before any of this talk of prophecy and stuff occurred. What do you think of their views, and how would you resolve their discussion, retaining a right emphasis on both the Bible's teaching of the last things, and the practical outworking of God's reign for them today?

CONTENT

God's Reign Consummated

Segment 1

Rev. Dr. Don L. Davis

Summary of Segment 1

We intend to define eschatology and its significance, outline briefly the biblical conception of death, and then discuss together the Bible's teachings on the intermediate state.

page 339 📖 4

Our objectives for this first segment of *God's Reign Consummated* is to enable you to:

- Define and understand the importance of the doctrine of last things (eschatology) in the Scriptures, and its relationship to discipleship and Church life.
- Articulate what the Bible teaches about death, both for the Christian and non-Christian.
- Recite what the Scriptures teach on the intermediate state, that period between the death of an individual and the final end of all humankind at the consummation of God's Kingdom.

Video Segment 1 Outline

I. What Is the Definition of Eschatology?

page 341 📖 5

A. Eschatology, Greek for "the study of last things"

B. Why must we be diligent and careful to study the events and truths associated with our Lord's coming again? Two reasons are given:

1. To comfort us regarding the loss of believing loved ones

a. Paul's counsel to the Thessalonians, 1 Thess. 4

Though believers may physically die in this age, our hope is absolutely certain that in his own time and manner, the Lord will bring to pass the prophetic and apostolic promise to reign forever as King, in a new heaven and new earth where his justice and truth will endure unto the ages.

b. Believers, because of the Kingdom's consummation, need not grieve as the lost do, who have no hope of God's reign returning in power to the earth.

c. Paul instructs the Thessalonians in the truths of Jesus' return, then suggests that they comfort each other with those words, 1 Thess. 4.18.

2. To encourage us to remain ever watchful, sober, and alert in light of the soon appearing of Jesus Christ

a. Jesus' constant word to his disciples to watch and stay ready for his appearing, Luke 12.35-40

b. Paul suggests in Romans 13.11-12 that the time of the end approaches quickly, calling for sober readiness and alertness.

c. Further, Paul proclaimed to the Thessalonians, as children of the light that they ought to be sober, staying alert for his coming, 1 Thess. 5.6-9.

d. Peter tells the persecuted Christians of Asia Minor to be sober and rest their hope fully on the grace to come at Jesus' revelation, 1 Pet. 1.13.

e. Peter reiterates the need to be sober and watchful since the end of all things is at hand, 1 Pet. 4.7.

f. The power of the word of prophecy to impact one's discipleship, 2 Pet. 1.19

g. Keep ourselves in God's love looking for the mercy of Jesus unto eternal life, Jude 1.20-21

C. Eschatology's importance: God's Kingdom will soon be fulfilled, and we ought to stand ready and be alert for its final, glorious appearing.

II. What Is the Relationship between the Issue of Death and the Consummation of God's Kingdom Reign?

page 342 📖 6

A. Note the difference between individual and cosmic eschatology.

1. Individual eschatology - those experiences awaiting the future of individuals

2. Cosmic eschatology - those experiences awaiting the future of the human race and all creation

B. What are the essential biblical tenets regarding death in Scripture?

1. Death is real and inevitable for every person.

a. Death is certain for every human being.

b. It is appointed for all people to die once, and then to face judgment, Heb. 9.27.

c. The wages of our sin is death, but the gift of God is eternal life in Christ Jesus our Lord, Rom. 6.23.

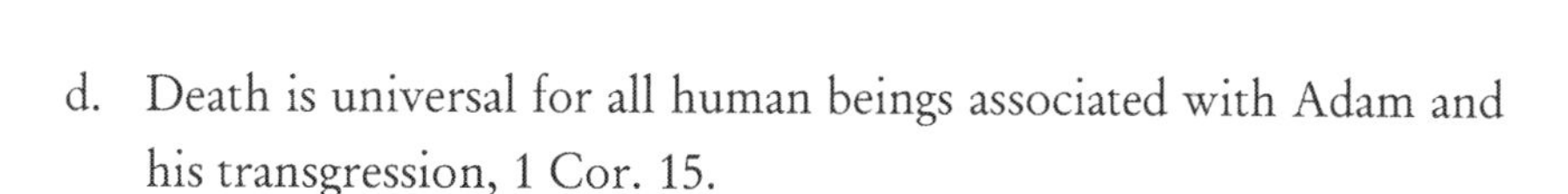

d. Death is universal for all human beings associated with Adam and his transgression, 1 Cor. 15.

e. The Apostles spoke of and anticipated their own death, as in Paul's case in 2 Timothy 4.7-8.

f. Until Christ comes and finally consummates his kingdom work, death will remain an inevitable fact for all of us.

2. The nature of our death is both physical and spiritual.

a. The physical nature of death: the ending of life and separation of the soul from the body

(1) Jesus distinguished between the death of the body and the soul, Matt. 10.28.

(2) Physical death is separation of the body from the soul and the spirit.

(3) The body returns to dust, the spirit to the God who gave it, Eccles. 12.7.

(4) The body without the spirit is dead, James 2.26.

(5) Death is not the end of our existence, but a movement to a different mode of being.

b. The spiritual nature of death: separation of the person from God

(1) To be dead spiritually refers to the state of being alienated and separated from the life in God.

(2) The second death, spoken of in Revelation 21.8, is the eternal death that represents for the one who is lost for all eternity their disconnection and separation from God forever.

(3) This is distinct from and comes after physical death.

3. Physical and spiritual death are both the result of sin, Rom. 6.23; Eph. 2.1-2.

4. That which is called the "second death," (the eternal separation of a human being from the presence of God) does not apply to believers.

   a. Over those chosen to enter into Christ's Kingdom, the second death has no power, Rev. 20.6.

   b. Since Jesus is the resurrection and the life, those believing in him shall not die in the second death, John 11.25-26.

5. Jesus' mighty kingdom work overcomes the power of death for the believer.

   a. Through his coming to earth to defeat the devil

   b. Through his overcoming of the curse

   c. Through his payment for the penalty for our sin on the cross through his shed blood

   d. Because of these, none who believe in him will ever experience the second death or eternal separation from the Lord.

C. What, then, are the effects of death?

1. For the unbeliever, death is a tragedy, a curse, and a penalty.

a. It is a tragedy, because all hope of salvation is lost.

b. It is a curse, because death is directly associated with the wages of sin.

c. It is a penalty, because a holy and infinite God will have his vengeance upon sin.

2. For the believer, however, all curses associated with death are gone.

a. Christ has become a curse for us, Gal. 3.13.

b. Because of Christ's kingdom work, the perishable will put on the imperishable, the mortal will put on immortality, and the sting of death will be overcome, 1 Cor. 15.54-55.

c. While physical death may be certain, to die as a Christian is to be placed into the presence of the Lord.

(1) To be away from the body is to be at home (present) with the Lord, 2 Cor. 5.6-9.

(2) For the Christian to live is Christ, and to die is actually gain, since death means instant transportation into the presence of Jesus, Phil. 1.20-23.

III. What Is the Nature of the "Intermediate State," and How Does it Relate to Our Understanding of the Kingdom's Consummation?

page 343 📖 7

A. To what does the term "intermediate state" refer?

1. Intermediate state - the condition or state of human beings between their physical death and the resurrection

2. It is important because it enables us to more effectively minister to those who have lost family and friends in the city.

3. Difficult subject to resolve: few texts and much heated debate

B. The intermediate state as "soul sleep"

1. Soul sleep is the view that the soul is asleep during the period between death and resurrection, in a state of repose and unconsciousness.

2. What is the biblical evidence for this view?

a. Stephen's martyrdom is described as sleep, Acts 7.60.

b. Paul refers to David having fallen asleep (or died) after he served God in his generation, Acts 13.36.

c. The image of sleep is used four times in 1 Corinthians 15, vv. 6, 18, 20, 51.

d. The image of sleep is used three times in 1 Thessalonians 4.13-15.

e. Soul sleep is a view that takes this imagery literally for the state of the soul after death and before the resurrection.

3. Is this view persuasive? It is a simple view, but has some serious problems.

a. The Bible tends to suggest that the soul survives death, and that we are not merely one united component (body-soul-spirit), but that the soul and body are separate.

b. The Bible teaches in several places of personal conscious existence after death.

(1) The rich man and Lazarus, Luke 16.19-31

(2) Jesus' word to the thief on the cross, "Truly, I say to you, today you will be with me in Paradise," Luke 23.43

(3) Jesus' committal of his own Spirit to God, Luke 23.46

(4) Paul desires to depart and be with Christ, which signifies conscious communion with Jesus after death, Phil. 1.23.

c. We must take seriously the texts which suggest that to be absent from the body is to be present with the Lord, that is, in conscious communion with him, 2 Cor. 5.8.

C. The intermediate state as purgatory

1. Overview of the Catholic view of death

a. Immediately after a person dies, their eternal status is determined.

b. Those who die in a state of wickedness go directly to hell, the place of torment, while those in a state of grace and purified at the time of death go directly to heaven.

c. Those in a state of grace, who are not yet spiritually perfect go to purgatory, a place of temporal punishment, for those who are not entirely free from their venial sins or their transgressions.

d. Thomas Aquinas, the premiere Catholic scholar of the 12th century, tells how those in purgatory can be helped.

(1) Through the Mass

(2) Through the prayers of the saints

(3) Through the good works of living believers

2. Biblical evidence: "But whoever speaks against the Holy Spirit will not be forgiven, either in this age or in the age to come," Matt. 12.32.

a. This text is read to suggest that there are gradations (degrees) among sins.

b. That would mean that some sins (other than speaking against the Holy Spirit) will be forgiven in the world to come.

c. Purgatory is a doctrine which appears to be a logical result of this interpretation of Scripture.

3. Is this view persuasive? No, for several reasons:

   a. It implies a kind of works righteousness which is contrary to many clear teachings of the New Testament, especially Galatians 3.1-14 and Ephesians 2.8-9.

   b. The heart of the New Testament's teaching is that we are saved by grace through faith, not through our works.

   c. A theology of purgatory actually speaks of a kind of spiritual probation and personal contribution and aiding in one's own righteousness, and therefore cannot be accepted.

D. The intermediate state as the believer's hope: transported into the presence of the Lord

1. General overview of intermediate state

   a. The state of the unrighteous dead is not entirely clear from Scripture, although Jesus' teaching of the rich man in Luke 16 would argue against soul sleep, but a kind of conscious misery and torment in Hades.

   b. The Bible does provide, however, indications that the righteous dead do not go into unconsciousness or a state of gloom in Hades.

2. What is the view of the believers hope of the presence of the Lord?

a. It appears that at death, the souls of the righteous are received into paradise, Luke 23.43.

b. To be absent from the body is to be found immediately in the presence of the Lord, 2 Cor. 5.1-10.

c. It seems clear that believers go immediately to a place of blessedness into God's presence, while those who do not believe go to a place of misery, awaiting the final judgment.

d. Again, while the evidence for the various views is scarce, it seems clear that Paul's desire to depart and to be with Christ is a hope that every Christian can readily share.

Conclusion

» Eschatology, the doctrine of last things, is critically important to understand, not only to be personally watchful in one's own discipleship, but to provide comfort to those who have lost loved ones in death.

» Death is inevitable and certain for all people, but Jesus of Nazareth, through his work on the cross, has overcome the power of death for those who believe.

» The intermediate state for those who cling to the Kingdom's hope is to know that, at the moment of death, the believer will be transported instantly into the presence of the Lord, awaiting the resurrection of the dead.

Segue 1

Student Questions and Response

page 345 8

Undoubtedly you have some questions on the study of eschatology, and the biblical teaching on death and the intermediate state. Please take as much time as you have available to answer these and other questions that the video brought out. Be clear and concise in your answers, and where possible, support with Scripture!

1. What is the meaning of the theological term *eschatology*? Why should the preaching and study of eschatology be a priority in the curricula of any Christian worker, pastor, or urban missionary?
2. What are some of the reasons that Scripture gives to the Church that we must study the doctrine of last things in conjunction with the consummation of the Kingdom?
3. Should Christians grieve the death of loved ones like those who do not know the Lord? Why or why not?
4. Why is it necessary for believers who cling to the hope of the Kingdom consummated to be sober and watchful regarding the time of Christ's appearing?
5. Explain the difference between *individual* and *cosmic* eschatology.
6. What are some of the general elements taught in Scripture in regards to death? What is the difference between physical and spiritual death? How are they the same?
7. What are the key effects of death outlined in Scripture? What are some of the differences between what death means for the non-Christian over against the Christian?
8. What is the meaning of the theological term *intermediate state*, and why is it important for ministering to the bereaved?
9. How would you define the view of the intermediate state as "soul sleep" and as "purgatory?" What is the biblical evidence for these views, and do you find them persuasive?
10. Define the view of the intermediate state as the presence of the Lord for Christians only. Do you find the biblical evidence here compelling? Why or why not?

God's Reign Consummated

Segment 2

Rev. Dr. Don L. Davis

Summary of Segment 2

The general elements associated with the consummation of the Kingdom of God are the Second Coming of Jesus Christ, the resurrection of the dead and the final judgment, and God becoming All-in-all.

page 345 9

Our objectives for this second segment of *God's Reign Consummated* is to enable you to:

- Define the essential elements related to the Second Coming of Jesus Christ to consummate the Kingdom of God in the earth.
- Articulate clearly the teachings of the Scriptures associated with the resurrection of the dead and the final judgment.
- Recite the final condition of the consummated Kingdom, when God Almighty becomes our All-in-all.

Video Segment 2 Outline

4

I. The Kingdom Will Be Consummated in the Second Coming of Jesus Christ.

A. The coming of Jesus Christ (the *parousia*) will certainly occur, and will be definite.

1. *Parousia*, which can be translated as either "presence" or "coming" is oftentimes associated with Jesus' return, which he mentioned often in his teaching, such as in Matthew 24.30 and 26.64.

2. Peter refers to the definiteness of Jesus coming, Acts 3.19-21.

3. Paul is unequivocal by the Spirit of the Lord to assert the certainty of Christ's coming, 1 Thess. 4.15-16.

4. For Jesus and the Apostles, the Second Coming of Jesus was certain, definite, and absolutely sure.

B. The Second Coming of Jesus Christ is also imminent (able to occur at any time).

1. The *parousia* is both imminent and unknown.

a. Jesus said that neither he, nor angels, nor anyone knows the time of his coming except his Father, Mark 13.32-33 and Matt. 24.36-44.

b. The Father has set the time in his own authority, Acts 1.7.

c. Since the coming was unknown, the Apostles gave numerous reminders to be alert, sober, and ready for his imminent, yet unknown return, 1 Thess. 5.6-9.

4

page 346 📖 *10*

C. The Second Coming of Jesus Christ will be glorious and magnificent. What will be its character?

1. His coming will be **personal**.

a. Jesus' promise to the disciples, John 14.3

b. Paul's testimony of the Lord's coming, 1 Thess. 4.16

c. Jesus will send no proxies, substitutes, or messengers in his place when it comes time to consummate God's Kingdom. He will come himself, personally.

2. His coming will be **physical**.

a. His coming will be bodily, real, not spiritual or psychic, Acts 1.11.

b. The personal coming will be in the same body with which he ascended to the heavens.

3. His coming will be **visible**.

a. Jesus says his coming will appear in the sky, and that the nations will mourn when they see him coming on the clouds of the sky, with power and great glory, Matt. 24.30.

b. The coming of Christ will be visible to the eyesight of all those on the earth.

4. His coming will be **full of splendor and glory**.

a. It is described in the Synoptic Gospels as our Lord Jesus coming on the clouds with great power and glory, Matt. 24.30; Mark 13.26; Luke 21.27.

b. It will be heralded by the archangel's trumpet blast, 1 Thess. 4.16.

c. It will be accompanied by the presence of angels, Matt. 24.31.

d. It will be associated with Christ Jesus taking up his kingly authority on his throne, judging and reigning over the nations, Matt. 25.31-46.

5. His coming will be **unexpected**.

a. It is portrayed as coming swiftly, like a thief in the night, with many being completely unaware of his return, 1 Thess. 5.1.

b. The parable of the ten virgins in Matthew 25 suggests this truth.

c. Peter suggests that his delayed coming may cause some to scoff, but the promise is sure, 2 Pet. 3.3-4.

d. Jesus says that it will come with surprise like in the days of Noah, and the time of Lot - swiftly, unexpectedly, and with great surprise, Luke 17.26-30.

6. His coming will be a **unified event**.

a. Some believers profess a kind of dual coming (one in secret "for the saints," and a second phase in public, after the seven year tribulation period, a "coming with the saints").

b. Yet texts like 1 Thessalonians 4.16, 2 Thessalonians 2.8, and Matthew 24.27 associate the term *parousia* to a powerful, single, and unified public event.

c. Saints await the one blessed hope (not hopes) and the appearing (not appearings) of the glory of our Great God and Savior Jesus Christ, Titus 2.13.

II. The Various Millennial and Tribulation Views Associated with the Second Coming of Jesus Christ

page 347 11

A. The disputed millennial question is whether or not there will be a millennium (a 1,000 year earthly reign of Jesus Christ), and if so, will it occur before or after his coming.

1. **Postmillennialism** is founded on the idea that the preaching of Jesus will be so successful that the world will be converted, and the reign of Christ will be complete and universal.

a. Appeals to verses like Isaiah 45.22-25

b. Most popular at times when the Church has been succeeding in political or social transformation

c. Has lost support in the wake of the world wars of the 20th century and mass devastation and injustice of modern times

2. **Premillennialism** believes in a literal earthly reign of Christ for approximately one thousand years after his return.

a. Called "*chialism*" (Greek for 1,000); this view was the dominant view of the Church's first three centuries, and grew in popularity in conservative circles in the 19th century.

b. Key text: Revelation 20.4-6

(1) A literal thousand year reign

(2) Two resurrections (one before the millennium for the righteous, and the second after, for the wicked)

c. The 1,000 year period occurs after the great tribulation, where Christ will come and establish a time of peace and justice.

3. **Amillennialism** suggests that there will be no millennium, no earthly reign of Christ.

a. The great and final judgment comes after his Second Coming.

b. The eternal states of the believing and unbelieving commence at that time.

c. Revelation is interpreted, by this view, as largely symbolic.

d. Asserts that this view is simpler than either post- or pre-millennial views, and takes the mention of a millennium, as many other items in Revelation, as a largely symbolic reference.

4. Resolution of these views of the millennium

a. The case for the premillennial view

(1) The **postmillennial** view seems to go against the plain teaching of Jesus that great ungodliness and apostasy would accompany his Second Coming.

(2) The **amillennial** view struggles, in some places, with taking the prophetic words seriously, relegating all prophetic Scripture to symbolic meanings.

(3) To its credit, the **premillennial** position tends to harmonize a large number of Scriptures, and there appear to be no biblical passages with which this view cannot cope.

(4) Perhaps the strongest point is the Bible's clues as to resurrections of a select group or stage, Luke 14.14; 20.35; 1 Cor. 15.23; 1 Thess. 4.16; Dan. 12.2, and John 5.29.

b. Understanding the bigger picture: the Kingdom will be consummated by Jesus in God's own time.

(1) Students of Scripture differ in their views here.

(2) More important than any one view is the certainty of our Lord's return, and the surety that he will consummate the Kingdom, in God's time.

B. The disputed tribulation question asks if Jesus Christ will remove his people from the world before the great tribulation (called pretribulationism), or if Jesus will return after the tribulation (posttribulationism), or if perhaps he will return in the middle of the great tribulation period (midtribulationism).

page 347 📖 12

1. **Pretribulationists** maintain that there will be two phases of Christ's coming.

a. Phase one occurs first at the resurrection of the believing dead and translation of Christians who are alive at the "rapture," which occurs before the "great tribulation" of Matthew 24, a period of unparalleled terror and judgment on the earth.

(1) The world will experience God's wrath and judgment during the tribulation.

(2) The Church will be judged and issued rewards in the heavenlies for its faithfulness.

b. Phase two occurs at the end of this 7 years; Christ will return with a resurrection of those saints who died during the tribulation.

c. The heart of this view is Christ's intent to deliver the Church from the great tribulation, 1 Thess. 5.10.

2. **Posttribulationists** hold that the coming of Christ for his people takes place at the end of the tribulation.

a. They reject any kind of "rapture" notion of Christ's coming.

b. The Church will be present through the great tribulation.

c. This view also makes a difference between God's wrath and the tribulation.

(1) God's wrath is God's judgment on the wicked, John 3.36.

(2) Tribulation, on the other hand, is a distinct element in the faith of the saints, John 16.33.

d. The **posttribulation** view believes that God will sustain his people in the midst of the great tribulation.

3. **Midtribulationism** seeks to resolve the conflict between pre- and post-tribulation views. It asserts that the Church will experience the less-severe first-half of the tribulation, and then be removed for the second half, when God pours out his wrath on the earth.

   a. The Church, in this view, then experiences tribulation but avoids the wrath of God.

   b. Represents a mid-point between the pre- and post-tribulation viewpoints

4. The bigger picture: God's ability to sustain his own in the time of crisis

   a. The general flavor of the Bible's teaching in regards to trials and testings seem to align with the posttribulational view.

   b. Scripture is full of warnings of the inevitability of believers to go through various trials, James 1.3 and 1 Pet. 4.12ff.

   c. We must be ready to endure whatever God may outline for us.

   d. We can be confident that whatever God demands, his grace will supply the strength to endure.

III. The Kingdom of God Will Be Directly Connected with the Resurrection and the Judgment Associated with Jesus' Return. What Is the Character of that Resurrection?

A. The resurrection is **definite.**

1. It is spoken of in both the Old and New Testaments directly.

2. Old Testament citations of the resurrection:

a. Isa. 26.19

b. Dan. 12.2

c. Ps. 49.15

d. Ps. 71.15

3. New Testament citations of the resurrection:

a. John 5.28-29

b. The epistles are filled with citations as to a literal, physical resurrection of the dead, perhaps the most well known being 1 Corinthians 15.51-52.

B. The resurrection is the **work of the triune God, the Lord (Father, Son, and Holy Spirit).** Each member of the trinity is connected to the resurrection.

1. The Father through the Spirit, Rom. 8.11

2. Jesus Christ as the firstborn from the dead, Col. 1.18

C. The resurrection is a **literal, bodily raising of the dead.**

1. Rom. 8.11

2. 1 Corinthians 15.20ff speaks to the certainty of the physical raising from the dead, Jesus' resurrection being the prototype of all to come.

D. The resurrection will be a resurrection of both **the righteous and the unrighteous.**

1. The resurrection for the righteous.

a. Spoken of oftentimes as a certainty

b. In connection to a reward, Isa. 26.9; Luke 14.14; Phil. 3.11

2. The resurrection of unbelievers

a. Associated with everlasting shame and contempt, Dan. 12:2

b. Associated with God's judgment, Rev. 20.12-15

page 348 📖 13

IV. The Character of the Final Judgment

A. The final judgment is yet to occur; it is **a future judgment.**

1. This judgment is associated with the totality of a person's life, after their death.

2. Judgment to follow after the death of a person, and after the Second Coming itself, Heb. 9.27

3. The Son of Man to reward each person for what they have done, Matt. 16.27.

4

B. The final judgment has Jesus Christ serving as **Judge of all.**

1. Jesus' testimony regarding his role in judgment, John 5.22,27

2. Paul's corroboration of Jesus's testimony occurs in several places in the New Testament:

a. 2 Cor. 5.10

b. 2 Tim. 4

3. Jesus' standard: the measure of knowledge one had of God's explicit will, Matt. 11.21-24.

C. The final judgment includes all of humanity: every human being **will be judged**, Matt. 25.32; 2 Cor. 5.10; Heb. 9.27.

1. Each person will give an account of themselves to God as Paul warns in Romans 14.10-12.

2. Both Christians and non-Christians will be judged, however, the judgment will be based on highly different measures.

D. The final judgment will be based on one's **relationship to God in Jesus Christ**.

1. This judgment is based on what a person believes in regard to the person and work of Jesus Christ, John 3.36.

2. The one who has the Son, and the one who does not have the Son, 1 John 5.11-13

3. The believer's work and the test to come, 1 Cor. 3.12-15

E. The final judgment will be **final**.

1. Those who do not know God will be subject to God's unending judgment.

2. The judgment will be irreversible, as is evident in Luke 16.19-31.

3. Note the terrifying reality of finality associated with this judgment in Matthew 25:41.

4. The doctrine of annihilationism

   a. This view suggests that although not everyone is saved (called "universalism"), the unrighteous will be destroyed, annihilated; they do not exist forever.

   b. It holds that the wicked simply cease to exist, while the righteous continue to enjoy God's endless blessing.

   c. While this view is enjoying some popularity now, we must grapple with the language associated with the judgment given in Scripture, speaking of its unending nature.

      (1) The judgment is associated with "unquenchable fire," Mark 9.48.

      (2) With everlasting burning, Matt. 25.41

      (3) With everlasting contempt, Dan. 12.2

      (4) With eternal destruction, 2 Thess. 1.9

      (5) With everlasting torment, Rev. 14.11

      (6) With everlasting punishment, Matt. 25.46

page 350 📖 14

V. The Final End of the Kingdom Consummated Will Be its Theocentric Character: God Will Become All-in-All.

A. The Kingdom's consummation will reflect the universal knowledge of God.

1. For the first time, we shall all see God and know God in a direct way, unencumbered by sin or evil, Isa. 11.1-9.

2. We will be like him, for we will see him as he is, 1 John 3.2.

B. The Kingdom's consummation will result in the removal of all evil, which will be eradicated and put down, under the feet of Jesus Christ.

1. All creation will be restored to its Edenic glory, Isa. 11.1-9.

2. All afflictions, evils, distresses, and sin will be put down, and its effects forever, Rev. 21:4.

3. Even the source of temptation and evil will be put down forever, Rev. 20:10.

C. The Kingdom's consummation will make the redeemed the sole possession of the Lord, those who will belong exclusively to God, called to the worship and service of God and the Lamb.

1. In the New Jerusalem, the city of God come down to humankind, Rev. 21.1-4.

2. The recreated earth will be full of the worship of the Lord and the Lamb as is evident in Rev. 19.1-4.

3. The saints of God will count it their blessedness to forever serve him, Rev. 22:3.

4. God's people will serve him forever, glorified in immortal bodies, in a redeemed earth where justice and peace will forever rule.

D. The Kingdom's consummation; after all enemies including death have been put under Christ's feet, then Christ will transfer the Kingdom to God, who will then become the universe's All-in-all.

1. In a deep mystery, the kingdom rule of God will be given over to God Godself.

2. Christ will wind up the story, turning over the Kingdom itself to the Lord God, who himself will become All-in-all.

3. After Jesus has destroyed all dominion, authority, and power, he will hand over the Kingdom to God the Father, 1 Cor. 15.24-28.

a. He must reign until he has put all enemies under his feet.

b. The last enemy to be destroyed is death.

c. When this has been accomplished, then Jesus himself will be made subject to God the Father.

d. God Almighty, the triune God, will become All-in-all.

Maranatha! Even so, come, Lord Jesus!

Conclusion

» The Kingdom will be consummated in the Second Coming of Jesus Christ.

» In that consummation, God Almighty in Jesus will conquer death, resulting in the resurrection of the dead and the final judgment on humankind.

» Finally, at the end, even the Kingdom itself will be made subject to God Godself, in order that God may become All-in-all.

Segue 2

Student Questions and Response

page 351 15

The following questions were designed to help you review the material in the second video segment related to the Second Coming of Jesus, as well as the issues of death, the intermediate state, the resurrection, the judgment, and the final consummation of the Kingdom with God as All-in-all. Answer the questions, concentrating on the "big ideas" and principles associated with the consummation, especially on Jesus' role in consummating the Kingdom at his Second Coming. Be clear and concise in your answers, and where possible, support with Scripture!

1. What is the meaning of the Greek term *parousia*? How does this term help us to understand the Second Coming of Christ?

2. In what ways do we know that the Second Coming of Jesus is definite, sure, and certain? What do we mean when we say that his coming is "imminent but unknown?"

3. Explain the various meanings associated with the glorious character of Jesus' soon return (e.g. it is personal, physical, visible, full of splendor and glory, and unexpected). Why are each of these important in order to understand the true nature of the *parousia*?

4. Explain the difference between the various millennial views (*postmillenial*, *premillenial*, and *amillennial*) of the Second Coming. Which view seems to reflect best what Scripture teaches on the millennium?

5. Explain the differences in the various views on the great tribulation (*pretribulation*, *posttribulation*, and *midtribulation* views). Which view seems to best reflect what Scripture teaches on the tribulation?

6. Discuss together some of the critical elements associated with the resurrection. What are the main contrasts between the resurrection of the righteous and the unjust?

7. What are some of the more critical characteristics spoken of in Scripture regarding the final judgment? What role does Jesus play in that judgment, and what will be the end of all those within that judgment?

8. What will characterize the restored universe and new heaven and earth at the Kingdom's consummation? How will creation change? What of the role of the saints in the new heaven and earth?

9. In the end itself, what will Jesus do with the Kingdom when all enemies have been put down under his feet? What will God's role be in the ages of ages to come?

Summary of Key Concepts

This lesson focuses upon the consummation of the Kingdom of God in the Second Coming of Jesus Christ, who is soon to be revealed and will establish his rule on earth. *Parousia* is the term associated with Jesus' return, which shall be personal, bodily, visible, glorious, and is imminent. The Kingdom's consummation is integrally tied into what the Bible teaches about death, the resurrection, and the final judgment. When all enemies have been placed under Jesus' feet, he will deliver the Kingdom over to God his Father in order that God may become All-in-all.

- *Eschatology* is the theological term associated with the study of last things, and *parousia* is the term associated with the Second Coming of Jesus Christ.

- We should be diligent and careful to study the doctrine of last things (the consummation of the Kingdom) because of its ability not only to affect our urgency, soberness, and holiness after God, but also our ability to minister and comfort those who are grieving because of lost loved ones.

- Individual eschatology deals with those experiences awaiting the future of individuals, while cosmic eschatology deals with those awaiting the entire human race and all creation.

4

- In regard to the biblical teaching on death, we know that death is real and inevitable for all people, that the nature of death is both physical (the ending of life and separation of the body from the soul) and spiritual (the separation of the person from God). All death, whether physical or spiritual, is the result of sins committed and God's judgment upon them.

- While death is a tragedy and a penalty for the unbeliever, death is no longer a curse for the Christian, since Jesus has become a curse for us. While physical death may be certain for believers, to die as a Christian is to be transported instantaneously into the presence of the Lord. For the unbeliever, neither soul sleep nor purgatory appear to be biblical alternatives to their intermediate states, but rather some kind of conscious torment in Hades awaiting judgment.

- The Kingdom of God will be consummated in the Second Coming of Jesus Christ, which will be definite, imminent, unknown to all but the Father, personal, physical, visible, full of splendor and glory, and unexpected. It is to be a unified event, although the one event of his coming may involve different phases and stages.

- The millennial question seeks to answer whether there will be a millennium (a 1,000 year period of earthly reign of Jesus Christ), and if so, when will it occur (before or after his coming). *Postmillennialism* believes the preaching of Jesus will be so successful that the world will be converted. *Premillennialism* believes Jesus will return before the 1,000 year period, resulting in a literal earthly reign on the earth. *Amillennialism* suggests that there will be no millennium or earthly reign of Christ. While all views hold some difficulty, the premillennial view appears to harmonize the scriptural teaching best.

- The tribulation question asks whether Jesus will remove his people from the world before, (*pretribulationism*) during (*midtribulationism*), or after (*posttribulationism*) the tribulation. Regardless of the timing, God has promised to supply his people with all the strength needed to endure trials for his greater glory.

- The Bible teaches unequivocally the resurrection of the dead. This resurrection will be definite, will involve the work of the triune God, and be a literal and physical resurrection. There will also be a resurrection of the righteous and the unrighteous. In the same vein, the final judgment will be future, with Jesus Christ serving as Judge, involving every human being, based on their relationship to God in Christ, with the results being final.

- The final end of the Kingdom's consummation will result in the removal of all evil, affliction, and distress, and the judgment of the devil. The redeemed will become the sole possession of God, the city of God will enter into the domain of humankind, with the putting down of all authorities, dominions, and powers contrary to the rule of God. God's *shalom* shall completely and finally come to earth.

- In the end, Jesus will put down all enemies under his feet with all authority, dominion, and power. Once this is accomplished, he will deliver the Kingdom over to God his Father, and in the ages of the ages, God will become All-in-all.

Student Application and Implications

Now, in this last lesson on the consummation of the Kingdom of God, you have the opportunity to explore with your fellow students your own questions about the Kingdom of God and its soon consummation in Jesus' Second Coming. Time will not allow for a full and unlimited treatment of your questions, so think hard. What are those particular issues, concerns, and themes which you would like to explore in regards to the Kingdom's consummation? This is your time to discuss them. Maybe some of the questions below might help you form your own, more specific and critical questions.

- What are we to make of all the detail in the symbolism and imagery associated with the biblical prophecies regarding the Second Coming? Is there some way we can focus on the main things, and not get lost in the minutia?

- What is the best way to emphasize eschatological themes in your ongoing ministry of evangelism, discipling, and church preaching and growth?

- In light of all the differing views about death and dying, especially now with so much talk of spirituality in common culture, what ought we to emphasize when we discuss death in public arenas?

- Is it important to emphasize the prospect of eternal damnation to those who do not know God? (Many churches employing a "seeker sensitivity" viewpoint would shun this kind of presentation to the lost.)

* What are we to make of all the millions who do not know God in Christ? What is their state when they die - what intermediate state do they experience, and what will their final outcome be?

* Can there be an emphasis on eschatological things, that is, a focus on the end times, that does not produce the kind of sobriety and alertness spoken of in the Bible? When does a discussion of these things become a problem, or even a waste of time?

* Do you have to believe in an eternal hell in order to be historically orthodox in faith?

* Are issues like the millennium and tribulation critical for urban Christian leaders to know and be able to defend? Is there a line drawn on what is really important here?

CASE STUDIES

Drawing the Lines in the Right Places

1

A large, urban, mixed-race church has become an extremely popular place for the young, spiritually sensitive minorities who live in the city. Every Sunday, hundreds of urban Blacks, Browns, and Yellows come to worship in this fast-growing, lively urban church. With the resignation of their senior pastor, the church has elected a committee to search for a new pastor to replace their fine leader who was called by God to another place. In interviewing a number of pastoral candidates, the committee believes it has found a leader for its next phase. A godly man of prayer and the Word, this dear brother loves the church and is ready to come, if the church agrees to call him. The only "drawback" that the committee sees is that the pastoral candidate loves to teach and preach about Bible prophecy, especially on the prospect of eternal life for the saved, and eternal damnation for the lost. The church is "seeker sensitive" in its orientation, that is, it seeks through love, service, and friendship to build bridges of connection before they share the "hard data" of the Gospel. He has been clear that he wants to have the freedom to speak of the final judgment, the resurrection, and hope of heaven freely. Some are concerned that he will intimidate and frighten many people from the church, and from possible commitments to God. How would you counsel the pastoral search committee?

page 351 16

Annihilation Versus Eternal Judgment

2 In a striking sermon on sin, forgiveness, and reconciliation, the pastor of a church suggests that he no longer believes that judgment is eternal, that is, that the lost will be tormented forever and ever. While he is certain that God's judgment will be final, and that only those who believe in Christ will live in the forever Kingdom of God, he is adamant in suggesting that all of the citations in the Bible on the eternal judgment of the lost are not that people will be tormented eternally, but only that their judgment will never be able to be overturned eternally. He now believes that the lost will be annihilated, never to return to earth or enjoy the blessings of God. This so-called "new view" has disturbed many in the church, and even some of the elders are thinking about calling a special meeting to deal with the pastor's perspective on hell. What should the church do now with their pastor's new view regarding eternal damnation?

The Right Word for the Right Time

3 You have been asked to give a word of eulogy at the funeral of a dear acquaintance at work, whose family know you to be a minister, or at the very least, a "religious person." From conversations with the deceased, you are fairly certain that she did not know the Lord; as a matter of fact, in the last exchange you had about the Lord with her, she was very hostile and aggressive. They are hoping you can offer them some comforting words about their loved one at the service. What do you believe, in light of what you know about the consummation of the Kingdom, should be the "word of the Lord" for the family of this dear sister?

Restatement of the Lesson's Thesis

The Kingdom of God will be consummated at the Second Coming of Jesus Christ. Eschatology, the study of last things, deals with the notion of the Kingdom's consummation. The consummation of the Kingdom of God will occur at the Second Coming of Jesus Christ, who is soon to be revealed and will establish his rule on earth. *Parousia* is the term associated with Jesus' return, which shall be personal, bodily, visible, glorious, and is imminent. The Kingdom's consummation is integrally tied into what the Bible teaches about death, the resurrection, and the final judgment. When all enemies have been placed under Jesus' feet, he will deliver the Kingdom over to God his Father in order that God may become All-in-all.

Resources and Bibliographies

If you are interested in pursuing some of the ideas about the end times, and issues such as the rapture and tribulation, you might want to give these books a try:

Archer, Gleason L. Jr., Feinberg, Paul D. et al. *Three Views on the Rapture: Pre, Mid, or Post Tribulational?* Grand Rapids: Zondervan, 1984.

Ladd, G. E. *The Blessed Hope: A Biblical Study of the Second Advent and the Rapture*. Grand Rapids: Eerdmans, 1956.

Ministry Connections

You will be responsible to now apply the insights of your module in a practicum that you and your mentor agreed to. The ramifications of Jesus' return are numerous and rich: think of all the ways that this teaching can influence your devotional life, your prayers, your response to your church leaders and friends, your attitude at work, and on and on and on. What is significant is that you seek to correlate this teaching of the Kingdom with your life, work, and ministry. The ministry project is designed for this, and in the next days you will have the opportunity to share these insights in real-life, actual ministry environments. Pray that God will give you insight into his ways as you share your insight in your project.

Counseling and Prayer

4

Are there any issues, persons, situations, or opportunities that need to be prayed for as a result of your studies in this lesson? What particular issues or people has God laid upon your heart that require focused supplication and prayer for in this lesson? Take the time to ponder this, and receive the necessary support in counsel and prayer for what the Spirit has shown you.

Scripture Memory

No assignment due.

Reading Assignment

No assignment due.

Other Assignments

page 352 17

Your ministry project and your exegetical project should now be outlined, determined, and accepted by your instructor. Make sure that you plan ahead, so you will not be late in turning in your assignments.

Final Exam Notice

The final will be a take home exam, and will include questions taken from the first three quizzes, new questions on material drawn from this lesson, and essay questions which will ask for your short answer responses to key integrating questions. Also, you should plan on reciting or writing out the verses memorized for the course on the exam. When you have completed your exam, please notify your mentor and make certain that they get your copy.

Please note: Your module grade cannot be determined if you do not take the final exam and turn in all outstanding assignments to your mentor (ministry project, exegetical project, and final exam).

The Last Word about this Module

page 352 18

Praise God, you have completed the Capstone module on the Kingdom of God, but you have only begun to explore the rich biblical resources on the Kingdom of God. May God give you the grace and wisdom to seek first the Kingdom of God, and his righteousness, in order that all that you need for life and ministry may be added to you. Amen.

Appendices

APPENDIX 1

The Nicene Creed

We believe in one God, *(Deut. 6.4-5; Mark 12.29; 1 Cor. 8.6)*
the Father Almighty, *(Gen. 17.1; Dan. 4.35; Matt. 6.9; Eph. 4.6; Rev. 1.8)*
Maker of heaven and earth *(Gen 1.1; Isa. 40.28; Rev. 10.6)*
and of all things visible and invisible. *(Ps. 148; Rom. 11.36; Rev. 4.11)*

We believe in one Lord Jesus Christ, the only Begotten Son of God,
begotten of the Father before all ages,
God from God, Light from Light, True God from True God,
begotten not created,
of the same essence as the Father, *(John 1.1-2; 3.18; 8.58; 14.9-10; 20.28; Col. 1.15, 17; Heb. 1.3-6)*
through whom all things were made. *(John 1.3; Col. 1.16)*

Who for us men and for our salvation came down from heaven
and was incarnate by the Holy Spirit and the virgin Mary
and became human. *(Matt. 1.20-23; John 1.14; 6.38; Luke 19.10)*
Who for us too, was crucified under Pontius Pilate,
suffered, and was buried. *(Matt. 27.1-2; Mark 15.24-39, 43-47; Acts 13.29; Rom. 5.8; Heb. 2.10; 13.12)*
The third day he rose again
according to the Scriptures, *(Mark 16.5-7; Luke 24.6-8; Acts 1.3; Rom. 6.9; 10.9; 2 Tim. 2.8)*
ascended into heaven,
and is seated at the right hand of the Father. *(Mark 16.19; Eph. 1.19-20)*
He will come again in glory
to judge the living and the dead,
and his Kingdom will have no end.
(Isa. 9.7; Matt. 24.30; John 5.22; Acts 1.11; 17.31; Rom. 14.9; 2 Cor. 5.10; 2 Tim. 4.1)

We believe in the Holy Spirit, the Lord and life-giver,
(Gen. 1.1-2; Job 33.4; Ps. 104.30; 139.7-8; Luke 4.18-19; John 3.5-6; Acts 1.1-2; 1 Cor. 2.11; Rev. 3.22)
who proceeds from the Father and the Son, *(John 14.16-18, 26; 15.26; 20.22)*
who together with the Father and Son
is worshiped and glorified, *(Isa. 6.3; Matt. 28.19; 2 Cor. 13.14; Rev. 4.8)*
who spoke by the prophets. *(Num. 11.29; Mic. 3.8; Acts 2.17-18; 2 Pet. 1.21)*

We believe in one holy, catholic, and apostolic Church.
(Matt. 16.18; Eph. 5.25-28; 1 Cor. 1.2; 10.17; 1 Tim. 3.15; Rev. 7.9)

We acknowledge one baptism for the forgiveness of sin, *(Acts 22.16; 1 Pet. 3.21; Eph. 4.4-5)*
And we look for the resurrection of the dead
And the life of the age to come. *(Isa. 11.6-10; Mic. 4.1-7; Luke 18.29-30; Rev. 21.1-5; 21.22-22.5)*

Amen.

Memory Verses ⇩

Rev. 4.11 (ESV) *Worthy are you, our Lord and God, to receive glory and honor and power, for you created all things, and by your will they existed and were created.*

John 1.1 (ESV) *In the beginning was the Word, and the Word was with God, and the Word was God.*

1 Cor.15.3-5 (ESV) *For what I received I passed on to you as of first importance: that Christ died for our sins according to the Scriptures, that he was buried, that he was raised on the third day according to the Scriptures, and that he appeared to Peter, and then to the Twelve.*

Rom. 8.11 (ESV) *If the Spirit of him who raised Jesus from the dead dwells in you, he who raised Christ Jesus from the dead will also give life to your mortal bodies through his Spirit who dwells in you.*

1 Pet. 2.9 (ESV) *But you are a chosen race, a royal priesthood, a holy nation, a people for his own possession, that you may proclaim the excellencies of him who called you out of darkness into his marvelous light.*

1 Thess. 4.16-17 (ESV) *For the Lord himself will descend from heaven with a cry of command, with the voice of an archangel, and with the sound of the trumpet of God. And the dead in Christ will rise first. Then we who are alive, who are left, will be caught up together with them in the clouds to meet the Lord in the air, and so we will always be with the Lord.*

APPENDIX 2

We Believe: Confession of the Nicene Creed (Common Meter*)

* This song is adapted from the Nicene Creed, and set to Common Meter (8.6.8.6.), meaning it can be sung to tunes of the same meter, such as: *O, for a Thousand Tongues to Sing; Alas, and Did My Savior Bleed?; Amazing Grace; All Hail the Power of Jesus' Name; There Is a Fountain; Joy to the World*

The Father God Almighty rules, Maker of earth and heav'n.
Yes, all things seen and those unseen, by him were made, and given!

We hold to one Lord Jesus Christ, God's one and only Son,
Begotten, not created, too, he and our Lord are one!

Begotten from the Father, same, in essence, God and Light;
Through him all things were made by God, in him were given life.

Who for us all, for salvation, came down from heav'n to earth,
Was incarnate by the Spirit's pow'r, and the Virgin Mary's birth.

Who for us too, was crucified, by Pontius Pilate's hand,
Suffered, was buried in the tomb, on third day rose again.

According to the Sacred text all this was meant to be.
Ascended to heav'n, to God's right hand, now seated high in glory.

He'll come again in glory to judge all those alive and dead.
His Kingdom rule shall never end, for he will reign as Head.

We worship God, the Holy Spirit, our Lord, Life-giver known,
With Fath'r and Son is glorified, Who by the prophets spoke.

And we believe in one true Church, God's people for all time,
Cath'lic in scope, and built upon the apostolic line.

Acknowledging one baptism, for forgiv'ness of our sin,
We look for Resurrection day–the dead shall live again.

We look for those unending days, life of the Age to come,
When Christ's great Reign shall come to earth, and God's will shall be done!

APPENDIX 3

The Story of God: Our Sacred Roots

Rev. Dr. Don L. Davis

The Alpha and the Omega	Christus Victor	Come, Holy Spirit	Your Word Is Truth	The Great Confession	His Life in Us	Living in the Way	Reborn to Serve
The LORD God is the source, sustainer, and end of all things in the heavens and earth. All things were formed and exist by his will and for his eternal glory, the triune God, Father, Son, and Holy Spirit, Rom. 11.36.							
The Triune God's Unfolding Drama God's Self-Revelation in Creation, Israel, and Christ				The Church's Participation in God's Unfolding Drama Fidelity to the Apostolic Witness to Christ and His Kingdom			
The Objective Foundation: The Sovereign Love of God *God's Narration of His Saving Work in Christ*				The Subjective Practice: Salvation by Grace through Faith *The Redeemed's Joyous Response to God's Saving Work in Christ*			
The Author of the Story	*The Champion* of the Story	*The Interpreter* of the Story	*The Testimony* of the Story	*The People* of the Story	*Re-enactment* of the Story	*Embodiment* of the Story	*Continuation* of the Story
The Father as *Director*	Jesus as *Lead Actor*	The Spirit as *Narrator*	Scripture as *Script*	As Saints, *Confessors*	As Worshipers, *Ministers*	As Followers, *Sojourners*	As Servants, *Ambassadors*
Christian *Worldview*	Communal *Identity*	Spiritual *Experience*	Biblical *Authority*	Orthodox *Theology*	Priestly *Worship*	Congregational *Discipleship*	Kingdom *Witness*
Theistic and Trinitarian Vision	Christ-centered Foundation	Spirit-Indwelt and -Filled Community	Canonical and Apostolic Witness	Ancient Creedal Affirmation of Faith	Weekly Gathering in Christian Assembly	Corporate, Ongoing Spiritual Formation	Active Agents of the Reign of God
Sovereign Willing	Messianic Representing	Divine Comforting	Inspired Testifying	Truthful Retelling	Joyful Excelling	Faithful Indwelling	Hopeful Compelling
Creator True Maker of the Cosmos	Recapitulation Typos and Fulfillment of the Covenant	Life-Giver Regeneration and Adoption	Divine Inspiration God-breathed Word	The Confession of Faith Union with Christ	Song and Celebration Historical Recitation	Pastoral Oversight Shepherding the Flock	Explicit Unity Love for the Saints
Owner Sovereign Disposer of Creation	Revealer Incarnation of the Word	Teacher Illuminator of the Truth	Sacred History Historical Record	Baptism into Christ Communion of Saints	Homilies and Teachings Prophetic Proclamation	Shared Spirituality Common Journey through the Spiritual Disciplines	Radical Hospitality Evidence of God's Kingdom Reign
Ruler Blessed Controller of All Things	Redeemer Reconciler of All Things	Helper Endowment and the Power	Biblical Theology Divine Commentary	The Rule of Faith Apostles' Creed and Nicene Creed	The Lord's Supper Dramatic Re-enactment	Embodiment Anamnesis and Prolepsis through the Church Year	Extravagant Generosity Good Works
Covenant Keeper Faithful Promisor	Restorer Christ, the Victor over the powers of evil	Guide Divine Presence and Shekinah	Spiritual Food Sustenance for the Journey	The Vincentian Canon Ubiquity, antiquity, universality	Eschatological Foreshadowing The Already/Not Yet	Effective Discipling Spiritual Formation in the Believing Assembly	Evangelical Witness Making Disciples of All People Groups

APPENDIX 4

The Theology of Christus Victor

A Christ-Centered Biblical Motif for Integrating and Renewing the Urban Church

Rev. Dr. Don L. Davis

	The Promised Messiah	The Word Made Flesh	The Son of Man	The Suffering Servant	The Lamb of God	The Victorious Conqueror	The Reigning Lord in Heaven	The Bridegroom and Coming King
Biblical Framework	Israel's hope of Yahweh's anointed who would redeem his people	In the person of Jesus of Nazareth, the Lord has come to the world	As the promised king and divine Son of Man, Jesus reveals the Father's glory and salvation to the world	As Inaugurator of the Kingdom of God, Jesus demonstrates God's reign present through his words, wonders, and works	As both High Priest and Paschal Lamb, Jesus offers himself to God on our behalf as a sacrifice for sin	In his resurrection from the dead and ascension to God's right hand, Jesus is proclaimed as Victor over the power of sin and death	Now reigning at God's right hand till his enemies are made his footstool, Jesus pours out his benefits on his body	Soon the risen and ascended Lord will return to gather his Bride, the Church, and consummate his work
Scripture References	Isa. 9.6-7 Jer. 23.5-6 Isa. 11.1-10	John 1.14-18 Matt. 1.20-23 Phil. 2.6-8	Matt. 2.1-11 Num. 24.17 Luke 1.78-79	Mark 1.14-15 Matt. 12.25-30 Luke 17.20-21	2 Cor. 5.18-21 Isa. 52-53 John 1.29	Eph. 1.16-23 Phil. 2.5-11 Col. 1.15-20	1 Cor. 15.25 Eph. 4.15-16 Acts. 2.32-36	Rom. 14.7-9 Rev. 5.9-13 1 Thess. 4.13-18
Jesus' History	The pre-incarnate, only begotten Son of God in glory	His conception by the Spirit, and birth to Mary	His manifestation to the Magi and to the world	His teaching, exorcisms, miracles, and mighty works among the people	His suffering, crucifixion, death, and burial	His resurrection, with appearances to his witnesses, and his ascension to the Father	The sending of the Holy Spirit and his gifts, and Christ's session in heaven at the Father's right hand	His soon return from heaven to earth as Lord and Christ: the Second Coming
Description	The biblical promise for the seed of Abraham, the prophet like Moses, the son of David	In the Incarnation, God has come to us; Jesus reveals to humankind the Father's glory in fullness	In Jesus, God has shown his salvation to the entire world, including the Gentiles	In Jesus, the promised Kingdom of God has come visibly to earth, demonstrating his binding of Satan and rescinding the Curse	As God's perfect Lamb, Jesus offers himself up to God as a sin offering on behalf of the entire world	In his resurrection and ascension, Jesus destroyed death, disarmed Satan, and rescinded the Curse	Jesus is installed at the Father's right hand as Head of the Church, Firstborn from the dead, and supreme Lord in heaven	As we labor in his harvest field in the world, so we await Christ's return, the fulfillment of his promise
Church Year	**Advent**	**Christmas**	**Season after Epiphany** Baptism and Transfiguration	**Lent**	**Holy Week** Passion	**Eastertide** Easter, Ascension Day, Pentecost	**Season after Pentecost** Trinity Sunday	**Season after Pentecost** All Saints Day, Reign of Christ the King
	The Coming of Christ	*The Birth of Christ*	*The Manifestation of Christ*	*The Ministry of Christ*	*The Suffering and Death of Christ*	*The Resurrection and Ascension of Christ*	*The Heavenly Session of Christ*	*The Reign of Christ*
Spiritual Formation	As we await his Coming, let us proclaim and affirm the hope of Christ	O Word made flesh, let us every heart prepare him room to dwell	Divine Son of Man, show the nations your salvation and glory	In the person of Christ, the power of the reign of God has come to earth and to the Church	May those who share the Lord's death be resurrected with him	Let us participate by faith in the victory of Christ over the power of sin, Satan, and death	Come, indwell us, Holy Spirit, and empower us to advance Christ's Kingdom in the world	We live and work in expectation of his soon return, seeking to please him in all things

APPENDIX 5

Christus Victor

An Integrated Vision for the Christian Life

Rev. Dr. Don L. Davis

For the Church

- The Church is the primary extension of Jesus in the world
- Ransomed treasure of the victorious, risen Christ
- *Laos:* The people of God
- God's new creation: presence of the future
- Locus and agent of the Already/Not Yet Kingdom

For Theology and Doctrine

- The authoritative Word of Christ's victory: the Apostolic Tradition: the Holy Scriptures
- Theology as commentary on the grand narrative of God
- *Christus Victor* as core theological framework for meaning in the world
- The Nicene Creed: the Story of God's triumphant grace

For Spirituality

- The Holy Spirit's presence and power in the midst of God's people
- Sharing in the disciplines of the Spirit
- Gatherings, lectionary, liturgy, and our observances in the Church Year
- Living the life of the risen Christ in the rhythm of our ordinary lives

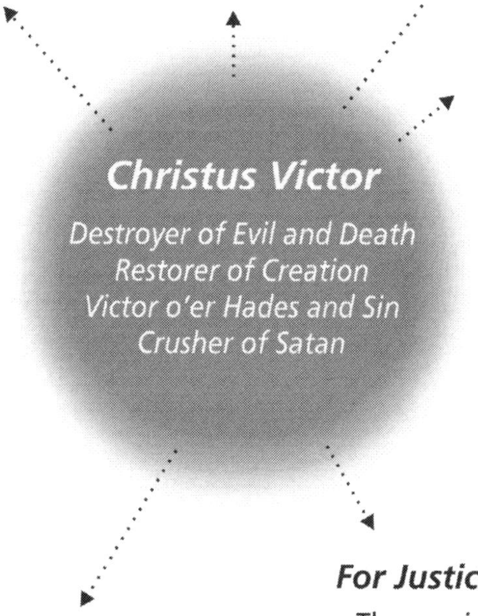

Christus Victor

Destroyer of Evil and Death
Restorer of Creation
Victor o'er Hades and Sin
Crusher of Satan

For Gifts

- God's gracious endowments and benefits from *Christus Victor*
- Pastoral offices to the Church
- The Holy Spirit's sovereign dispensing of the gifts
- Stewardship: divine, diverse gifts for the common good

For Worship

- People of the Resurrection: unending celebration of the people of God
- Remembering, participating in the Christ event in our worship
- Listen and respond to the Word
- Transformed at the Table, the Lord's Supper
- The presence of the Father through the Son in the Spirit

For Evangelism and Mission

- Evangelism as unashamed declaration and demonstration of *Christus Victor* to the world
- The Gospel as Good News of kingdom pledge
- We proclaim God's Kingdom come in the person of Jesus of Nazareth
- The Great Commission: go to all people groups making disciples of Christ and his Kingdom
- Proclaiming Christ as Lord and Messiah

For Justice and Compassion

- The gracious and generous expressions of Jesus through the Church
- The Church displays the very life of the Kingdom
- The Church demonstrates the very life of the Kingdom of heaven right here and now
- Having freely received, we freely give (no sense of merit or pride)
- Justice as tangible evidence of the Kingdom come

APPENDIX 6

Old Testament Witness to Christ and His Kingdom

Rev. Dr. Don L. Davis

Christ Is Seen in the OT's:	*Covenant Promise and Fulfillment*	*Moral Law*	*Christophanies*	*Typology*	*Tabernacle, Festival, and Levitical Priesthood*	*Messianic Prophecy*	*Salvation Promises*
Passage	Gen. 12.1-3	Matt. 5.17-18	John 1.18	1 Cor. 15.45	Heb. 8.1-6	Mic. 5.2	Isa. 9.6-7
Example	The Promised Seed of the Abrahamic covenant	The Law given on Mount Sinai	Commander of the Lord's army	Jonah and the great fish	Melchizedek, as both High Priest and King	The Lord's Suffering Servant	Righteous Branch of David
Christ As	Seed of the woman	The Prophet of God	God's present Revelation	Antitype of God's drama	Our eternal High Priest	The coming Son of Man	Israel's Redeemer and King
Where Illustrated	Galatians	Matthew	John	Matthew	Hebrews	Luke and Acts	John and Revelation
Exegetical Goal	To see Christ as heart of God's sacred drama	To see Christ as fulfillment of the Law	To see Christ as God's revealer	To see Christ as antitype of divine typos	To see Christ in the Temple *cultus*	To see Christ as true Messiah	To see Christ as coming King
How Seen in the NT	As fulfillment of God's sacred oath	As *telos* of the Law	As full, final, and superior revelation	As substance behind the historical shadows	As reality behind the rules and roles	As the Kingdom made present	As the One who will rule on David's throne
Our Response in Worship	God's veracity and faithfulness	God's perfect righteousness	God's presence among us	God's inspired Scripture	God's ontology: his realm as primary and determinative	God's anointed servant and mediator	God's resolve to restore his kingdom authority
How God Is Vindicated	God does not lie: he's true to his word	Jesus fulfills all righteousness	God's fulness is revealed to us in Jesus of Nazareth	The Spirit spoke by the prophets	The Lord has provided a mediator for humankind	Every jot and tittle written of him will occur	Evil will be put down, creation restored, under his reign

APPENDIX 7

Summary Outline of the Scriptures

Rev. Dr. Don L. Davis

1. GENESIS - Beginnings
   a. Adam
   b. Noah
   c. Abraham
   d. Isaac
   e. Jacob
   f. Joseph

2. EXODUS - Redemption, (out of)
   a. Slavery
   b. Deliverance
   c. Law
   d. Tabernacle

3. LEVITICUS - Worship and Fellowship
   a. Offerings, sacrifices
   b. Priests
   c. Feasts, festivals

4. NUMBERS - Service and Walk
   a. Organized
   b. Wanderings

5. DEUTERONOMY - Obedience
   a. Moses reviews history and law
   b. Civil and social laws
   c. Palestinian Covenant
   d. Moses' blessing and death

6. JOSHUA - Redemption (into)
   a. Conquer the land
   b. Divide up the land
   c. Joshua's farewell

7. JUDGES - God's Deliverance
   a. Disobedience and judgment
   b. Israel's twelve judges
   c. Lawless conditions

8. RUTH - Love
   a. Ruth chooses
   b. Ruth works
   c. Ruth waits
   d. Ruth rewarded

9. 1 SAMUEL - Kings, Priestly Perspective
   a. Eli
   b. Samuel
   c. Saul
   d. David

10. 2 SAMUEL - David
    a. King of Judah (9 years - Hebron)
    b. King of all Israel (33 years - Jerusalem)

11. 1 KINGS - Solomon's Glory, Kingdom's Decline
    a. Solomon's glory
    b. Kingdom's decline
    c. Elijah the prophet

12. 2 KINGS- Divided Kingdom
    a. Elisha
    b. Israel (N. Kingdom falls)
    c. Judah (S. Kingdom falls)

13. 1 CHRONICLES - David's Temple Arrangements
    a. Genealogies
    b. End of Saul's reign
    c. Reign of David
    d. Temple preparations

14. 2 CHRONICLES - Temple and Worship Abandoned
    a. Solomon
    b. Kings of Judah

15. EZRA - The Minority (Remnant)
    a. First return from exile - Zerubbabel
    b. Second return from exile - Ezra (priest)

16. NEHEMIAH - Rebuilding by Faith
    a. Rebuild walls
    b. Revival
    c. Religious reform

17. ESTHER - Female Savior
    a. Esther
    b. Haman
    c. Mordecai
    d. Deliverance: Feast of Purim

18. JOB - Why the Righteous Suffer
    a. Godly Job
    b. Satan's attack
    c. Four philosophical friends
    d. God lives

19. PSALMS - Prayer and Praise
    a. Prayers of David
    b. Godly suffer; deliverance
    c. God deals with Israel
    d. Suffering of God's people - end with the Lord's reign
    e. The Word of God (Messiah's suffering and glorious return)

20. PROVERBS - Wisdom
    a. Wisdom versus folly
    b. Solomon
    c. Solomon - Hezekiah
    d. Agur
    e. Lemuel

21. ECCLESIASTES - Vanity
    a. Experimentation
    b. Observation
    c. Consideration

22. SONG OF SOLOMON - Love Story

23. ISAIAH - The Justice (Judgment) and Grace (Comfort) of God
    a. Prophecies of punishment
    b. History
    c. Prophecies of blessing

24. JEREMIAH - Judah's Sin Leads to Babylonian Captivity
    a. Jeremiah's call; empowered
    b. Judah condemned; predicted Babylonian captivity
    c. Restoration promised
    d. Prophesied judgment inflicted
    e. Prophesies against Gentiles
    f. Summary of Judah's captivity

25. LAMENTATIONS - Lament over Jerusalem
    a. Affliction of Jerusalem
    b. Destroyed because of sin
    c. The prophet's suffering
    d. Present desolation versus past splendor
    e. Appeal to God for mercy

26. EZEKIEL - Israel's Captivity and Restoration
    a. Judgment on Judah and Jerusalem
    b. Judgment on Gentile nations
    c. Israel restored; Jerusalem's future glory

27. DANIEL - The Time of the Gentiles
    a. History; Nebuchadnezzar, Belshazzar, Daniel
    b. Prophecy

28. HOSEA - Unfaithfulness
    a. Unfaithfulness
    b. Punishment
    c. Restoration

29. JOEL - The Day of the Lord
    a. Locust plague
    b. Events of the future day of the Lord
    c. Order of the future day of the Lord

30. AMOS - God Judges Sin
    a. Neighbors judged
    b. Israel judged
    c. Visions of future judgment
    d. Israel's past judgment blessings

31. OBADIAH - Edom's Destruction
    a. Destruction prophesied
    b. Reasons for destruction
    c. Israel's future blessing

32. JONAH - Gentile Salvation
    a. Jonah disobeys
    b. Other suffer
    c. Jonah punished
    d. Jonah obeys; thousands saved
    e. Jonah displeased, no love for souls

33. MICAH - Israel's Sins, Judgment, and Restoration
    a. Sin and judgment
    b. Grace and future restoration
    c. Appeal and petition

34. NAHUM - Nineveh Condemned
    a. God hates sin
    b. Nineveh's doom prophesied
    c. Reasons for doom

35. HABAKKUK - The Just Shall Live by Faith
    a. Complaint of Judah's unjudged sin
    b. Chaldeans will punish
    c. Complaint of Chaldeans' wickedness
    d. Punishment promised
    e. Prayer for revival; faith in God

36. ZEPHANIAH - Babylonian Invasion Prefigures the Day of the Lord
    a. Judgment on Judah foreshadows the Great Day of the Lord
    b. Judgment on Jerusalem and neighbors foreshadows final judgment of all nations
    c. Israel restored after judgments

37. HAGGAI - Rebuild the Temple
    a. Negligence
    b. Courage
    c. Separation
    d. Judgment

38. ZECHARIAH - Two Comings of Christ
    a. Zechariah's vision
    b. Bethel's question; Jehovah's answer
    c. Nation's downfall and salvation

39. MALACHI - Neglect
    a. The priest's sins
    b. The people's sins
    c. The faithful few

Summary Outline of the Scriptures (continued)

1. MATTHEW - Jesus the King
   - a. The Person of the King
   - b. The Preparation of the King
   - c. The Propaganda of the King
   - d. The Program of the King
   - e. The Passion of the King
   - f. The Power of the King

2. MARK - Jesus the Servant
   - a. John introduces the Servant
   - b. God the Father identifies the Servant
   - c. The temptation initiates the Servant
   - d. Work and word of the Servant
   - e. Death, burial, resurrection

3. LUKE - Jesus Christ the Perfect Man
   - a. Birth and family of the Perfect Man
   - b. Testing of the Perfect Man; hometown
   - c. Ministry of the Perfect Man
   - d. Betrayal, trial, and death of the Perfect Man
   - e. Resurrection of the Perfect Man

4. JOHN - Jesus Christ is God
   - a. Prologue - the Incarnation
   - b. Introduction
   - c. Witness of Jesus to his Apostles
   - d. Passion - witness to the world
   - e. Epilogue

5. ACTS - The Holy Spirit Working in the Church
   - a. The Lord Jesus at work by the Holy Spirit through the Apostles at Jerusalem
   - b. In Judea and Samaria
   - c. To the uttermost parts of the Earth

6. ROMANS - The Righteousness of God
   - a. Salutation
   - b. Sin and salvation
   - c. Sanctification
   - d. Struggle
   - e. Spirit-filled living
   - f. Security of salvation
   - g. Segregation
   - h. Sacrifice and service
   - i. Separation and salutation

7. 1 CORINTHIANS - The Lordship of Christ
   - a. Salutation and thanksgiving
   - b. Conditions in the Corinthian body
   - c. Concerning the Gospel
   - d. Concerning collections

8. 2 CORINTHIANS - The Ministry in the Church
   - a. The comfort of God
   - b. Collection for the poor
   - c. Calling of the Apostle Paul

9. GALATIANS - Justification by Faith
   - a. Introduction
   - b. Personal - Authority of the Apostle and glory of the Gospel
   - c. Doctrinal - Justification by faith
   - d. Practical - Sanctification by the Holy Spirit
   - e. Autographed conclusion and exhortation

10. EPHESIANS - The Church of Jesus Christ
    - a. Doctrinal - the heavenly calling of the Church
      - A Body
      - A Temple
      - A Mystery
    - b. Practical - The earthly conduct of the Church
      - A New Man
      - A Bride
      - An Army

11. PHILIPPIANS - Joy in the Christian Life
    - a. Philosophy for Christian living
    - b. Pattern for Christian living
    - c. Prize for Christian living
    - d. Power for Christian living

12. COLOSSIANS - Christ the Fullness of God
    - a. Doctrinal - In Christ believers are made full
    - b. Practical - Christ's life poured out in believers, and through them

13. 1 THESSALONIANS - The Second Coming of Christ:
    - a. Is an inspiring hope
    - b. Is a working hope
    - c. Is a purifying hope
    - d. Is a comforting hope
    - e. Is a rousing, stimulating hope

14. 2 THESSALONIANS - The Second Coming of Christ
    - a. Persecution of believers now; judgment of unbelievers hereafter (at coming of Christ)
    - b. Program of the world in connection with the coming of Christ
    - c. Practical issues associated with the coming of Christ

15. 1 TIMOTHY - Government and Order in the Local Church
    - a. The faith of the Church
    - b. Public prayer and women's place in the Church
    - c. Officers in the Church
    - d. Apostasy in the Church
    - e. Duties of the officer of the Church

16. 2 TIMOTHY - Loyalty in the Days of Apostasy
    - a. Afflictions of the Gospel
    - b. Active in service
    - c. Apostasy coming; authority of the Scriptures
    - d. Allegiance to the Lord

17. TITUS - The Ideal New Testament Church
    - a. The Church is an organization
    - b. The Church is to teach and preach the Word of God
    - c. The Church is to perform good works

18. PHILEMON - Reveal Christ's Love and Teach Brotherly Love
    - a. Genial greeting to Philemon and family
    - b. Good reputation of Philemon
    - c. Gracious plea for Onesimus
    - d. Guiltless illustration of Imputation
    - e. General and personal requests

19. HEBREWS - The Superiority of Christ
    - a. Doctrinal - Christ is better than the Old Testament economy
    - b. Practical - Christ brings better benefits and duties

20. JAMES - Ethics of Christianity
    - a. Faith tested
    - b. Difficulty of controlling the tongue
    - c. Warning against worldliness
    - d. Admonitions in view of the Lord's coming

21. 1 PETER - Christian Hope in the Time of Persecution and Trial
    - a. Suffering and security of believers
    - b. Suffering and the Scriptures
    - c. Suffering and the sufferings of Christ
    - d. Suffering and the Second Coming of Christ

22. 2 PETER - Warning Against False Teachers
    - a. Addition of Christian graces gives assurance
    - b. Authority of the Scriptures
    - c. Apostasy brought in by false testimony
    - d. Attitude toward Return of Christ: test for apostasy
    - e. Agenda of God in the world
    - f. Admonition to believers

23. 1 JOHN - The Family of God
    - a. God is Light
    - b. God is Love
    - c. God is Life

24. 2 JOHN - Warning against Receiving Deceivers
    - a. Walk in truth
    - b. Love one another
    - c. Receive not deceivers
    - d. Find joy in fellowship

25. 3 JOHN - Admonition to Receive True Believers
    - a. Gaius, brother in the Church
    - b. Diotrephes
    - c. Demetrius

26. JUDE - Contending for the Faith
    - a. Occasion of the epistle
    - b. Occurrences of apostasy
    - c. Occupation of believers in the days of apostasy

27. REVELATION - The Unveiling of Christ Glorified
    - a. The person of Christ in glory
    - b. The possession of Jesus Christ - the Church in the World
    - c. The program of Jesus Christ - the scene in Heaven
    - d. The seven seals
    - e. The seven trumpets
    - f. Important persons in the last days
    - g. The seven vials
    - h. The fall of Babylon
    - i. The eternal state

APPENDIX 8

From Before to Beyond Time:

The Plan of God and Human History

Adapted from: Suzanne de Dietrich. ***God's Unfolding Purpose.*** *Philadelphia: Westminster Press, 1976.*

I. Before Time (Eternity Past) 1 Cor. 2.7

A. The Eternal Triune God
B. God's Eternal Purpose
C. The Mystery of Iniquity
D. The Principalities and Powers

II. Beginning of Time (Creation and Fall) Gen. 1.1

A. Creative Word
B. Humanity
C. Fall
D. Reign of Death and First Signs of Grace

III. Unfolding of Time (God's Plan Revealed Through Israel) Gal. 3.8

A. Promise (Patriarchs)
B. Exodus and Covenant at Sinai
C. Promised Land
D. The City, the Temple, and the Throne (Prophet, Priest, and King)
E. Exile
F. Remnant

IV. Fullness of Time (Incarnation of the Messiah) Gal. 4.4-5

A. The King Comes to His Kingdom
B. The Present Reality of His Reign
C. The Secret of the Kingdom: the Already and the Not Yet
D. The Crucified King
E. The Risen Lord

V. The Last Times (The Descent of the Holy Spirit) Acts 2.16-18

A. Between the Times: the Church as Foretaste of the Kingdom
B. The Church as Agent of the Kingdom
C. The Conflict Between the Kingdoms of Darkness and Light

VI. The Fulfillment of Time (The Second Coming) Matt. 13.40-43

A. The Return of Christ
B. Judgment
C. The Consummation of His Kingdom

VII. Beyond Time (Eternity Future) 1 Cor. 15.24-28

A. Kingdom Handed Over to God the Father
B. God as All in All

From Before to Beyond Time

Scriptures for Major Outline Points

I. Before Time (Eternity Past)

1 Cor. 2.7 (ESV) - But we impart a secret and hidden wisdom of God, *which God decreed before the ages* for our glory (cf. Titus 1.2).

II. Beginning of Time (Creation and Fall)

Gen. 1.1 (ESV) - *In the beginning*, God created the heavens and the earth.

III. Unfolding of Time (God's Plan Revealed Through Israel)

Gal. 3.8 (ESV) - And the Scripture, foreseeing that God would justify the Gentiles by faith, *preached the Gospel beforehand to Abraham*, saying, "In you shall all the nations be blessed" (cf. Rom. 9.4-5).

IV. Fullness of Time (The Incarnation of the Messiah)

Gal. 4.4-5 (ESV) - *But when the fullness of time had come*, God sent forth his Son, born of woman, born under the law, to redeem those who were under the law, so that we might receive adoption as sons.

V. The Last Times (The Descent of the Holy Spirit)

Acts 2.16-18 (ESV) - But this is what was uttered through the prophet Joel: "'*And in the last days it shall be*,' God declares, 'that I will pour out my Spirit on all flesh, and your sons and your daughters shall prophesy, and your young men shall see visions, and your old men shall dream dreams; even on my male servants and female servants in those days I will pour out my Spirit, and they shall prophesy.'"

VI. The Fulfillment of Time (The Second Coming)

Matt. 13.40-43 (ESV) - Just as the weeds are gathered and burned with fire, *so will it be at the close of the age*. The Son of Man will send his angels, and they will gather out of his kingdom all causes of sin and all lawbreakers, and throw them into the fiery furnace. In that place there will be weeping and gnashing of teeth. Then the righteous will shine like the sun in the Kingdom of their Father. He who has ears, let him hear.

VII. Beyond Time (Eternity Future)

1 Cor. 15.24-28 (ESV) - Then comes the end, when he delivers the Kingdom to God the Father after destroying every rule and every authority and power. For he must reign until he has put all his enemies under his feet. The last enemy to be destroyed is death. For "God has put all things in subjection under his feet." But when it says, "all things are put in subjection," it is plain that he is excepted who put all things in subjection under him. When all things are subjected to him, then the Son himself will also be subjected to him who put all things in subjection under him, that God may be all in all.

APPENDIX 9

"There Is a River"

Identifying the Streams of a Revitalized Authentic Christian Community in the City[1]

Rev. Dr. Don L. Davis • Psalm 46.4 (ESV) - There is a river whose streams make glad the city of God, the holy habitation of the Most High.

Tributaries of Authentic Historic Biblical Faith			
Recognized Biblical Identity	*Revived Urban Spirituality*	*Reaffirmed Historical Connectivity*	*Refocused Kingdom Authority*
*The Church Is **One***	*The Church Is **Holy***	*The Church Is **Catholic***	*The Church Is **Apostolic***
A Call to Biblical Fidelity *Recognizing the Scriptures as the anchor and foundation of the Christian faith and practice*	A Call to the Freedom, Power, and Fullness of the Holy Spirit *Walking in the holiness, power, gifting, and liberty of the Holy Spirit in the body of Christ*	A Call to Historic Roots and Continuity *Confessing the common historical identity and continuity of authentic Christian faith*	A Call to the Apostolic Faith *Affirming the apostolic tradition as the authoritative ground of the Christian hope*
A Call to Messianic Kingdom Identity *Rediscovering the story of the promised Messiah and his Kingdom in Jesus of Nazareth*	A Call to Live as Sojourners and Aliens as the People of God *Defining authentic Christian discipleship as faithful membership among God's people*	A Call to Affirm and Express the Global Communion of Saints *Expressing cooperation and collaboration with all other believers, both local and global*	A Call to Representative Authority *Submitting joyfully to God's gifted servants in the Church as undershepherds of true faith*
A Call to Creedal Affinity *Embracing the Nicene Creed as the shared rule of faith of historic orthodoxy*	A Call to Liturgical, Sacramental, and Catechetical Vitality *Experiencing God's presence in the context of the Word, sacrament, and instruction*	A Call to Radical Hospitality and Good Works *Expressing kingdom love to all, and especially to those of the household of faith*	A Call to Prophetic and Holistic Witness *Proclaiming Christ and his Kingdom in word and deed to our neighbors and all peoples*

[1] *This schema is an adaptation and is based on the insights of the **Chicago Call** statement of May 1977, where various leading evangelical scholars and practitioners met to discuss the relationship of modern evangelicalism to the historic Christian faith.*

APPENDIX 10

A Schematic for a Theology of the Kingdom and the Church

The Urban Ministry Institute

The Reign of the One, True, Sovereign, and Triune God, the LORD God, Yahweh, God the Father, Son, and Holy Spirit		
The Father Love - 1 John 4.8 Maker of heaven and earth and of all things visible and invisible	**The Son** Faith - Heb. 12.2 Prophet, Priest, and King	**The Spirit** Hope - Rom. 15.13 Lord of the Church
Creation All that exists through the creative action of God.	**Kingdom** The Reign of God expressed in the rule of his Son Jesus the Messiah.	**Church** The one, holy, apostolic community which functions as a witness to (Acts 28.31) and a foretaste of (Col. 1.12; James 1.18; 1 Pet. 2.9; Rev. 1.6) the Kingdom of God.
Rom. 8.18-21 → The eternal God, sovereign in power, infinite in wisdom, perfect in holiness, and steadfast in love, is the source and goal of all things.	**Freedom** (Slavery) Jesus answered them, "Truly, truly, I say to you, everyone who commits sin is a slave to sin. The slave does not remain in the house forever; the son remains forever. So if the Son sets you free, you will be free indeed." - John 8.34-36 (ESV)	*The Church is an Apostolic Community Where the Word is Rightly Preached, Therefore it is a Community of:* **Calling** - For freedom Christ has set us free; stand firm therefore, and do not submit again to a yoke of slavery. - Gal. 5.1 (ESV) (cf. Rom. 8.28-30; 1 Cor. 1.26-31; Eph. 1.18; 2 Thess. 2.13-14; Jude 1.1) **Faith** - ". . . for unless you believe that I am he you will die in your sins". . . . So Jesus said to the Jews who had believed in him, "If you abide in my word, you are truly my disciples, and you will know the truth, and the truth will set you free." - John 8.24b, 31-32 (ESV) (cf. Ps. 119.45; Rom. 1.17; 5.1-2; Eph. 2.8-9; 2 Tim. 1.13-14; Heb. 2.14-15; James 1.25) **Witness** - The Spirit of the Lord is upon me, because he has anointed me to proclaim good news to the poor. He has sent me to proclaim liberty to the captives and recovering of sight to the blind, to set at liberty those who are oppressed, to proclaim the year of the Lord's favor. - Luke 4.18-19 (ESV) (cf. Lev. 25.10; Prov. 31.8; Matt. 4.17; 28.18-20; Mark 13.10; Acts 1.8; 8.4, 12; 13.1-3; 25.20; 28.30-31)
Rev. 21.1-5 → O, the depth of the riches and wisdom and knowledge of God! How unsearchable are his judgments, and how inscrutable his ways! For who has known the mind of the Lord, or who has been his counselor? Or who has ever given a gift to him, that he might be repaid?" For from him and through him and to him are all things. To him be glory forever! Amen! - Rom. 11.33-36 (ESV) (cf. 1 Cor. 15.23-28; Rev.)	**Wholeness** (Sickness) But he was wounded for our transgressions; he was crushed for our iniquities; upon him was the chastisement that brought us peace, and with his stripes we are healed. - Isa. 53.5 (ESV)	*The Church is One Community Where the Sacraments are Rightly Administered, Therefore it is a Community of:* **Worship** - You shall serve the Lord your God, and he will bless your bread and your water, and I will take sickness away from among you. - Exod. 23.25 (ESV) (cf. Ps. 147.1-3; Heb. 12.28; Col. 3.16; Rev. 15.3-4; 19.5) **Covenant** - And the Holy Spirit also bears witness to us; for after the saying, "This is the covenant that I will make with them after those days, declares the Lord: I will put my laws on their hearts, and write them on their minds," then he adds, "I will remember their sins and their lawless deeds no more." - Heb. 10.15-17 (ESV) (cf. Isa. 54.10-17; Ezek. 34.25-31; 37.26-27; Mal. 2.4-5; Luke 22.20; 2 Cor. 3.6; Col. 3.15; Heb. 8.7-13; 12.22-24; 13.20-21) **Presence** - In him you also are being built together into a dwelling place for God by his Spirit. - Eph. 2.22 (ESV) (cf. Exod. 40.34-38; Ezek. 48.35; Matt. 18.18-20)
Isa. 11.6-9 →	**Justice** (Selfishness) Behold, my servant whom I have chosen, my beloved with whom my soul is well pleased. I will put my Spirit upon him, and he will proclaim justice to the Gentiles. He will not quarrel or cry aloud, nor will anyone hear his voice in the streets; a bruised reed he will not break, and a smoldering wick he will not quench, until he brings justice to victory. - Matt. 12.18-20 (ESV)	*The Church is a Holy Community Where Discipline is Rightly Ordered, Therefore it is a Community of:* **Reconciliation** - For he himself is our peace, who has made us both one and has broken down in his flesh the dividing wall of hostility by abolishing the law of commandments and ordinances, that he might create in himself one new man in place of the two, so making peace, and might reconcile us both to God in one body through the cross, thereby killing the hostility. And he came and preached peace to you who were far off and peace to those who were near. For through him we both have access in one Spirit to the Father. - Eph. 2.14-18 (ESV) (cf. Exod. 23.4-9; Lev. 19.34; Deut. 10.18-19; Ezek. 22.29; Mic. 6.8; 2 Cor. 5.16-21) **Suffering** - Since therefore Christ suffered in the flesh, arm yourselves with the same way of thinking, for whoever has suffered in the flesh has ceased from sin, so as to live for the rest of the time in the flesh no longer for human passions but for the will of God. - 1 Pet. 4.1-2 (ESV) (cf. Luke 6.22; 10.3; Rom. 8.17; 2 Tim. 2.3; 3.12; 1 Pet. 2.20-24; Heb. 5.8; 13.11-14) **Service** - But Jesus called them to him and said, "You know that the rulers of the Gentiles lord it over them, and their great ones exercise authority over them. It shall not be so among you. But whoever would be great among you must be your servant, and whoever would be first among you must be your slave even as the Son of Man came not to be served but to serve, and to give his life as a ransom for many." - Matt. 20.25-28 (ESV) (cf. 1 John 4.16-18; Gal. 2.10)

APPENDIX 11

Living in the Already and the Not Yet Kingdom

Rev. Dr. Don L. Davis

The Spirit: The pledge of the inheritance ***(arrabon)***
The Church: The foretaste ***(aparche)*** of the Kingdom
"In Christ": The rich life ***(en Christos)*** we share as citizens of the Kingdom

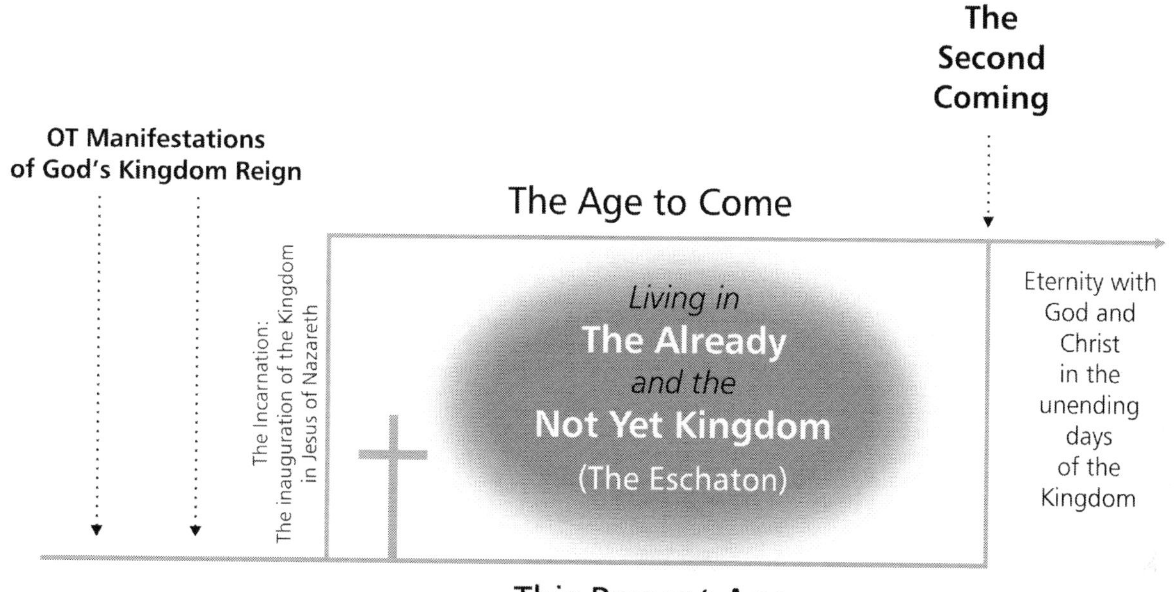

Internal enemy: The flesh (*sarx*) and the sin nature
External enemy: The world (*kosmos*) the systems of greed, lust, and pride
Infernal enemy: The devil (*kakos*) the animating spirit of falsehood and fear

Jewish View of Time

This Present Age

The Age to Come

The Coming of Messiah

The restoration of Israel
The end of Gentile oppression
The return of the earth to Edenic glory
Universal knowledge of the Lord

APPENDIX 12

Jesus of Nazareth: The Presence of the Future

Rev. Dr. Don L. Davis

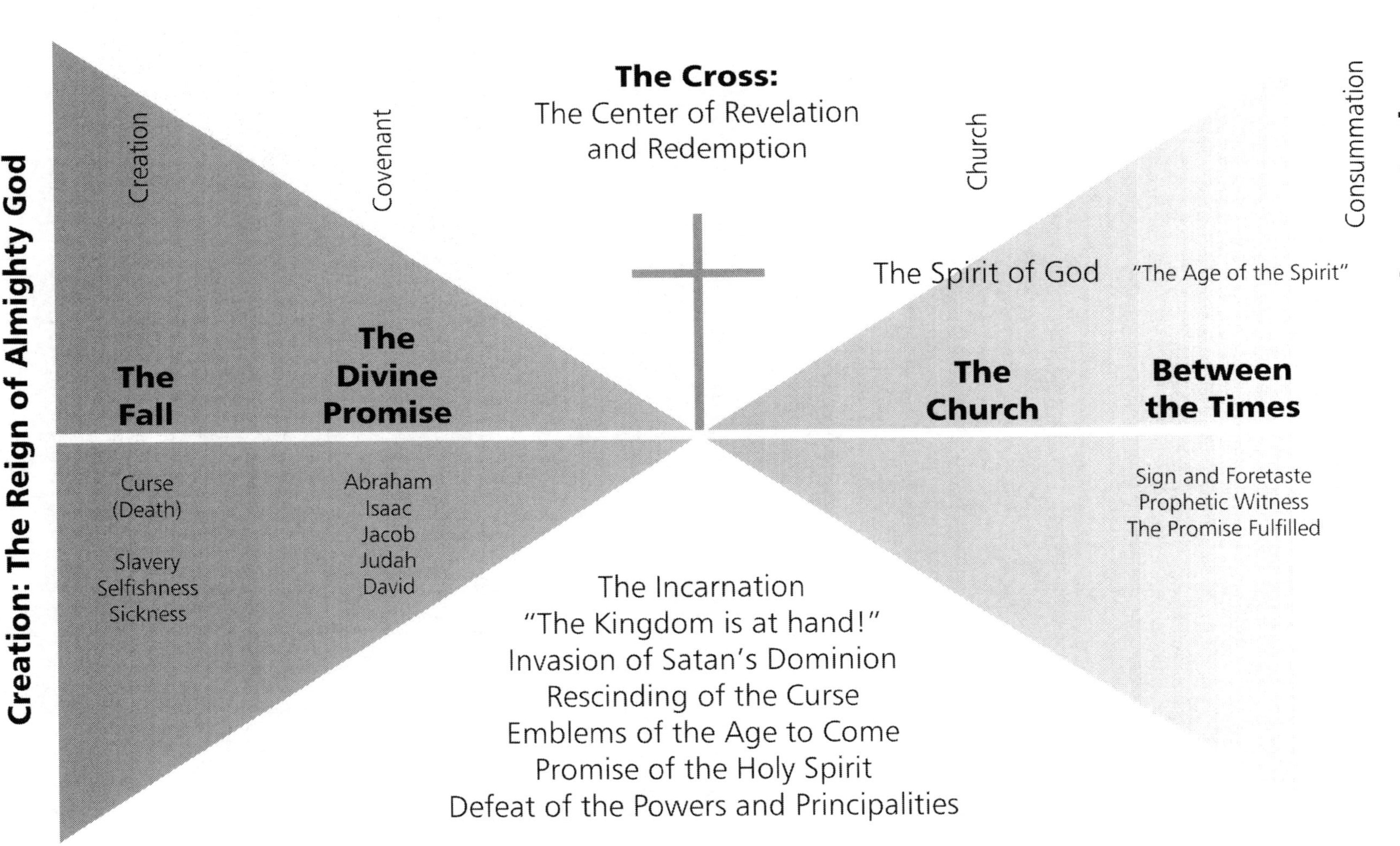

APPENDIX 13

Traditions

(Paradosis)

Dr. Don L. Davis and Rev. Terry G. Cornett

Strong's Definition

Paradosis. Transmission, i.e. (concretely) a precept; specifically, the Jewish traditionary law

Vine's Explanation

denotes "a tradition," and hence, by metonymy, (a) "the teachings of the rabbis," . . . (b) "apostolic teaching," . . . of instructions concerning the gatherings of believers, of Christian doctrine in general . . . of instructions concerning everyday conduct.

1. The concept of tradition in Scripture is essentially positive.

Jer. 6.16 (ESV) - Thus says the Lord: "Stand by the roads, and look, and ask for the ancient paths, where the good way is; and walk in it, and find rest for your souls. But they said, 'We will not walk in it'" (cf. Exod. 3.15; Judg. 2.17; 1 Kings 8.57-58; Ps. 78.1-6).

2 Chron. 35.25 (ESV) - Jeremiah also uttered a lament for Josiah; and all the singing men and singing women have spoken of Josiah in their laments to this day. They made these a rule in Israel; behold, they are written in the Laments (cf. Gen. 32.32; Judg. 11.38-40).

Jer. 35.14-19 (ESV) - The command that Jonadab the son of Rechab gave to his sons, to drink no wine, has been kept, and they drink none to this day, for they have obeyed their father's command. I have spoken to you persistently, but you have not listened to me. I have sent to you all my servants the prophets, sending them persistently, saying, 'Turn now every one of you from his evil way, and amend your deeds, and do not go after other gods to serve them, and then you shall dwell in the land that I gave to you and your fathers.' But you did not incline your ear or listen to me. The sons of Jonadab the son of Rechab have kept the command that their father gave them, but this people has not obeyed me. Therefore, thus says the

Traditions (continued)

Lord, the God of hosts, the God of Israel: Behold, I am bringing upon Judah and all the inhabitants of Jerusalem all the disaster that I have pronounced against them, because I have spoken to them and they have not listened, I have called to them and they have not answered." But to the house of the Rechabites Jeremiah said, "Thus says the Lord of hosts, the God of Israel: Because you have obeyed the command of Jonadab your father and kept all his precepts and done all that he commanded you, therefore thus says the Lord of hosts, the God of Israel: Jonadab the son of Rechab shall never lack a man to stand before me."

2. Godly tradition is a wonderful thing, but not all tradition is godly.

Any individual tradition must be judged by its faithfulness to the Word of God and its usefulness in helping people maintain obedience to Christ's example and teaching.[1] In the Gospels, Jesus frequently rebukes the Pharisees for establishing traditions that nullify rather than uphold God's commands.

Mark 7.8 (ESV) - You leave the commandment of God and hold to the tradition of men" (cf. Matt. 15.2-6; Mark 7.13).

Col. 2.8 (ESV) - See to it that no one takes you captive by philosophy and empty deceit, according to human tradition, according to the elemental spirits of the world, and not according to Christ.

3. Without the fullness of the Holy Spirit, and the constant edification provided to us by the Word of God, tradition will inevitably lead to dead formalism.

Those who are spiritual are filled with the Holy Spirit, whose power and leading alone provides individuals and congregations a sense of freedom and vitality in all they practice and believe. However, when the practices and teachings of any given tradition are no longer infused by the power of the Holy Spirit and the Word of God, tradition loses its effectiveness, and may actually become counterproductive to our discipleship in Jesus Christ.

Eph. 5.18 (ESV) - And do not get drunk with wine, for that is debauchery, but be filled with the Spirit.

[1] "All Protestants insist that these traditions must ever be tested against Scripture and can never possess an independent apostolic authority over or alongside of Scripture." (J. Van Engen, "Tradition," ***Evangelical Dictionary of Theology****, Walter Elwell, Gen. ed.) We would add that Scripture is itself the "authoritative tradition" by which all other traditions are judged. See "Appendix A, The Founders of Tradition: Three Levels of Christian Authority," p. 4.*

Traditions (continued)

Gal. 5.22-25 (ESV) - But the fruit of the Spirit is love, joy, peace, patience, kindness, goodness, faithfulness, gentleness, self-control; against such things there is no law. And those who belong to Christ Jesus have crucified the flesh with its passions and desires. If we live by the Spirit, let us also walk by the Spirit.

2 Cor. 3.5-6 (ESV) - Not that we are sufficient in ourselves to claim anything as coming from us, but our sufficiency is from God, who has made us competent to be ministers of a new covenant, not of the letter but of the Spirit. For the letter kills, but the Spirit gives life.

4. **Fidelity to the Apostolic tradition (teaching and modeling) is the essence of Christian maturity.**

2 Tim. 2.2 (ESV) - and what you have heard from me in the presence of many witnesses entrust to faithful men who will be able to teach others also.

1 Cor. 11.1-2 (ESV) - Be imitators of me, as I am of Christ. Now I commend you because you remember me in everything and maintain the traditions even as I delivered them to you (cf.1 Cor. 4.16-17, 2 Tim. 1.13-14, 2 Thess. 3.7-9, Phil. 4.9).

1 Cor. 15.3-8 (ESV) - For I delivered to you as of first importance what I also received: that Christ died for our sins in accordance with the Scriptures, that he was buried, that he was raised on the third day in accordance with the Scriptures, and that he appeared to Cephas, then to the twelve. Then he appeared to more than five hundred brothers at one time, most of whom are still alive, though some have fallen asleep. Then he appeared to James, then to all the apostles. Last of all, as to one untimely born, he appeared also to me.

5. **The Apostle Paul often includes an appeal to the tradition for support in doctrinal practices.**

1 Cor. 11.16 (ESV) - If anyone is inclined to be contentious, we have no such practice, nor do the churches of God (cf. 1 Cor. 1.2, 7.17, 15.3).

Traditions (continued)

1 Cor. 14.33-34 (ESV) - For God is not a God of confusion but of peace. As in all the churches of the saints, the women should keep silent in the churches. For they are not permitted to speak, but should be in submission, as the Law also says.

6. When a congregation uses received tradition to remain faithful to the "Word of God," they are commended by the Apostles.

1 Cor. 11.2 (ESV) - Now I commend you because you remember me in everything and maintain the traditions even as I delivered them to you.

2 Thess. 2.15 (ESV) - So then, brothers, stand firm and hold to the traditions that you were taught by us, either by our spoken word or by our letter.

2 Thess. 3.6 (ESV) - Now we command you, brothers, in the name of our Lord Jesus Christ, that you keep away from any brother who is walking in idleness and not in accord with the tradition that you received from us.

Appendix A

The Founders of Tradition: Three Levels of Christian Authority

Exod. 3.15 (ESV) - God also said to Moses, "Say this to the people of Israel, 'The Lord, the God of your fathers, the God of Abraham, the God of Isaac, and the God of Jacob, has sent me to you.' This is my name forever, and thus I am to be remembered throughout all generations."

1. The Authoritative Tradition: the Apostles and the Prophets (The Holy Scriptures)

Eph. 2.19-21 (ESV) - So then you are no longer strangers and aliens, but you are fellow citizens with the saints and members of the household of God, built on the foundation of the apostles and prophets, Christ Jesus himself being the cornerstone, in whom the whole structure, being joined together, grows into a holy temple in the Lord.

~ The Apostle Paul

Traditions (continued)

Those who gave eyewitness testimony to the revelation and saving acts of Yahweh, first in Israel, and ultimately in Jesus Christ the Messiah. This testimony is binding for all people, at all times, and in all places. It is the authoritative tradition by which all subsequent tradition is judged.

2. The Great Tradition: The Ecumenical Councils and their Creeds[2]

What has been believed everywhere, always, and by all.

~ Vincent of Lerins

The Great Tradition is the core dogma (doctrine) of the Church. It represents the teaching of the Church as it has understood the Authoritative Tradition (the Holy Scriptures), and summarizes those essential truths that Christians of all ages have confessed and believed. To these doctrinal statements the whole church, (Catholic, Orthodox, and Protestant)[3] gives its assent. The worship and theology of the church reflects this core dogma, which finds its summation and fulfillment in the person and work of Jesus Christ. From earliest times, Christians have expressed their devotion to God in its Church calendar, a yearly pattern of worship which summarizes and reenacts the events of Christ's life.

3. Specific Church Traditions: the Founders of Denominations and Orders

The Presbyterian Church (U.S.A.) has approximately 2.5 million members, 11,200 congregations and 21,000 ordained ministers. Presbyterians trace their history to the 16th century and the Protestant Reformation. Our heritage, and much of what we believe, began with the French lawyer John Calvin (1509-1564), whose writings crystallized much of the Reformed thinking that came before him.

~ The Presbyterian Church, U.S.A.

Christians have expressed their faith in Jesus Christ in various ways through specific movements and traditions which embrace and express the Authoritative Tradition and the Great Tradition in unique ways. For instance,

[2] *See Appendix B, "Defining the Great Tradition."*

[3] *Even the more radical wing of the Protestant reformation (Anabaptists) who were the most reluctant to embrace the creeds as dogmatic instruments of faith, did not disagree with the essential content found in them. "They assumed the Apostolic Creed–they called it 'The Faith,'* **Der Glaube***, as did most people." See John Howard Yoder,* ***Preface to Theology: Christology and Theological Method.*** *Grand Rapids: Brazos Press, 2002. pp. 222-223.*

Traditions (continued)

Catholic movements have arisen around people like Benedict, Francis, or Dominic, and among Protestants people like Martin Luther, John Calvin, Ulrich Zwingli, and John Wesley. Women have founded vital movements of Christian faith (e.g., Aimee Semple McPherson of the Foursquare Church), as well as minorities (e.g., Richard Allen of the African Methodist Episcopal Church or Charles H. Mason of the Church of God in Christ, who also helped to spawn the Assemblies of God), all which attempted to express the Authoritative Tradition and the Great Tradition in a specific way consistent with their time and expression.

The emergence of vital, dynamic movements of the faith at different times and among different peoples reveal the fresh working of the Holy Spirit throughout history. Thus, inside Catholicism, new communities have arisen such as the Benedictines, Franciscans, and Dominicans; and outside Catholicism, new denominations have emerged (Lutherans, Presbyterians, Methodists, Church of God in Christ, etc.). Each of these specific traditions have "founders," key leaders whose energy and vision helped to establish a unique expression of Christian faith and practice. Of course, to be legitimate, these movements must adhere to and faithfully express both the Authoritative Tradition and the Great Tradition. Members of these specific traditions embrace their own unique practices and patterns of spirituality, but these unique features are not necessarily binding on the Church at large. They represent the unique expressions of that community's understanding of and faithfulness to the Authoritative and Great Traditions.

Specific traditions seek to express and live out this faithfulness to the Authoritative and Great Traditions through their worship, teaching, and service. They seek to make the Gospel clear within new cultures or sub-cultures, speaking and modeling the hope of Christ into new situations shaped by their own set of questions posed in light of their own unique circumstances. These movements, therefore, seek to contextualize the Authoritative tradition in a way that faithfully and effectively leads new groups of people to faith in Jesus Christ, and incorporates those who believe into the community of faith that obeys his teachings and gives witness of him to others.

Traditions (continued)

Appendix B

Defining the "Great Tradition"

The Great Tradition (sometimes called the "classical Christian tradition") is defined by Robert E. Webber as follows:

> *[It is] the broad outline of Christian belief and practice developed from the Scriptures between the time of Christ and the middle of the fifth century*
>
> ~ Webber. **The Majestic Tapestry**.
> Nashville: Thomas Nelson Publishers, 1986. p. 10.

This tradition is widely affirmed by Protestant theologians both ancient and modern.

> *Thus those ancient Councils of Nicea, Constantinople, the first of Ephesus, Chalcedon, and the like, which were held for refuting errors, we willingly embrace, and reverence as sacred, in so far as relates to doctrines of faith, for they contain nothing but the pure and genuine interpretation of Scripture, which the holy Fathers with spiritual prudence adopted to crush the enemies of religion who had then arisen.*
>
> ~ John Calvin. **Institutes**. IV, ix. 8.

> *. . . most of what is enduringly valuable in contemporary biblical exegesis was discovered by the fifth century.*
>
> ~ Thomas C. Oden. **The Word of Life**.
> San Francisco: HarperSanFrancisco, 1989. p. xi

> *The first four Councils are by far the most important, as they settled the orthodox faith on the Trinity and the Incarnation.*
>
> ~ Philip Schaff. **The Creeds of Christendom**. Vol. 1.
> Grand Rapids: Baker Book House, 1996. p. 44.

Our reference to the Ecumenical Councils and Creeds is, therefore, focused on those Councils which retain a widespread agreement in the Church among Catholics, Orthodox, and Protestants. While Catholic and Orthodox share common agreement on the first seven councils, Protestants tend to affirm and use primarily the first four. Therefore, those councils which continue to be shared by the whole Church are completed with the Council of Chalcedon in 451.

Traditions (continued)

It is worth noting that each of these four Ecumenical Councils took place in a pre-European cultural context and that none of them were held in Europe. They were councils of the whole Church and they reflected a time in which Christianity was primarily an eastern religion in it's geographic core. By modern reckoning, their participants were African, Asian, and European. The councils reflected a church that ". . . has roots in cultures far distant from Europe and preceded the development of modern European identity, and [of which] some of its greatest minds have been African" (Oden, *The Living God*, San Francisco: HarperSanFrancisco, 1987, p. 9).

Perhaps the most important achievement of the Councils was the creation of what is now commonly called the Nicene Creed. It serves as a summary statement of the Christian faith that can be agreed on by Catholic, Orthodox, and Protestant Christians.

The first four Ecumenical Councils are summarized in the following chart:

Name/Date/Location	Purpose
First Ecumenical Council *325 A.D.* *Nicea, Asia Minor*	Defending against: *Arianism* Question answered: *Was Jesus God?* Action: *Developed the initial form of the Nicene Creed to serve as a summary of the Christian faith*
Second Ecumenical Council *381 A.D.* *Constantinople, Asia Minor*	Defending against: *Macedonianism* Question answered: *Is the Holy Spirit a personal and equal part of the Godhead?* Action: *Completed the Nicene Creed by expanding the article dealing with the Holy Spirit*
Third Ecumenical Council *431 A.D.* *Ephesus, Asia Minor*	Defending against: *Nestorianism* Question answered: *Is Jesus Christ both God and man in one person?* Action: *Defined Christ as the Incarnate Word of God and affirmed his mother Mary as* **theotokos** *(God-bearer)*
Fourth Ecumenical Council *451 A.D.* *Chalcedon, Asia Minor*	Defending against: *Monophysitism* Question answered: *How can Jesus be both God and man?* Action: *Explained the relationship between Jesus' two natures (human and Divine)*

APPENDIX 14

A Theology of the Church in Kingdom Perspective

Don Davis and Terry Cornett

APPENDIX 15

Kingdom Texts in the New Testament

Matt. 3.2 (ESV) - Repent, for the kingdom of heaven is at hand.

Matt. 4.17 (ESV) - From that time Jesus began to preach saying, "Repent, for the kingdom of heaven is at hand."

Matt. 4.23 (ESV) - And he went throughout all Galilee, teaching in their synagogues and proclaiming the gospel of the kingdom and healing every disease and every affliction among the people.

Matt. 5.3 (ESV) - Blessed are the poor in spirit, for theirs is the kingdom of heaven.

Matt. 5.10 (ESV) - Blessed are those who are persecuted for righteousness' sake, for theirs is the kingdom of heaven.

Matt. 5.19-20 (ESV) - Therefore whoever relaxes one of the least of these commandments and teaches others to do the same will be called least in the kingdom of heaven, but whoever does them and teaches them will be called great in the kingdom of heaven. [20] For I tell you, unless your righteousness exceeds that of the scribes and Pharisees, you will never enter the kingdom of heaven..

Matt. 6.10 (ESV) - Your kingdom come, your will be done, on earth as it is in heaven.

Matt. 6.33 (ESV) - But seek first the kingdom of God and his righteousness, and all these things will be added to you.

Matt. 7.21 (ESV) - Not everyone who says to me, "Lord, Lord," will enter the kingdom of heaven, but the one who does the will of my Father who is in heaven.

Matt. 8.11-12 (ESV) - I tell you, many will come from east and west and recline at table with Abraham, Isaac, and Jacob in the kingdom of heaven, [12] while the sons of the kingdom will be thrown into the outer darkness. In that place there will be weeping and gnashing of teeth.

Matt. 9.35 (ESV) - And Jesus went throughout all the cities and villages, teaching in their synagogues and proclaiming the gospel of the kingdom and healing every disease and every affliction.

Kingdom Texts in the New Testament (continued)

Matt. 10.7 (ESV) - And proclaim as you go, saying, "The kingdom of heaven is at hand."

Matt. 11.11-12 (ESV) - Truly, I say to you, among those born of women there has arisen no one greater than John the Baptist. Yet the one who is least in the kingdom of heaven is greater than he. [12] From the days of John the Baptist until now the kingdom of heaven has suffered violence, and the violent take it by force.

Matt. 12.25-26 (ESV) - Knowing their thoughts, he said to them, "Every kingdom divided against itself is laid waste, and no city or house divided against itself will stand. [26] And if Satan casts out Satan, he is divided against himself. How then will his kingdom stand?"

Matt. 12.28 (ESV) - But if it is by the Spirit of God that I cast out demons, then the kingdom of God has come upon you.

Matt. 13.11 (ESV) - And he answered them, "To you it has been given to know the secrets of the kingdom of heaven, but to them it has not been given."

Matt. 13.19 (ESV) - When anyone hears the word of the kingdom, and does not understand it, the evil one comes and snatches away what has been sown in his heart. This is what was sown along the path.

Matt. 13.24 (ESV) - He put another parable before them, saying, "The kingdom of heaven may be compared to a man who sowed good seed in his field."

Matt. 13.31 (ESV) - He put another parable before them, saying, "The kingdom of heaven is like a grain of mustard seed that a man took and sowed in his field."

Matt. 13.33 (ESV) - He told them another parable. "The kingdom of heaven is like leaven, that a woman took and hid in three measures of flour, till it was all leavened."

Matt. 13.38 (ESV) - The field is the world, and the good seed is the children of the kingdom. The weeds are the sons of the evil one.

Matt. 13.41 (ESV) - The Son of Man will send his angels, and they will gather out of his kingdom all causes of sin and all law-breakers.

Kingdom Texts in the New Testament (continued)

Matt. 13.43-45 (ESV) - Then the righteous will shine like the sun in the kingdom of their Father. He who has ears, let him hear. The kingdom of heaven is like treasure hidden in a field, which a man found and covered up. Then in his joy he goes and sells all that he has and buys that field. Again, the kingdom of heaven is like a merchant in search of fine pearls.

Matt. 13.47 (ESV) - Again, the kingdom of heaven is like a net that was thrown into the sea and gathered fish of every kind.

Matt. 13.52 (ESV) - And he said to them, "Therefore every scribe who has been trained for the kingdom of heaven is like a master of a house, who brings out of his treasure what is new and what is old."

Matt. 16.19 (ESV) - I will give you the keys of the kingdom of heaven, and whatever you bind on earth shall be bound in heaven, and whatever you loose on earth shall be loosed in heaven.

Matt. 16.28 (ESV) - Truly I say to you, there are some standing here who will not taste death until they see the Son of Man coming in his kingdom.

Matt. 18.1, 3-4 (ESV) - At that time the disciples came to Jesus, saying, "Who is greatest in the kingdom of heaven?" . . . "Truly, I say to you, unless you turn and become like children, you will never enter the kingdom of heaven. Whoever humbles himself like this child is the greatest in the kingdom of heaven."

Matt. 18.23 (ESV) - Therefore the kingdom of heaven may be compared to a king who wished to settle accounts with his servants.

Matt. 19.12 (ESV) - For there are eunuchs who have been so from birth, and there are eunuchs who have been made eunuchs by men, and there are eunuchs who have made themselves eunuchs for the sake of the kingdom of heaven. Let the one who is able to receive this receive it.

Matt. 19.14 (ESV) - . . . but Jesus said, "Let the little children come to me and do not hinder them, for to such belongs the kingdom of heaven."

Matt. 19.23-24 (ESV) - And Jesus said to his disciples, "Truly, I say to you, only with difficulty will a rich person enter the kingdom of heaven. Again I tell you, it is easier for a camel to go through the eye of a needle than for a rich person to enter the kingdom of God."

Kingdom Texts in the New Testament (continued)

Matt. 20.1 (ESV) - For the kingdom of heaven is like a master of a house who went out early in the morning to hire laborers for his vineyard.

Matt. 20.21 (ESV) - And he said to her, "What do you want?" She said to him, "Say that these two sons of mine are to sit, one at your right hand and one at your left, in your kingdom."

Matt. 21.31 (ESV) - "Which of the two did the will of his father?" They said, "The first." Jesus said to them, "Truly, I say to you, the tax collectors and the prostitutes go into the kingdom of God before you."

Matt. 21.43 (ESV) - Therefore I tell you, the kingdom of God will be taken away from you and given to a people producing its fruits.

Matt. 22.2 (ESV) - The kingdom of heaven may be compared to a king who gave a wedding feast for his son.

Matt. 23.13 (ESV) - But woe to you, scribes and Pharisees, hypocrites! For you shut the kingdom of heaven in people's faces. For you neither enter yourselves nor allow those who would enter to go in.

Matt. 24.7 (ESV) - For nation will rise against nation, and kingdom against kingdom, and there will be famines and earthquakes in various places.

Matt. 24.14 (ESV) - And this gospel of the kingdom will be proclaimed throughout the whole world as a testimony to all nations, and then the end will come.

Matt. 25.1 (ESV) - Then the kingdom of heaven will be like ten virgins who took their lamps and went to meet the bridegroom.

Matt. 25.34 (ESV) - Then the King will say to those on his right, "Come, you who are blessed by my Father, inherit the kingdom prepared for you from the foundation of the world."

Matt. 26.29 (ESV) - I tell you, I will not drink again of this fruit of the vine until that day when I drink it new with you in my Father's kingdom.

Mark 1.15 (ESV) - . . . and saying, "The time is fulfilled, and the kingdom of God is at hand; repent and believe in the gospel."

Mark 3.24 (ESV) - And if a kingdom is divided against itself, that kingdom cannot stand.

Kingdom Texts in the New Testament (continued)

Mark 4.11 (ESV) - And he said to them, "To you has been given the secret of the kingdom of God, but for those outside everything is in parables."

Mark 4.26 (ESV) - And he said, "The kingdom of God is as if a man should scatter seed on the ground."

Mark 4.30 (ESV) - And he said, "With what can we compare the kingdom of God, or what parable shall we use for it?"

Mark 6.23 (ESV) - And he vowed to her, "Whatever you ask of me, I will give you, up to half of my kingdom."

Mark 9.1 (ESV) - And he said to them, "Truly, I say to you, there are some standing here who will not taste death until they see the kingdom of God after it has come with power."

Mark 9.47 (ESV) - And if your eye causes you to sin, tear it out; it is better for you to enter the kingdom of God with one eye than with two eyes to be thrown into hell.

Mark 10.14-15 (ESV) - But when Jesus saw it, he was indignant and said to them, "Let the children to come to me; do not hinder them, for to such belongs kingdom of God. Truly, I say to you, whoever does not receive the kingdom of God like a child shall not enter it."

Mark 10.23-25 (ESV) - And Jesus looked around and said to his disciples, "How difficult it will be for those who have wealth to enter the kingdom of God!" And the disciples were amazed at his words. But Jesus said to them again, "Children, how difficult it is to enter the Kingdom of God! It is easier for a camel to go through the eye of a needle than for a rich person to enter the kingdom of God."

Mark 11.10 (ESV) - Blessed is the coming kingdom of our father David! Hosanna in the highest!

Mark 12.34 (ESV) - And when Jesus saw that he answered wisely, he said to him, "You are not far from the kingdom of God." And after that, no one dared to ask him any more questions.

Mark 13.8 (ESV) - For nation will arise against nation, and kingdom against kingdom. There will be earthquakes in various places; there will be famines. These are but the beginning of the birth pains.

Kingdom Texts in the New Testament (continued)

Mark 14.25 (ESV) - Truly, I say to you, I will not drink again of the fruit of the vine until that day when I drink it new in the kingdom of God.

Mark 15.43 (ESV) - Joseph of Arimathea, a respected member of the Council, who was also himself looking for the kingdom of God, took courage and went to Pilate and asked for the body of Jesus.

Luke 1.33 (ESV) - . . . and he will reign over the house of Jacob forever, and of his kingdom there will be no end.

Luke 4.43 (ESV) - . . . but he said to them, "I must preach the good news of the kingdom of God to the other towns as well; for I was sent for this purpose."

Luke 6.20 (ESV) - And he lifted up his eyes on his disciples, and said, "Blessed are you who are poor, for yours is the kingdom of God."

Luke 7.28 (ESV) - I tell you, among those born of women none is greater than John. Yet the one who is least in the kingdom of God is greater than he.

Luke 8.1 (ESV) - Soon afterwards he went on through cities and villages, proclaiming and bringing the good news of the kingdom of God. And the twelve were with him.

Luke 8.10 (ESV) - . . . he said, "To you it has been given to know the secrets of the kingdom of God, but for others they are in parables, so that 'Seeing they may not see, and hearing they may not understand.'"

Luke 9.2 (ESV) - . . . and he sent them out to proclaim the kingdom of God and to heal.

Luke 9.11 (ESV) - When the crowds learned it, they followed him; and he welcomed them and spoke to them of the kingdom of God and cured those who had need of healing.

Luke 9.27 (ESV) - But I tell you truly, there are some standing here who will not taste death until they see the kingdom of God.

Luke 9.60 (ESV) - And Jesus said to him, "Leave the dead to bury their own dead; but as for you, go and proclaim everywhere the kingdom of God."

Luke 9.62 (ESV) - Jesus said to him, "No one who puts his hand to the plow and looks back is fit for the kingdom of God."

Kingdom Texts in the New Testament (continued)

Luke 10.9 (ESV) - Heal the sick in it and say to them, "The kingdom of God has come near to you."

Luke 10.11 (ESV) - Even the dust of your town that clings to our feet we wipe off against you. Nonetheless know this, that the kingdom of God has come near.

Luke 11.2 (ESV) - And he said to them, "When you pray, say: 'Father, hallowed be your name. Your kingdom come.'"

Luke 11.17-18 (ESV) - But he, knowing their thoughts, said to them, "Every kingdom divided against itself is laid waste, and a divided household falls. And if Satan also is divided against himself, how will his kingdom stand? For you say that I cast out demons by Beelzebul."

Luke 11.20 (ESV) - But if it is by the finger of God that I cast out demons, then the kingdom of God has come upon you.

Luke 12.31-32 (ESV) - Instead, seek his kingdom, and these things will be added to you. Fear not, little flock, for it is your Father's good pleasure to give you the kingdom.

Luke 13.18 (ESV) - He said therefore, "What is the kingdom of God like? And to what shall I compare it?"

Luke 13.20 (ESV) - And again he said, "To what shall I compare the kingdom of God?"

Luke 13.28-29 (ESV) - In that place there will be weeping and gnashing of teeth, when you see Abraham and Isaac and Jacob and all the prophets in the kingdom of God but you yourselves cast out. And people will come from east and west, and from north and south, and will recline at table in the kingdom of God.

Luke 14.15 (ESV) - When one of those who reclined at table with him heard these things, he said to him, "Blessed is everyone who will eat bread in the kingdom of God!"

Luke 16.16 (ESV) - The Law and the Prophets were until John; since then the good news of the kingdom of God is preached, and everyone forces his way into it.

Kingdom Texts in the New Testament (continued)

Luke 17.20-21 (ESV) - Being asked by the Pharisees when the kingdom of God would come, he answered them, "The kingdom of God is not coming with signs to be observed, nor will they say, 'Look, here it is!' or 'There!' for behold, the kingdom of God is in the midst of you."

Luke 18.16-17 (ESV) - But Jesus called them to him, saying, "Let the children come to me, and do not hinder them, for to such belongs the kingdom of God. Truly, I say to you, whoever does not receive the kingdom of God like a child shall not enter it."

Luke 18.24-25 (ESV) - Jesus, looking at him with sadness, said, "How difficult it is for those who have wealth to enter the kingdom of God! For it is easier for a camel to go through the eye of a needle than for a rich person to enter the kingdom of God."

Luke 18.29 (ESV) - And he said to them, "Truly I say to you, there is no one who has left house or wife or brothers or parents or children, for the sake of the kingdom of God . . ."

Luke 19.11-12 (ESV) - As they heard these things, he proceeded to tell a parable, because he was near to Jerusalem, and because they supposed that the kingdom of God was to appear immediately. He said therefore, "A nobleman went into a far country to receive for himself a kingdom for himself and then return."

Luke 19.15 (ESV) - When he returned, having received the kingdom, he ordered these servants to whom he had given the money to be called to him, that he might know what they had gained by doing business.

Luke 21.10 (ESV) - Then he said to them, "Nation will rise against nation, and kingdom against kingdom."

Luke 21.31 (ESV) - So also, when you see these things taking place, you know that the kingdom of God is near.

Luke 22.16 (ESV) - For I tell you, I will not eat it until it is fulfilled in the kingdom of God.

Luke 22.18 (ESV) - For I tell you that from now on I will not drink of the fruit of the vine until the kingdom of God comes.

Kingdom Texts in the New Testament (continued)

Luke 22.29-30 (ESV) - . . . and I assign to you, as my Father assigned to me, a kingdom, that you may eat and drink at my table in my kingdom, and sit on thrones judging the twelve tribes of Israel.

Luke 23.42 (ESV) - And he said, "Jesus, remember me when you come into your kingdom."

Luke 23.51 (ESV) - . . . who had not consented to their decision and action; and he was looking for the kingdom of God.

John 3.3 (ESV) - Jesus answered him, "Truly, truly, I say to you, unless one is born again, he cannot see the kingdom of God."

John 3.5 (ESV) - Jesus answered, "Truly, truly, I say to you, unless one is born of water and the Spirit, he cannot enter the kingdom of God."

John 18.36 (ESV) - Jesus answered, "My kingdom is not of this world. If my kingdom were of this world, my servants would have been fighting, that I might not be delivered over to the Jews. But my kingdom is not from the world."

Acts 1.3 (ESV) - To them he presented himself alive after his suffering by many proofs, appearing to them during forty days and speaking about the kingdom of God.

Acts 1.6 (ESV) - So when they had come together, they asked him, "Lord, will you at this time restore the kingdom to Israel?"

Acts 8.12 (ESV) - But when they believed Philip as he preached good news about the kingdom of God and the name of Jesus Christ, they were baptized, both men and women.

Acts 14.22 (ESV) - . . . strengthening the souls of the disciples, encouraging them to continue in the faith, and saying that through many tribulations we must enter the kingdom of God.

Acts 20.25 (ESV) - And now, behold, I know that none of you among whom I have gone about proclaiming the kingdom will see my face again.

Acts 28.23 (ESV) - When they had appointed a day for him, they came to him at his lodging in greater numbers. From morning till evening he expounded to them, testifying to the kingdom of God and trying to convince them about Jesus both from the Law of Moses and from the Prophets.

Kingdom Texts in the New Testament (continued)

Acts 28.31 (ESV) - . . . proclaiming the kingdom of God and teaching about the Lord Jesus Christ with all openness and without hindrance.

Rom. 14.17 (ESV) - . . . for the kingdom of God is not eating and drinking, but righteousness and peace and joy in the Holy Spirit.

1 Cor. 4.20 (ESV) - For the kingdom of God does not consist in words, but in power.

1 Cor. 6.9-10 (ESV) - Do you not know that the unrighteous will not inherit the kingdom of God? Do not be deceived: neither the sexually immoral, nor idolaters, nor adulterers, nor men who practice homosexuality, [10] nor thieves, nor the greedy, nor drunkards, nor revilers, nor swindlers will inherit the kingdom of God.

1 Cor. 15.24 (ESV) - Then comes the end, when he delivers the kingdom to God the Father after destroying every rule and every authority and power.

1 Cor. 15.50 (ESV) - I tell you this, brothers: flesh and blood cannot inherit the kingdom of God, nor does the perishable inherit the imperishable.

Gal. 5.21 (ESV) - . . . envy, drunkenness, orgies, and things like these. I warn you, as I warned you before, that those who do such things will not inherit the kingdom of God.

Eph. 5.5 (ESV) - For you may be sure of this, that everyone who is sexually immoral or impure, or who is covetous (that is, an idolater), has no inheritance in the kingdom of Christ and God.

Col. 1.13 (ESV) - He has delivered us from the domain of darkness and transferred us to the kingdom of his beloved Son.

Col. 4.11 (ESV) - . . . and Jesus who is called Justus. These are the only men of the circumcision among my fellow workers for the kingdom of God, and they have been a comfort to me.

1 Thess. 2.12 (ESV) - . . . we exhorted each one of you and encouraged you and charged you to walk in a manner worthy of God, who calls you into his own kingdom and glory.

2 Thess. 1.5 (ESV) - This is evidence of the righteous judgment of God, that you may be considered worthy of the kingdom of God, for which you are also suffering.

Kingdom Texts in the New Testament (continued)

2 Tim. 4.1 (ESV) - I charge you in the presence of God and of Christ Jesus, who is to judge the living and the dead, and by his appearing and his kingdom.

2 Tim. 4.18 (ESV) - The Lord will rescue me from every evil deed and bring me safely into his heavenly kingdom. To him be the glory forever and ever. Amen.

Heb. 1.8 (ESV) - But of the Son he says, "Your throne, O God, is forever and ever, the scepter of uprightness is the scepter of your kingdom.

Heb. 12.28 (ESV) - Therefore let us be grateful for receiving a kingdom that cannot be shaken, and thus let us offer to God acceptable worship, with reverence and awe.

James 2.5 (ESV) - Listen, my beloved brothers, has not God chosen those who are poor in the world to be rich in faith and heirs of the kingdom, which he has promised to those who love him?

2 Pet. 1.11 (ESV) - For in this way there will be richly provided for you an entrance into the eternal kingdom of our Lord and Savior Jesus Christ.

Rev. 1.6 (ESV) - . . . and made us a kingdom, priests to his God and Father, to him be glory and dominion forever and ever. Amen.

Rev. 1.9 (ESV) - I, John, your brother and partner in the tribulation and the kingdom and the patient endurance that are in Jesus, was on the island called Patmos on account of the word of God and the testimony of Jesus.

Rev. 5.10 (ESV) - . . . and you have made them a kingdom and priests to our God, and they shall reign on the earth.

Rev. 11.15 (ESV) - Then the seventh angel blew his trumpet, and there were loud voices in heaven, saying, "The kingdom of the world has become the kingdom of our Lord and of his Christ, and he shall reign forever and ever."

Rev. 12.10 (ESV) - And I heard a loud voice in heaven, saying, "Now the salvation and the power and the kingdom of our God and the authority of his Christ have come, for the accuser of our brothers has been thrown down, who accuses them day and night before our God.

Rev. 16.10 (ESV) - The fifth angel poured out his bowl on the throne of the beast, and its kingdom was plunged into darkness. People gnawed their tongues in anguish.

Kingdom Texts in the New Testament (continued)

Rev. 17.12 (ESV) - And the ten horns that you saw are ten kings who have not yet received royal power, but they are to receive authority as kings for one hour, together with the beast.

Rev. 17.17 (ESV) - . . . for God has put it into their hearts to carry out his purpose by being of one mind and handing over their royal power to the beast, until the words of God are fulfilled.

APPENDIX 16

Kingdom Texts in the Old Testament

Exod. 19.3-6 (ESV) - . . . while Moses went up to God. The LORD called to him out of the mountain, saying, "Thus you shall say to the house of Jacob, and tell the people of Israel: [4] You yourselves have seen what I did to the Egyptians, and how I bore you on eagles' wings and brought you to myself. [5] Now therefore, if you will indeed obey my voice and keep my covenant, you shall be my treasured possession among all peoples, for all the earth is mine; [6] and you shall be to me a kingdom of priests and a holy nation. These are the words that you shall speak to the people of Israel."

2 Sam. 7.12-16 (ESV) - When your days are fulfilled and you lie down with your fathers, I will raise up your offspring after you, who shall come from your body, and I will establish his kingdom. [13] He shall build a house for my name, and I will establish the throne of his kingdom forever. [14] I will be to him a father, and he shall be to me a son. When he commits iniquity, I will discipline him with the rod of men, with the stripes of the sons of men, [15] but my steadfast love will not depart from him, as I took it from Saul, whom I put away from before you. [16] And your house and your kingdom shall be made sure forever before me. Your throne shall be established forever.'"

1 Chron. 14.2 (ESV) - And David knew that the LORD had established him as king over Israel, and that his kingdom was highly exalted for the sake of his people Israel.

1 Chron. 16.20 (ESV) - . . . wandering from nation to nation, from one kingdom to another people . . .

1 Chron. 17.11-14 (ESV) - When your days are fulfilled to walk with your fathers, I will raise up your offspring after you, one of your own sons, and I will establish his kingdom. [12] He shall build a house for me, and I will establish his throne forever. [13] I will be to him a father, and he shall be to me a son. I will not take my steadfast love from him, as I took it from him who was before you, [14] but I will confirm him in my house and in my kingdom forever, and his throne shall be established forever.

1 Chron. 22.10 (ESV) - He shall build a house for my name. He shall be my son, and I will be his father, and I will establish his royal throne in Israel forever.

Kingdom Texts in the Old Testament (continued)

1 Chron. 28.7 (ESV) - I will establish his kingdom forever if he continues strong in keeping my commandments and my rules, as he is today.

1 Chron. 29.10-12 (ESV) - Therefore David blessed the LORD in the presence of all the assembly. And David said: "Blessed are you, O LORD, the God of Israel our father, forever and ever. [11] Yours, O LORD, is the greatness and the power and the glory and the victory and the majesty, for all that is in the heavens and in the earth is yours. Yours is the kingdom, O LORD, and you are exalted as head above all. [12] Both riches and honor come from you, and you rule over all. In your hand are power and might, and in your hand it is to make great and to give strength to all."

2 Chron. 32.15 (ESV) - Now, therefore, do not let Hezekiah deceive you or mislead you in this fashion, and do not believe him, for no god of any nation or kingdom has been able to deliver his people from my hand or from the hand of my fathers. How much less will your God deliver you out of my hand!

2 Chron. 33.13 (ESV) - He prayed to him, and God was moved by his entreaty and heard his plea and brought him again to Jerusalem into his kingdom. Then Manasseh knew that the LORD was God.

Neh. 9.32-35 (ESV) - Now, therefore, our God, the great, the mighty, and the awesome God, who keeps covenant and steadfast love, let not all the hardship seem little to you that has come upon us, upon our kings, our princes, our priests, our prophets, our fathers, and all your people, since the time of the kings of Assyria until this day. [33] Yet you have been righteous in all that has come upon us, for you have dealt faithfully and we have acted wickedly. [34] Our kings, our princes, our priests, and our fathers have not kept your law or paid attention to your commandments and your warnings that you gave them. [35] Even in their own kingdom, enjoying your great goodness that you gave them, and in the large and rich land that you set before them, they did not serve you or turn from their wicked works.

Ps. 9.7-8 (ESV) - But the Lord sits enthroned forever; he has established his throne for justice, [8] and he judges the world with righteousness; he judges the peoples with uprightness.

Kingdom Texts in the Old Testament (continued)

Ps. 22.27-28 (ESV) - All the ends of the earth shall remember and turn to the LORD, and all the families of the nations shall worship before you. [28] For kingship belongs to the LORD, and he rules over the nations.

Ps. 45.6 (ESV) - Your throne, O God, is forever and ever. The scepter of your kingdom is a scepter of uprightness.

Ps. 47.7-8 (ESV) - For God is the King of all the earth; sing praises with a psalm! [8] God reigns over the nations; God sits on his holy throne.

Ps. 103.17-19 (ESV) - But the steadfast love of the LORD is from everlasting to everlasting on those who fear him, and his righteousness to children's children, [18] to those who keep his covenant and remember to do his commandments. [19] The LORD has established his throne in the heavens, and his kingdom rules over all.

Ps. 105.13 (ESV) - . . . wandering from nation to nation, from one kingdom to another people.

Ps. 145.9-13 (ESV) - The LORD is good to all, and his mercy is over all that he has made. [10] All your works shall give thanks to you, O LORD, and all your saints shall bless you! [11] They shall speak of the glory of your kingdom and tell of your power, [12] to make known to the children of man your [2] mighty deeds, and the glorious splendor of your kingdom. [13] Your kingdom is an everlasting kingdom, and your dominion endures throughout all generations.

Isa. 2.2-5 (ESV) - It shall come to pass in the latter days that the mountain of the house of the LORD shall be established as the highest of the mountains, and shall be lifted up above the hills; and all the nations shall flow to it, [3] and many peoples shall come, and say: "Come, let us go up to the mountain of the LORD, to the house of the God of Jacob, that he may teach us his ways and that we may walk in his paths." For out of Zion shall go the law, and the word of the LORD from Jerusalem. [4] He shall judge between the nations, and shall decide disputes for many peoples; and they shall beat their swords into plowshares, and their spears into pruning hooks; nation shall not lift up sword against nation, neither shall they learn war anymore. [5] O house of Jacob, come, let us walk in the light of the LORD.

Kingdom Texts in the Old Testament (continued)

Isa. 9.6-7 (ESV) - For to us a child is born, to us a son is given; and the government shall be upon his shoulder, and his name shall be called Wonderful Counselor, Mighty God, Everlasting Father, Prince of Peace. [7] Of the increase of his government and of peace there will be no end, on the throne of David and over his kingdom, to establish it and to uphold it with justice and with righteousness from this time forth and forevermore. The zeal of the LORD of hosts will do this.

Isa. 11.1-12.6 (ESV) - There shall come forth a shoot from the stump of Jesse, and a branch from his roots shall bear fruit. [2] And the Spirit of the LORD shall rest upon him, the Spirit of wisdom and understanding, the Spirit of counsel and might, the Spirit of knowledge and the fear of the LORD. [3] And his delight shall be in the fear of the LORD. He shall not judge by what his eyes see, or decide disputes by what his ears hear, [4] but with righteousness he shall judge the poor, and decide with equity for the meek of the earth; and he shall strike the earth with the rod of his mouth, and with the breath of his lips he shall kill the wicked. [5] Righteousness shall be the belt of his waist, and faithfulness the belt of his loins. [6] The wolf shall dwell with the lamb, and the leopard shall lie down with the young goat, and the calf and the lion and the fattened calf together; and a little child shall lead them. [7] The cow and the bear shall graze; their young shall lie down together; and the lion shall eat straw like the ox. [8] The nursing child shall play over the hole of the cobra, and the weaned child shall put his hand on the adder's den. [9] They shall not hurt or destroy in all my holy mountain; for the earth shall be full of the knowledge of the LORD as the waters cover the sea. [10] In that day the root of Jesse, who shall stand as a signal for the peoples—of him shall the nations inquire, and his resting place shall be glorious. [11] In that day the Lord will extend his hand yet a second time to recover the remnant that remains of his people, from Assyria, from Egypt, from Pathros, from Cush, [1] from Elam, from Shinar, from Hamath, and from the coastlands of the sea. [12] He will raise a signal for the nations and will assemble the banished of Israel, and gather the dispersed of Judah from the four corners of the earth. [13] The jealousy of Ephraim shall depart, and those who harass Judah shall be cut off; Ephraim shall not be jealous of Judah, and Judah shall not harass Ephraim. [14] But they shall swoop down on the shoulder of the Philistines in the west, and together they shall plunder the people of the east. They shall put out their hand against Edom and Moab, and the Ammonites shall obey them. [15] And the LORD will utterly destroy the tongue of the Sea of Egypt, and will

Kingdom Texts in the Old Testament (continued)

wave his hand over the River with his scorching breath, and strike it into seven channels, and he will lead people across in sandals. [16] And there will be a highway from Assyria for the remnant that remains of his people, as there was for Israel when they came up from the land of Egypt.

[XII.] You will say in that day: "I will give thanks to you, O LORD, for though you were angry with me, your anger turned away, that you might comfort me. [2] "Behold, God is my salvation; I will trust, and will not be afraid; for the LORD GOD [2] is my strength and my song, and he has become my salvation." [3] With joy you will draw water from the wells of salvation. [4] And you will say in that day: "Give thanks to the LORD, call upon his name, make known his deeds among the peoples, proclaim that his name is exalted. [5] "Sing praises to the LORD, for he has done gloriously; let this be made known in all the earth. [6] Shout, and sing for joy, O inhabitant of Zion, for great in your midst is the Holy One of Israel."

Isa. 19.2 (ESV) - And I will stir up Egyptians against Egyptians, and they will fight, each against another and each against his neighbor, city against city, kingdom against kingdom.

Isa. 51.4-5 (ESV) - Give attention to me, my people, and give ear to me, my nation; for a law will go out from me, and I will set my justice for a light to the peoples. [5] My righteousness draws near, my salvation has gone out, and my arms will judge the peoples; the coastlands hope for me, and for my arm they wait.

Isa. 60.9-13 (ESV) - For the coastlands shall hope for me, the ships of Tarshish first, to bring your children from afar, their silver and gold with them, for the name of the LORD your God, and for the Holy One of Israel, because he has made you beautiful. [10] Foreigners shall build up your walls, and their kings shall minister to you; for in my wrath I struck you, but in my favor I have had mercy on you. [11] Your gates shall be open continually; day and night they shall not be shut, that people may bring to you the wealth of the nations, with their kings led in procession. [12] For the nation and kingdom that will not serve you shall perish; those nations shall be utterly laid waste. [13] The glory of Lebanon shall come to you, the cypress, the plane, and the pine, to beautify the place of my sanctuary, and I will make the place of my feet glorious.

Kingdom Texts in the Old Testament (continued)

Isa. 61.1-4 (ESV) - The Spirit of the Lord GOD is upon me, because the LORD has anointed me to bring good news to the poor; he has sent me to bind up the brokenhearted, to proclaim liberty to the captives, and the opening of the prison to those who are bound; [2] to proclaim the year of the LORD's favor, and the day of vengeance of our God; to comfort all who mourn; [3] to grant to those who mourn in Zion—to give them a beautiful headdress instead of ashes, the oil of gladness instead of mourning, the garment of praise instead of a faint spirit; that they may be called oaks of righteousness, the planting of the LORD, that he may be glorified. [4] They shall build up the ancient ruins; they shall raise up the former devastations; they shall repair the ruined cities, the devastations of many generations.

Jer. 23.5-6 (ESV) - Behold, the days are coming, declares the LORD, when I will raise up for David a righteous Branch, and he shall reign as king and deal wisely, and shall execute justice and righteousness in the land. [6] In his days Judah will be saved, and Israel will dwell securely. And this is the name by which he will be called: "The LORD is our righteousness."

Lam. 2.2 (ESV) - The Lord has swallowed up without mercy all the habitations of Jacob; in his wrath he has broken down the strongholds of the daughter of Judah; he has brought down to the ground in dishonor the kingdom and its rulers.

Dan. 2.37 (ESV) - You, O king, the king of kings, to whom the God of heaven has given the kingdom, the power, and the might, and the glory.

Dan. 2.44 (ESV) - And in the days of those kings the God of heaven will set up a kingdom that shall never be destroyed, nor shall the kingdom be left to another people. It shall break in pieces all these kingdoms and bring them to an end, and it shall stand forever.

Dan. 4.34-36 (ESV) - At the end of the days I, Nebuchadnezzar, lifted my eyes to heaven, and my reason returned to me, and I blessed the Most High, and praised and honored him who lives forever, for his dominion is an everlasting dominion, and his kingdom endures from generation to generation; [35] all the inhabitants of the earth are accounted as nothing, and he does according to his will among the host of heaven and among the inhabitants of the earth; and none can stay his hand or say to him, "What have you done?" [36] At the same time

Kingdom Texts in the Old Testament (continued)

my reason returned to me, and for the glory of my kingdom, my majesty and splendor returned to me. My counselors and my lords sought me, and I was established in my kingdom, and still more greatness was added to me.

Dan. 5.26-28 (ESV) - This is the interpretation of the matter: MENE, God has numbered the days of your kingdom and brought it to an end; [27] TEKEL, you have been weighed in the balances and found wanting; [28] PERES, your kingdom is divided and given to the Medes and Persians.

Dan. 6.25-27 (ESV) - Then King Darius wrote to all the peoples, nations, and languages that dwell in all the earth: "Peace be multiplied to you. [26] I make a decree, that in all my royal dominion people are to tremble and fear before the God of Daniel, for he is the living God, enduring forever; his kingdom shall never be destroyed, and his dominion shall be to the end. [27] He delivers and rescues; he works signs and wonders in heaven and on earth, he who has saved Daniel from the power of the lions."

Dan. 7.13-14 (ESV) - I saw in the night visions, and behold, with the clouds of heaven there came one like a son of man, and he came to the Ancient of Days and was presented before him. [14] And to him was given dominion and glory and a kingdom, that all peoples, nations, and languages should serve him; his dominion is an everlasting dominion, which shall not pass away, and his kingdom one that shall not be destroyed.

Dan. 7.18 (ESV) - But the saints of the Most High shall receive the kingdom and possess the kingdom forever, forever and ever.

Dan. 7.22 (ESV) - . . . until the Ancient of Days came, and judgment was given for the saints of the Most High, and the time came when the saints possessed the kingdom.

Dan. 7.27 (ESV) - And the kingdom and the dominion and the greatness of the kingdoms under the whole heaven shall be given to the people of the saints of the Most High; their kingdom shall be an everlasting kingdom, and all dominions shall serve and obey them.

Mic. 4.1-3 (ESV) - It shall come to pass in the latter days that the mountain of the house of the LORD shall be established as the highest of the mountains, and it shall be lifted up above the hills; and peoples shall flow to it, [2] and many nations shall come, and say: "Come, let us go up to the mountain of the LORD,

Kingdom Texts in the Old Testament (continued)

to the house of the God of Jacob, that he may teach us his ways and that we may walk in his paths." For out of Zion shall go forth the law, and the word of the LORD from Jerusalem. [3] He shall judge between many peoples, and shall decide for strong nations afar off; and they shall beat their swords into plowshares, and their spears into pruning hooks; nation shall not lift up sword against nation, neither shall they learn war anymore.

Mic. 5.4-5 (ESV) - And he shall stand and shepherd his flock in the strength of the LORD, in the majesty of the name of the LORD his God. And they shall dwell secure, for now he shall be great to the ends of the earth. [5] And he shall be their peace. When the Assyrian comes into our land and treads in our palaces, then we will raise against him seven shepherds and eight princes of men.

Hos. 1.4 (ESV) - And the LORD said to him, "Call his name Jezreel, for in just a little while I will punish the house of Jehu for the blood of Jezreel, and I will put an end to the kingdom of the house of Israel.

Amos 9.8 (ESV) - "Behold, the eyes of the Lord God are upon the sinful kingdom, and I will destroy it from the surface of the ground, except that I will not utterly destroy the house of Jacob," declares the LORD.

Obad. 1.21 (ESV) - Saviors shall go up to Mount Zion to rule Mount Esau, and the kingdom shall be the LORD's.

Joel 2.26-32 (ESV) - You shall eat in plenty and be satisfied, and praise the name of the LORD your God, who has dealt wondrously with you. And my people shall never again be put to shame. [27] You shall know that I am in the midst of Israel, and that I am the LORD your God and there is none else. And my people shall never again be put to shame. [28] And it shall come to pass afterward, that I will pour out my Spirit on all flesh; your sons and your daughters shall prophesy, your old men shall dream dreams, and your young men shall see visions. [29] Even on the male and female servants in those days I will pour out my Spirit. [30] And I will show wonders in the heavens and on the earth, blood and fire and columns of smoke. [31] The sun shall be turned to darkness, and the moon to blood, before the great and awesome day of the LORD comes. [32] And it shall come to pass that everyone who calls on the name of the LORD shall be saved. For in Mount Zion and in Jerusalem there shall be those who escape, as the LORD has said, and among the survivors shall be those whom the LORD calls.

Kingdom Texts in the Old Testament (continued)

Zech. 8.22 (ESV) - Many peoples and strong nations shall come to seek the LORD of hosts in Jerusalem and to entreat the favor of the LORD.

Zech. 14.9 (ESV) - And the LORD will be king over all the earth. On that day the Lord will be one and his name one.

APPENDIX 17

Suffering: The Cost of Discipleship and Servant-Leadership

Don L. Davis

To be a disciple is to bear the stigma and reproach of the One who called you into service (2 Tim. 3.12). Practically, this may mean the loss of comfort, convenience, and even life itself (John 12.24-25).

All of Christ's Apostles endured insults, rebukes, lashes, and rejections by the enemies of their Master. Each of them sealed their doctrines with their blood in exile, torture, and martyrdom. Listed below are the fates of the Apostles according to traditional accounts.

- Matthew suffered martyrdom by being slain with a sword at a distant city of Ethiopia.
- Mark expired at Alexandria, after being cruelly dragged through the streets of that city.
- Luke was hanged upon an olive tree in the classic land of Greece.
- John was put in a caldron of boiling oil, but escaped death in a miraculous manner, and was afterward branded at Patmos.
- Peter was crucified at Rome with his head downward.
- James, the Greater, was beheaded at Jerusalem.
- James, the Less, was thrown from a lofty pinnacle of the temple, and then beaten to death with a fuller's club.
- Bartholomew was flayed alive.
- Andrew was bound to a cross, whence he preached to his persecutors until he died.
- Thomas was run through the body with a lance at Coromandel in the East Indies.
- Jude was shot to death with arrows.
- Matthias was first stoned and then beheaded.
- Barnabas of the Gentiles was stoned to death at Salonica.
- Paul, after various tortures and persecutions, was at length beheaded at Rome by the Emperor Nero.

APPENDIX 18

Kingdom of God Timeline

Rev. Dr. Don L. Davis

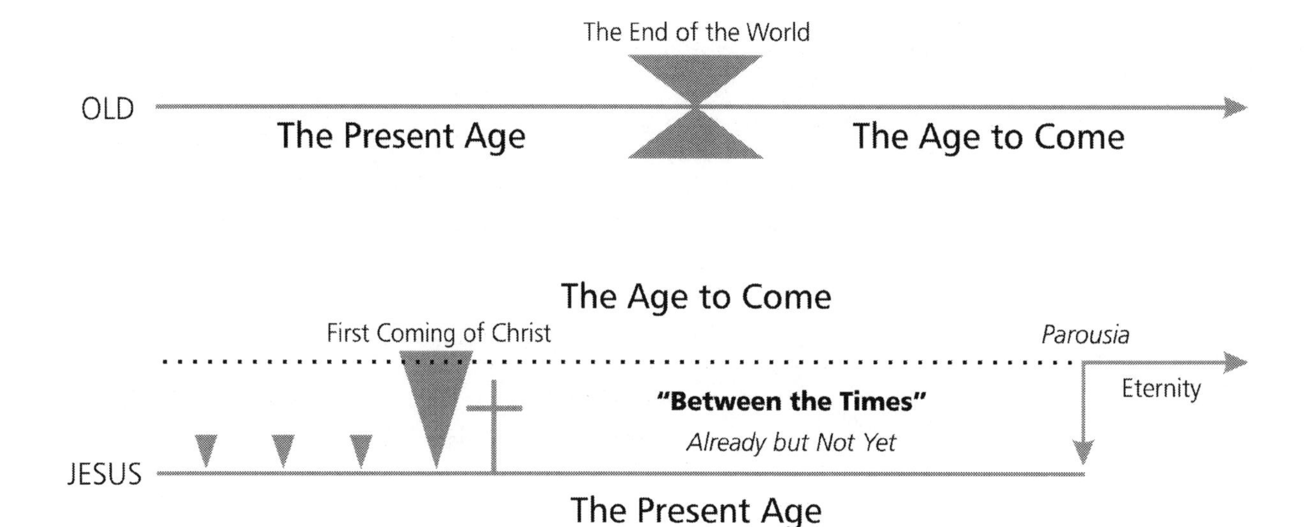

The "***malkuth***" **of Yahweh, the "*basileia tou Theou.*"** First century Palestinian Jews saw God as King, of his people Israel and all the earth. Yet, due to the rebellion of humankind and Satan and his angels, God's reign in the earth is **yet future**. It shall be: 1) nationalistic--the salvation and sovereignty of Israel over her enemies, 2) universal knowledge and reign of God, 3) *tsidkenu* (righteousness, justice) and *shalom* (peace), 4) obedience to the Law of God, 5) the final battle with the Gentile nations - Armageddon, 6) occur by a supernatural cataclysm realized at the end of time, 7) transformation of the heavens and earth to pre-Edenic splendor, 8) rule by the son of David-son of Man, 9) rescinding the effects of the curse, 10) the resurrection of the dead, 11) and judgment and destruction of all of God's enemies - sin, death, evil, the "world," the devil and his angels, and 12) eternal life.

Jesus' proclamation: **The Kingdom of God has now appeared in the life, person, and ministry of Messiah Jesus.** In Jesus' words (*kerygma*), his deeds of compassion (*diakinia*), his miracles, his exorcisms of demons, his passion, death, and resurrection, and the sending of the Spirit, **the promised-for Kingdom has come.** The Kingdom is **both** present and future; he announces **the presence of the future.** Present kingdom blessings include 1) the Church as sign and foretaste, 2) the pledge of the Holy Spirit, 3) the forgiveness of sin, 4) the proclamation of the Kingdom worldwide, 5) reconciliation and peace with God, 6) the binding of Satan, with authority given to Christ's disciples.

APPENDIX 19

33 Blessings in Christ

Rev. Dr. Don L. Davis

Did you know that 33 things happened to you at the moment you became a believer in Jesus Christ? Lewis Sperry Chafer, the first president of Dallas Theological Seminary, listed these benefits of salvation in his *Systematic Theology, Volume III* (pp. 234-266). These points, along with brief explanations, give the born-again Christian a better understanding of the work of grace accomplished in his life as well as a greater appreciation of his new life.

1. In the eternal plan of God, the believer is:

    a. ***Foreknown*** - Acts 2.23; 1 Pet. 1.2, 20. God knew from all eternity every step in the entire program of the universe.

    b. ***Predestined*** - Rom. 8.29-30. A believer's destiny has been appointed through foreknowledge to the unending realization of all God's riches of grace.

    c. ***Elected*** - Rom. 8.38; Col. 3.12. He/she is chosen of God in the present age and will manifest the grace of God in future ages.

    d. ***Chosen*** - Eph. 1.4. God has separated unto himself his elect who are both foreknown and predestined.

    e. ***Called*** - 1 Thess. 5.23-24. God invites man to enjoy the benefits of his redemptive purposes. This term may include those whom God has selected for salvation, but who are still in their unregenerate state.

2. A believer has been ***redeemed*** - Rom. 3.24. The price required to set him/her free from sin has been paid.

3. A believer has been ***reconciled*** - 2 Cor. 5.18-21; Rom. 5.10. He/she is both restored to fellowship by God and restored to fellowship with God.

4. A believer is related to God through ***propitiation*** - Rom. 3.24-26. He/she has been set free from judgment by God's satisfaction with his Son's death for sinners.

5. A believer has been ***forgiven*** all trespasses - Eph. 1.7. All his/her sins are taken care of - past, present, and future.

6. A believer is vitally ***conjoined to Christ*** for the judgment of the old man "unto a new walk" - Rom. 6.1-10. He/she is brought into a union with Christ.

33 Blessings in Christ (continued)

7. A believer is ***"free from the law"*** - Rom. 7.2-6. He/she is both dead to its condemnation, and delivered from its jurisdiction.

8. A believer has been made a ***child of God*** - Gal. 3.26. He/she is born anew by the regenerating power of the Holy Spirit into a relationship in which God the First Person becomes a legitimate Father and the saved one becomes a legitimate child with every right and title - an heir of God and a joint heir with Jesus Christ.

9. A believer has been ***adopted as an adult child*** into the Father's household - Rom. 8.15, 23.

10. A believer has been ***made acceptable to God*** by Jesus Christ - Eph. 1.6. He/she is made ***righteous*** (Rom. 3.22), ***sanctified*** (set apart) positionally (1 Cor. 1.30, 6.11); ***perfected forever in his/her standing and position*** (Heb. 10.14), and ***made acceptable*** in the Beloved (Col. 1.12).

11. A believer has been ***justified*** - Rom. 5.1. He/she has been declared righteous by God's decree.

12. A believer is ***"made right"*** - Eph. 2.13. A close relation is set up and exists between God and the believer.

13. A believer has been ***delivered from the power of darkness*** - Col. 1.13; 2.13. A Christian has been delivered from Satan and his evil spirits. Yet the disciple must continue to wage a warfare against these powers.

14. A believer has been ***translated into the Kingdom of God*** - Col. 1.13. The Christian has been transferred from Satan's kingdom to Christ's Kingdom.

15. A believer is ***planted*** on the Rock, Jesus Christ - 1 Cor. 3.9-15. Christ is the foundation on which the believer stands and on which he/she builds his/her Christian life.

16. A believer is ***a gift from God to Jesus Christ*** - John 17.6, 11, 12, 20. He/she is the Father's love gift to Jesus Christ.

17. A believer is ***circumcised in Christ*** - Col. 2.11. He/she has been delivered from the power of the old sin nature.

18. A believer has been made a ***partaker of the Holy and Royal Priesthood*** - 1 Pet. 2.5, 9. He/she is a priest because of his/her relation to Christ, the High Priest, and will reign on earth with Christ.

33 Blessings in Christ (continued)

19. A believer is part of a ***chosen generation, a holy nation and a peculiar people*** - 1 Pet. 2.9. This is the company of believers in this age.

20. A believer is a ***heavenly citizen*** - Phil. 3.20. Therefore he/she is called a stranger as far as his/her life on earth is concerned (1 Pet. 2.13), and will enjoy his/her true home in heaven forever.

21. A believer is in ***the family and household of God*** - Eph. 2.1, 9. He/she is part of God's "family" which is composed only of true believers.

22. A believer is in ***the fellowship of the saints.*** John 17.11, 21-23. He/she can be a part of the fellowship of believers with one another.

23. A believer is in ***a heavenly association*** - Col. 1.27; 3.1; 2 Cor. 6.1; Col. 1.24; John 14.12-14; Eph. 5.25-27; Titus 2.13. He/she is ***a partner with Christ*** now in life, position, service, suffering, prayer, betrothal as a bride to Christ, and expectation of the coming again of Christ.

24. A believer has ***access to God*** - Eph. 2.18. He/she has access to God's grace which enables him/her to grow spiritually, and he/she has unhindered approach to the Father (Heb. 4.16).

25. A believer is within ***the "much more" care of God*** - Rom. 5.8-10. He/she is an object of God's love (John 3.16), God's grace (Eph. 2.7-9), God's power (Eph. 1.19), God's faithfulness (Phil. 1.6), God's peace (Rom. 5.1), God's consolation (2 Thess. 2.16-17), and God's intercession (Rom. 8.26).

26. A believer is ***God's inheritance*** - Eph. 1.18. He/she is given to Christ as a gift from the Father.

27. A believer ***has the inheritance of God himself*** and all that God bestows - 1 Pet. 1.4.

28. A believer has ***light in the Lord*** - 2 Cor. 4.6. He/she not only has this light, but is commanded to walk in the light.

29. A believer is ***vitally united to the Father, the Son and the Holy Spirit*** - 1 Thess. 1.1; Eph. 4.6; Rom. 8.1; John 14.20; Rom. 8.9; 1 Cor. 2.12.

30. A believer is blessed with ***the earnest or firstfruits of the Spirit*** - Eph. 1.14; 8.23. He/she is born of the Spirit (John 3.6), and baptized by the Spirit (1 Cor. 12.13), which is a work of the Holy Spirit by which the believer is joined to Christ's body and comes to be "in Christ," and therefore is a partaker of all that Christ is.

33 Blessings in Christ (continued)

The disciple is also indwelt by the Spirit (Rom. 8.9), sealed by the Spirit (2 Cor. 1.22), making him/her eternally secure, and filled with the Spirit (Eph. 5.18) whose ministry releases his power and effectiveness in the heart in which he dwells.

31. A believer is ***glorified*** - Rom. 8.18. He/she will be a partaker of the infinite story of the Godhead.
32. A believer is ***complete in God*** - Col. 2.9, 10. He/she partakes of all that Christ is.
33. A believer ***possesses every spiritual blessing*** - Eph. 1.3. All the riches tabulated in the other 32 points made before are to be included in this sweeping term, "all spiritual blessings."

Come Thou Fount of every blessing
Tune my heart to sing Thy grace;
Streams of mercy, never ceasing,
Call for songs of loudest praise
Teach me some melodious sonnet,
Sung by flaming tongues above.
Praise the mount! I'm fixed upon it,
Mount of God's unchanging love.

Here I raise my Ebenezer;
Hither by Thy help I'm come;
And I hope, by Thy good pleasure,
Safely to arrive at home.
Jesus sought me when a stranger,
Wandering from the fold of God;
He, to rescue me from danger,
Interposed His precious blood.

O to grace how great a debtor
Daily I'm constrained to be!
Let that grace now like a fetter,
Bind my wandering heart to Thee.
Prone to wander, Lord, I feel it,
Prone to leave the God I love;
Here's my heart, O take and seal it,
Seal it for Thy courts above.

Come, Thou Fount of Every Blessing,
Robert Robinson, 1757

APPENDIX 20

Models of the Kingdom

Howard A Snyder, March 2002.

1. The Kingdom as Future Hope - the Future Kingdom

This has been a dominant model in the history of the Church. The emphasis is strongly on the future: a final culmination and reconciliation of all things which is more than merely the eternal existence of the soul. The model draws heavily on NT material. While some of the following models also represent future hope, here the note of futurity is determinative.

2. The Kingdom as Inner Spiritual Experience - the Interior Kingdom

A "spiritual kingdom" to be experienced in the heart or soul; "beatific vision." Highly mystical, therefore individualistic; an experience that can't really be shared with others. Examples: Julian of Norwich, other mystics; also some contemporary Protestant examples.

3. The Kingdom as Mystical Communion - the Heavenly Kingdom

The "communion of saints"; the Kingdom as essentially identified with heaven. Less individualistic. Often centers especially in worship and liturgy. Examples: John of Damascus, John Tauler; in somewhat different ways, Wesley and 19th and 20th-century revivalistic and Evangelical Protestantism. Kingdom is primarily other-worldly and future.

4. The Kingdom as Institutional Church - the Ecclesiastical Kingdom

The dominant view of medieval Christianity; dominant in Roman Catholicism until Vatican II. Pope as Vicar of Christ rules on earth in Christ's stead. The tension between the Church and the Kingdom largely dissolves. Traces to Augustine's City of God, but was developed differently from what Augustine believed. Protestant variations appear whenever the Church and Kingdom are too closely identified. Modern "Church Growth" thinking has been criticized at this point.

Models of the Kingdom (continued)

5. The Kingdom as Counter-System - the Subversive Kingdom

May be a protest to #4; sees the Kingdom as a reality which prophetically judges the sociopolitical order as well as the Church. One of the best examples: Francis of Assisi; also 16th century Radical Reformers; "Radical Christians" today; Sojourners magazine. Sees Church as counter-culture embodying the new order of the Kingdom.

6. The Kingdom as Political State - the Theocratic Kingdom

Kingdom may be seen as a political theocracy; Church and society not necessarily to be organized democratically. Tends to work from O.T. models, especially the Davidic Kingdom. Constantinian model; Byzantine Christianity a good example. Calvin's Geneva, perhaps, in a somewhat different sense. Problem of Luther's "two kingdoms" view.

7. The Kingdom as Christianized Society - the Transforming Kingdom

Here also the Kingdom provides a model for society, but more in terms of values & principles to be worked out in society. Kingdom in its fullness would be society completely leavened by Christian values. Post-millennialism; many mid-19th-century Evangelicals; early 20th-century Social Gospel. Kingdom manifested progressively in society, in contrast to premillennialism.

8. The Kingdom as Earthly Utopia - the Earthly Kingdom

May be seen as #7 taken to extreme. This view of the Kingdom is literally utopian. Tends to deny or downplay sin, or see evil as purely environmental. The view of many utopian communities (Cohn, *Pursuit of the Millennium*) including 19th-century U.S. and British examples. In a different way, the view of many of America's Founding Fathers. Most influential 20th-century example: Marxism. Liberation theology, to some degree. In a starkly different way: U.S. Fundamentalist premillennialism, combining this model with #1, #2 and/or #3 -Kingdom has no contemporary relevance, but will be literal utopia in the future. Thus similarities between Marxism and Fundamentalism.

APPENDIX 21

Thy Kingdom Come!

Readings on the Kingdom of God

Edited by Terry G. Cornett and Don L. Davis

Taken from "The Agony and The Ecstasy" in Why We Haven't Changed the World, *by Peter E. Gillquist. Old Tappan, New Jersey: Fleming H. Revell Company, 1982. pp. 47-48.*

A Tale of Two Kingdoms

Hear the parable of a kingdom, a usurper-prince of the realm of this world. By means of a masterful program of clever deception, he has managed to bring millions of subjects under his powerful rule. Granted, he has enticed them from the realm of another Monarch, but he considers them his. After all, they have been under his dominion for some considerable time now, and the Enemy hasn't yet taken them back. Yes, in the mind of this prince, these people are legally his people and this land *his* land. Possession is, after all, he says, nine-tenths of the law.

Suddenly, without much warning, the rival Government takes action. The Son of the Enemy Monarch is dispatched to the prince's very own turf (well, yes, he did steal it, but. . .) to take back those who would resubmit to his reign. The Monarch's plan is to draw these people out from under the prince's authority, philosophy, and life-style.

Most outrageous of all, the Monarch sets up his Government on the prince's own real estate. And instead of immediately removing his restored subjects from the country, he is keeping them there until a disease called *death* (a consequence of the prince's regime which eventually claims everyone) brings about a change in their state of existence. To make the matter even more aggravating, the Son even promises people that he will save them from death, and become the firstfruits by dying and coming back to life again himself.

Unsettled, but undefeated (he thinks), the prince launches an all fronts counterattack. Plainly, he is no match for the other King one on One. So he launches a renewed program of deception, simply lying to his citizens about the other Government. That doesn't always work, for the Monarch's Son keeps taking subjects back. Since they are such weak creatures, however, the prince sees no reason to give up hope for their eventual return. Consequently, even after they become citizens of that other kingdom, he keeps the pressure on.

Falsehood is the prince's most common weapon. He uses it at the most strategic points. Since the most committed people are the most dangerous, he attacks the zealots among his former subjects by spreading rumors about them and

Thy Kingdom Come! Readings on the Kingdom of God (continued)

intimidating them by hints of his power. By and large his successes are few, however, for these people demonstrate an almost supernatural attachment to the Enemy Monarch.

Still, the prince in encouraged by one relatively small, though nonetheless significant, source of help he had not counted on.

There are some servants of the Monarch's Son, mostly honest and well intentioned, who mis-state his promises. These servants are so intent upon winning people back from the realm of the evil prince, that they leave out of their messages some very important facts concerning responsible citizenship in that Domain. They rarely, if ever, mention warfare, or the prince's subversive devices, or the residual effects of the dread diseases caught under his reign. Frankly, they portray the Son's Government as sort of a spiritual welfare state, where there are free goodies for all, with little work or responsibility. One gets the picture of a sort of laid-back paradise, with the Monarch running a giant handout program.

Gleefully, the wicked prince capitalizes on this unexplained chink in their armor. All he has to do is let them preach these omissions, and then cash in on the contradictions the people experience in their daily lives. After all, his best source of returnees just might turn out to be the disappointed hearers who listen to these enthusiastic servants.

The Kingdom as a Key to All of Scripture

Excerpted from "Introduction and Chapter One" in A Kingdom Manifesto, *by Howard A. Snyder. Downers Grove: InterVarsity Press, 1985. pp. 11-25*

Jesus was always full of surprises, even with his disciples. Perhaps the biggest surprise was his news about the Kingdom of God.

Jesus came announcing the Kingdom, creating a stir. Through a brief span of public ministry he kept showing his disciples what the Kingdom was really like. They understood only in part.

Later, risen from the dead, Jesus spent six weeks teaching his disciples more about the Kingdom (Acts 1.3). He explained that his own suffering, death and resurrection were all part of the kingdom plan foretold by Old Testament prophets (Luke 24.44-47).

Now, after the resurrection, his disciples ask, "Are *you finally* going to set up your Kingdom?" (paraphrasing Acts 1.6). How does Jesus respond? He says, in effect,

Thy Kingdom Come! Readings on the Kingdom of God (continued)

"The time for the full flowering of the new order still remains a mystery to you; it's in God's hands. But. . . . the Holy Spirit will give you the power to live the kingdom life now. So you are to be witnesses of the Kingdom and its power from here to the very ends of the earth" (Acts 1.7-8).

And so it was, and so it has been. Today we are finally nearing the fulfillment of Jesus' prophecy that "this gospel of the Kingdom will be preached in the whole world as a testimony to all nations" (Matt. 24.14 [NIV]).

And so, as never before, it is time to speak of God's Kingdom now!

This is no attempt to outguess God or pre-empt the sovereign mystery of the Kingdom. The Kingdom still and always remains in God's hands. So this book is not about "times or dates" (Acts 1.7) - a tempting but disastrous detour - but about the plain kingdom teachings which run throughout Scripture. My point is simply this: The Bible is full of teaching on the Kingdom of God, and the Church has largely missed it. But in the providence of God we may now have reached a time when the good news of the Kingdom can be heard and understood as never before. This is due not to any one person, not to any human wisdom or insight, but to God's own working in our day, bringing a new kingdom consciousness.

Thus the theme of this book: The Kingdom of God in Scripture and its meaning for us today.

The Kingdom of God is a key thread in Scripture, tying the whole Bible together. It is not the only unifying theme, nor should it replace other themes which are clearly biblical. Yet it is a critically important theme, especially today. And its recent resurgence in the Church is, I believe, one of the most significant developments of this century!

Once you begin to look in Scripture for the theme of God's reign or Kingdom, it turns up everywhere! Take an example I recently encountered in my own devotional study:

> All you have made will praise you, O LORD; your saints will extol you. They will tell of the glory of your kingdom and speak of your might, so that all men may know of your mighty acts and the glorious splendor of your kingdom. Your kingdom is an everlasting kingdom, and your dominion endures through all generations.
>
> ~ Psalm 145.10-13 (NIV)

Thy Kingdom Come! Readings on the Kingdom of God (continued)

This one psalm in fact contains a substantial theology of the Kingdom, stressing God's sovereign reign, his mighty acts, his compassion and nearness to those who seek him, his righteousness and justice.

The Kingdom is such a key theme of Scripture that Richard Lovelace can say, "The Messianic Kingdom is not only the main theme of Jesus' preaching; it is the central category unifying biblical revelation." And John Bright comments, "The concept of the Kingdom of God involves, in a real sense, the total message of the Bible. . . . To grasp what is meant by the Kingdom of God is to come very close to the heart of the Bible's gospel of salvation." As E. Stanley Jones wrote over four decades ago, Jesus' message "was the Kingdom of God. It was the center and circumference of all he taught and did. . . . The Kingdom of God is the master-conception, the master-plan, the master-purpose, the master-will that gathers everything up into itself and gives it redemption, coherence, purpose, goal."

True, seeing the Kingdom of God as the only unifying theme of Scripture could be misleading. Personally, I believe the overarching truth is the revelation of the nature and character of God (not merely his existence, which is clear from the created order - Romans 1.20). Here God's love, justice and holiness are central - the character of God's *person* in his tri-unity. Still the reign/rule of God is a key theme of Scripture, for the loving, just, holy God rules consistent with his character and in a way that produces the reflection of his character in all who willingly serve him.

So the Kingdom is indeed a key strand running through the Bible. If it seems less evident in Paul's writings, that is because Paul often speaks of the Kingdom in terms of the sovereign *plan* of God realized through Jesus Christ (as, for example, in Ephesians 1.10), and, for very good reasons, uses less kingdom language. But it is incorrect to say, as some have, that the kingdom theme "disappears" in Paul. . . .

The Bible is full of God's Kingdom. . . . We learn more about the Kingdom when we view all of Scripture as the history of God's "economy" or plan to restore a fallen creation, bringing all God has made - woman, man and their total environment - to the fulfillment of his purposes under his sovereign reign.

One evening my seven-year-old son and I walked through a little patch of woods and came out on an open field. The sun was westering; the sky was serenely laced with blue and gold. Birds flitted in the trees. We talked about peace, the future and the Kingdom of God. Somehow we both sensed, despite our differences in age and understanding, that God desires peace and that what he desires he will bring.

Thy Kingdom Come! Readings on the Kingdom of God (continued)

Someday, we said and knew, all the world will be like this magic moment. But not without cost and struggle.

Jesus urges: "Enter through the narrow gate." For "small is the gate and narrow the road that leads to life, and only a few find it" (Matthew 7.13-14). The Kingdom of God is life in abundance (John 10.10), but the way to life is through the narrow gate of faith and obedience to Jesus Christ. If Christians today want to experience the peaceable order of the Kingdom, they must learn and live God's way of peace.

The Preaching and Teaching of Jesus

Summary of Teaching, Vic Gordon

1. The most important thing in life is to be a disciple of Jesus Christ. To do that we must learn from him and then obey what we hear. He must be our Teacher and Lord (Matthew 7.24-27; 11.29; 28.18-20; John 13.13).

2. Obviously, we cannot follow Jesus if we do not know what he taught. The main theme of his preaching and teaching was the Kingdom of God. Most Christians do not know this, yet they call him Lord and Master Teacher!

3. But we are then faced with an immediate problem. As soon as we know the main theme of his teaching, we automatically misunderstand it. Kingdom means something different in the biblical idiom (Hebrew, Aramaic, Greek) than in contemporary English. To us "Kingdom" means "realm" (a place over which a king rules) or "a group of people who live in a king's realm" (the people over whom a king rules). In the Bible, however, the primary meaning of "Kingdom" is "reign" or "rule." The Kingdom of God thus means the reign of God or the rule of God. The Kingdom of God is not a place nor a people, but God's active, dynamic rule. The Kingdom is an act of God, i.e. something he does.

4. The burden and purpose of Jesus' three year public ministry leading up to his death and resurrection was to preach, proclaim and teach about the Kingdom of God (Mark 1.14ff; Matthew 4.17, 23; 9.35; Luke 4.42ff; 8.1; 9.2, 6, 11; 10.1, 9; Acts 1.3; 28.31).

5. Jesus was the original proclaimer of the Gospel, and he proclaimed it originally in terms of the Kingdom of God (Mark 1.14ff; Matthew 4.23; 9.35; 24.14; Luke 20.1). The good news is about God's reign. Of course this is a metaphor, a word picture describing a profound reality.

Thy Kingdom Come! Readings on the Kingdom of God (continued)

6. Jesus' teaching on the Kingdom of God as we will see, determines the basic structure of all his teaching, and indeed the structure of the teaching of the entire New Testament.

7. Why did Jesus choose the word picture "Kingdom of God" to proclaim the good news of God to the world? Two basic reasons:

   a. **It was biblical.** While the exact phrase "Kingdom of God" never occurs in the Old Testament (maybe once in 1 Chronicles 28.5), the idea is everywhere present in the Old Testament. God is always and everywhere King in the Old Testament, especially in the prophets. His kingship is not always realized in this sinful world. In fact the major emphasis in the Old Testament, stated in hundreds of ways and different word pictures, is on God's future, coming reign. The hope of the Old Testament is that God himself will come and bring salvation to his people and judgment/destruction to his enemies. (See e.g. 1 Chronicles 29.11; Psalms 22.28; 96.10-13; 103.19; 145.11-13; Isaiah 25ff; 65ff; Daniel 2.44; 4.3, 34; 6.26; 7.13ff, 27.)

   b. **It was understood and meaningful to the first century Palestinian Jews to whom he proclaimed the Good News.** In fact, the phrase "Kingdom of God" had developed a great deal in the 400 years between the Old Testament and the coming of Jesus. Kingdom of God now summarized the entire Old Testament hope! The first century Jews were expecting God to come as king and reign over the entire world, destroying his enemies and giving all his blessings to his people, Israel. This concept was especially meaningful to the Jews who, on the one hand, strongly believed that their God Yahweh was the one and only true God who ruled over all the universe, and who, on the other, experienced over 700 years of foreign domination at the hands of pagan rulers from Assyria, then Babylon, then Persia, then Greece and finally Rome. Jesus never defines the Kingdom of God for them, because they all knew what it meant. This is a great example for us in our ministries. Jesus went to the people where they were (the incarnation!), was faithful to the biblical message, and spoke it to them in terms they could understand. (See e.g. Luke 1.32ff; 19.11; 23.51; Mark 11.10; 15.43; Acts 1.6.) The phrase Kingdom of God summarized all of the Old

Thy Kingdom Come! Readings on the Kingdom of God (continued)

Testament hope and promise. "All that God has said and done in Israel's history is brought to completion in the Kingdom of God" (Dale Patrick).

8. But Jesus offers a new understanding of an already understood concept. He pours his own authoritative meaning into the Kingdom of God and offers a definitive new interpretation of the Old Testament promise and teaching. He makes it certain that the "Kingdom of God" is the interpretive key for the Old Testament. He agrees with the Jews that the Kingdom is God coming into history and reigning by giving salvation to his people and judgment to his enemies. But Jesus goes far beyond this in providing a grand new interpretation of God's reign.

9. Jesus startles and stuns his hearers by saying the Kingdom of God which they have all been waiting for is now present (Mark 1.15). The time of the fulfillment of the Old Testament promises has now arrived. He goes even further than this by teaching that the Kingdom is present in his own person and ministry. (Matthew 11.1-15; 12.28; Luke 10.23ff; 17.20ff.) This teaching that the Kingdom of God has arrived or is here is radically new. No Jewish rabbi had ever taught such a thing (Luke 10.23ff).

10. But Jesus, like most of the Jews of his day, also taught that the Kingdom of God was still future, i.e. it was yet to come (e.g. Matthew 6.10; 8.11ff; 25.31-34; Luke 21.31; 22.17ff. Cf. Matthew 5.3-12; Mark 9.47).

11. The solution to this strange teaching is to realize that Jesus' new perspective on the Kingdom of God contains both elements: the Kingdom is present and future. Jesus taught two comings of the Kingdom. First, the Kingdom came partially in his own person and ministry in history. Second, Jesus taught that there will be a future complete coming of his Kingdom when he returns at the end of human history.

12. Now we can understand what Jesus meant by the "mystery of the Kingdom" (Mark 4.10ff). This strange, new perspective on the Kingdom of God taught that the Old Testament promises could be fulfilled without being consummated. Thus, the mystery of the Kingdom is fulfillment without consummation. **The Kingdom of God has come into history in the person and ministry of Jesus Christ without consummation.** This mystery has been hidden until now revealed in Christ.

Thy Kingdom Come! Readings on the Kingdom of God (continued)

13. In one way or another, all of Jesus' kingdom parables ("The Kingdom of God is like. . .") proclaim and/or explain this mystery. This understanding of the Kingdom is radically new. The first century Palestinian Jews needed to hear this message, understand it and believe it. This is the major concern of Jesus' preaching and teaching.

14. Thus, we can understand Jesus' teaching on the coming of God's Kingdom as being both present and future. The Kingdom is now and it is not yet. Jesus announces the presence of the future.

15. This chart of the Kingdom of God in the teaching of Jesus can help us see more clearly what he is saying. The chart is a time line from Creation into an eternal future (eternal in the Bible means unending time).

    a. The age of the Kingdom is the age to come. We now live in both this age and the age to come.

    b. The Kingdom of God has two moments, each one characterized by a coming of Jesus as the Messianic King to bring God's reign.

16. The Kingdom of God brings the blessings of God. As the people of the Kingdom live now in the tension of both the presence and the future of the Kingdom, some of the blessings have already arrived for us and some await the consummation of the Kingdom in the future.

Present Blessings of the Kingdom

a. The Gospel is proclaimed.

b. The forgiveness of sin.

c. The Holy Spirit indwells God's people.

d. Sanctification has begun.

Thy Kingdom Come! Readings on the Kingdom of God (continued)

Future Blessings of the Kingdom

a. The Presence of God

b. Resurrection bodies

c. Full sanctification

d. Shalom: peace, righteousness, joy, health, wholeness

e. A new heaven and a new earth

f. Judgment and destruction of all God's enemies including sin, death, the devil and his demons, all evil

17. Let us not overlook the obvious fact that for Jesus his preaching about the Kingdom is fundamentally a proclamation about God. God brings his Kingdom as a seeking, inviting, gracious Abba Father. He also comes as judge to those who refuse his Kingdom.

18. The Kingdom of God is altogether God's work. He graciously comes into human history in the person of his Son Jesus Christ to bring his rule to the earth. The Kingdom is therefore completely supernatural and gracious. Humans cannot bring, build or accomplish the Kingdom. It is wholly God's act.

19. Jesus' miracles and exorcisms are signs that the Kingdom of God is present in him and his ministry (Matthew 11.1-6; 4.23; 9.35; 10.7ff; Luke 9.1, 2, 6, 11).

20. The Kingdom of God invades the kingdom of Satan when Jesus comes bringing the Kingdom (Matthew 12.22-29; 25.41; Mark 1.24, 34; Luke 10.17ff; 11.17-22).

21. The Kingdom of God is of great value, indeed the greatest thing by far in the whole world (Matthew 13.44-46). Therefore, we must ask, "How should we then respond to this Kingdom?" or "How do we receive this gift of the Kingdom of God?"

APPENDIX 22

Discipling the Faithful: Establishing Leaders for the Urban Church

Crowns of Beauty Conference. Don Davis. February 1998.

	Commission	Character	Competence	Community
Definition	Recognizes the call of God and replies with prompt obedience to his lordship and leading	Reflects the character of Christ in their personal convictions, conduct, and lifestyle	Responds in the power of the Spirit with excellence in carrying out their appointed tasks and ministry	Regards multiplying disciples in the body of Christ as the primary role of ministry
Key Scripture	2 Tim. 1.6-14; 1 Tim. 4.14; Acts 1.8; Matt. 28.18-20	John 15.4-5; 2 Tim. 2.2; 1 Cor. 4.2; Gal. 5.16-23	2 Tim. 2.15; 3.16-17; Rom. 15.14; 1 Cor. 12	Eph. 4.9-15; 1 Cor. 12.1-27
Critical Concept	The Authority of God: God's leader acts on God's recognized call and authority, acknowledged by the saints and God's leaders	The Humility of Christ: God's leader demonstrates the mind and lifestyle of Christ in his or her actions and relationships	The Power of the Spirit: God's leader operates in the gifting and anointing of the Holy Spirit	The Growth of the Church: God's leader uses all of his or her resources to equip and empower the body of Christ for his/her goal and task
Central Elements	A clear call from God Authentic testimony before God and others Deep sense of personal conviction based on Scripture Personal burden for a particular task or people Confirmation by leaders and the body	Passion for Christlikeness Radical lifestyle for the Kingdom Serious pursuit of holiness Discipline in the personal life Fulfills role-relationships as bondslave of Jesus Christ Provides an attractive model for others in their conduct, speech, and lifestyle (the fruit of the Spirit)	Endowments and gifts from the Spirit Sound discipling from an able mentor Skill in the spiritual disciplines Ability in the Word Able to evangelize, follow up, and disciple new converts Strategic in the use of resources and people to accomplish God's task	Genuine love for and desire to serve God's people Disciples faithful individuals Facilitates growth in small groups Pastors and equips believers in the congregation Nurtures associations and networks among Christians and churches Advances new movements among God's people locally
Satanic Strategy to Abort	Operates on the basis of personality or position rather than on God's appointed call and ongoing authority	Substitutes ministry activity and/or hard work and industry for godliness and Christlikeness	Functions on natural gifting and personal ingenuity rather than on the Spirit's leading and gifting	Exalts tasks and activities above equipping the saints and developing Christian community
Key Steps	Identify God's call Discover your burden Be confirmed by leaders	Abide in Christ Discipline for godliness Pursue holiness in all	Discover the Spirit's gifts Receive excellent training Hone your performance	Embrace God's Church Learn leadership's contexts Equip concentrically
Results	Deep confidence in God arising from God's call	Powerful Christlike example provided for others to follow	Dynamic working of the Holy Spirit	Multiplying disciples in the Church

APPENDIX 23

A Theology of the Church

Don L. Davis and Terry Cornett ©1996 World Impact Press

The Church Is an Apostolic Community Where the Word Is Rightly Preached

I. A Community of Calling

A. The essential meaning of Church is *Ekklesia*: those who have been "***called out***" in order to be "***called to***" a New Community.

1. Like the Thessalonians, the Church is called out from idolatry to serve the living God and ***called to*** wait for his Son from heaven.

2. The Church is ***called out*** in order that it may belong to Christ (Rom. 1.6). Jesus speaks of the Church as "my *ekklesia*" that is the "called out ones" who are his unique possession (Matt. 16.18; Gal. 5.24; James 2.7).

3. The components of God's call:

   a. The foundation is God's desire to save (John 3.16, 1 Tim. 2.4).

   b. The message is the good news of the Kingdom (Matt. 24.14).

   c. The recipients are "whosoever will" (John 3.15).

   d. The method is through faith in the shed blood of Christ and acknowledgment of his lordship (Rom. 3.25; 10.9-10; Eph. 2.8).

   e. The result is regeneration and placement into the body of Christ (2 Cor. 5.17; Rom. 12.4-5; Eph. 3.6; 5.30).

B. The Church is ***called out***.

1. Called out of the world:

   a. The world is under Satan's dominion and stands in opposition to God.

   b. Conversion and incorporation in Christ's Church involves repentance (*metanoia*) and a transfer of kingdom allegiances.

A Theology of the Church (continued)

c. The Church exists as strangers and aliens who are "in" but not "of" this world system.

2. Called out from sin:

a. Those in the Church are being sanctified, set apart for holy action, so that they may live out their calling as saints of God (1 Cor. 1.2; 2 Tim. 1.9, 1 Pet. 1.15).

b. The Church must be available for God's purpose and use (Rom. 8.28-29; Eph. 1.11; Rom. 6.13).

c. The Church must bring glory to God alone (Isa. 42.8; John 13.31-32; 17.1; Rom. 15.6; 1 Pet. 2.12).

d. The Church must now be characterized by obedience to God (2 Thess. 1.8; Heb. 5.8-9; 1 John 2.3).

C. The Church is ***called to***:

1. Salvation and new life

a. Forgiveness and cleansing from sin (Eph. 1.7; 5.26; 1 John 1.9).

b. Justification (Rom. 3.24; 8.30; Titus 3.7) in which God pronounces us guiltless as to the penalty of his divine law.

c. Regeneration (John 3.5-8; Col. 3.9-10) by which a "new self" is birthed in us through the Spirit.

d. Sanctification (John 17.19; 1 Cor. 1.2) in which we are "set apart" by God for holiness of life.

e. Glorification and Life Eternal (Rom. 8.30, 1 Tim. 6.12; 2 Thess. 2.14) in which we are changed to be like Christ and prepared to live forever in the presence of God (Rom. 8.23; 1 Cor. 15.51-53; 1 John 3.2).

2. Participation in a new community of God's chosen people (1 Pet. 2.9-10)

   a. Members of Christ's body (1 Cor. 10.16-17; 12.27).

   b. Sheep of God's flock under one Shepherd (John 10; Heb. 13.20; 1 Pet. 5.2-4).

   c. Members of God's family and household (Gal. 6.10; 1 Tim. 3.15).

   d. Children of Abraham and recipients of covenant promise (Rom. 4.16; Gal. 3.29; Eph. 2.12).

   e. Citizens of the New Jerusalem (Phil. 3.20; Rev. 3.12).

   f. The firstfruits of the Kingdom of God (Luke 12.32; James 1.18).

3. Freedom (Gal. 5.1, 13)

   a. Called out of the dominion of darkness which suppresses freedom (Col. 1.13-14).

   b. Called away from sin which enslaves (John 8.34-36).

   c. Called to God the Father who is the Liberator of his people (Exod. 6.6).

   d. Called to God the Son who gives the truth which sets free (John 8.31-36).

   e. Called to God the Spirit whose presence creates liberty (2 Cor. 3.17).

II. A Community of Faith

A. The Church is a community of faith, which has, by faith, confessed Jesus as Lord and Savior.

Faith refers both to ***the content of our belief*** and to ***the act of believing*** itself. Jesus is the object (content) of our faith and his life is received through faith (our belief) in him and his word. In both of these senses, the Church is a community of faith.

A Theology of the Church (continued)

1. The Church places its faith:

   a. in the Living Word (Jesus the Messiah),

   b. who is revealed in the written Word (Sacred Scripture),

   c. and who is now present, teaching and applying his Word to the Church (through the ministry of the Holy Spirit).

2. The Church guards the deposit of faith, given by Christ and the apostles, through sound teaching and the help of the Holy Spirit who indwells its members (2 Tim. 1.13-14).

B. Because it is a community of faith, the Church is also a community of grace.

1. The Church exists by grace-through faith rather than through human merit or works (Gal. 2.21; Eph. 2.8).

2. The Church announces, in faith, the grace of God to all humanity (Titus 2.11-15).

3. The Church lives by grace in all actions and relationships (Eph. 4.1-7).

C. The Church is a community where the Scriptures are preached, studied, meditated upon, memorized, believed, and obeyed (Ezek. 7.10; Jos. 1.8; Ps. 119; Col. 3.16; 1 Tim. 4.13; James 1.22-25).

1. The Church preaches the Gospel of the Kingdom, as revealed in Scripture, and calls people to repentance and faith which leads to obedience (Matt. 4.17; 28.19-20; Acts 2.38-40).

2. The Church studies and applies the Scriptures through teaching, rebuking, correcting, and training in righteousness so that all members of the community are equipped to live godly lives characterized by good works (2 Tim. 3.16-17; 4.2).

3. The Church intentionally reflects on the Scriptures in light of reason, tradition, and experience, learning and doing theology as a means of more fully understanding and acting upon truth (Ps. 119.97-99; 1 Tim. 4.16; 2 Tim. 2.15).

4. The Church functions as a listening community which is aware of the Spirit's presence and relies upon him to interpret and apply the Scriptures to the present moment (John 14.25-26).

D. The Church contends for the faith that was once for all entrusted to the saints (Jude 3).

III. A Community of Witness

A. The Church witnesses to the fact that in the incarnation, life, teaching, death and resurrection of Jesus the Christ, God's Kingdom has begun (Mark 1.15; Luke 4.43; 6.20; 11.20; Acts 1.3; 28.23; 1 Cor. 4.20; Col. 1.12-13).

1. The Church proclaims Jesus as *Christus Victor* whose reign will:

    a. Rescind the curse over creation and humankind (Rev. 22.3).

    b. Defeat Satan and the powers and destroy their work (1 John 3.8).

    c. Reverse the present order by defending and rewarding the meek, the humble, the despised, the lowly, the righteous, the hungry, and the rejected (Luke 1.46-55; 4.18-19; 6.20-22).

    d. Propitiate God's righteous anger (Gal. 3.10-14; 1 John 2.1-2).

    e. Create a new humanity (1 Cor. 15.45-49; Eph. 2.15; Rev. 5.9-10).

    f. Destroy the last enemy- death (1 Cor. 15.26).

2. Ultimately, the very Kingdom itself will be turned over to God the Father, and the freedom, wholeness, and justice of the Lord will abound throughout the universe (Isa. 10.2-7; 11.1-9; 53.5; Mic. 4.1-3; 6.8; Matt. 6.33; 23.23; Luke 4.18-19; John 8.34-36; 1 Cor. 15.28; Rev. 21).

A Theology of the Church (continued)

B. The Church witnesses by:

1. Functioning as a sign and foretaste of the Kingdom of God; the Church is a visible community where people see that:

   a. Jesus is acknowledged as Lord (Rom. 10.9-10).

   b. The truth and power of the Gospel is growing and producing fruit among every kindred, tribe, and nation (Acts 2.47; Rom. 1.16; Col. 1.6; Rev. 7.9-10).

   c. The values of God's Kingdom are accepted and acted upon (Matt. 6.33).

   d. God's commands are obeyed on earth as they are in heaven (Matt. 6.10; John 14.23-24).

   e. The presence of God is experienced (Matt. 18.20; John 14.16-21).

   f. The power of God is demonstrated (1 Cor. 4.20).

   g. The love of God is freely received and given (Eph. 5.1-2; 1 John 3.18; 4.7-8).

   h. The compassion of God is expressed in bearing each other's burdens, first within the Church, and then, in sacrificial service to the whole world (Matt. 5.44-45; Gal. 6.2, 10; Heb. 13.16).

   i. The redemptiveness of God transcends human frailty and sin so that the treasure of the Kingdom is evident in spite of being contained in earthen vessels (2 Cor. 4.7).

2. Performing signs and wonders which confirm the Gospel (Mark 16.20; Acts 4.30; 8.6,13; 14.3; 15.12; Rom. 15.18-19; Heb. 2.4)

3. Accepting the call to mission

   a. Going into all the world to preach the Gospel (Matt. 24.14; 28.18-20; Acts 1.8, Col. 1.6).

   b. Evangelizing and making disciples of Christ and his Kingdom (Matt. 28.18-20; 2 Tim. 2.2).

A Theology of the Church (continued)

c. Establishing churches among those unreached by the Gospel (Matt. 16.18; 28.19; Acts 2.41-42; 16.5; 2 Cor. 11.28; Heb. 12.22-23).

d. Displaying the excellencies of Christ's Kingdom by engendering freedom, wholeness, and justice in his Name (Isa. 53.5; Mic. 6.8; Matt. 5.16; 12.18-20; Luke 4.18-19; John 8.34-36; 1 Pet. 3.11).

4. Acting as a prophetic community

a. Speaking the Word of God into situations of error, confusion, and sin (2 Cor. 4.2; Heb. 4.12; James 5.20; Titus 2.15).

b. Speaking up for those who cannot speak up for themselves so that justice is defended (Prov. 31.8-9).

c. Announcing judgment against sin in all its forms (Rom. 2.5; Gal. 6.7-8; 1 Pet. 4.17).

d. Announcing hope in situations where sin has produced despair (Jer. 32.17; 2 Thess. 2.16; Heb. 10.22-23; 1 Pet. 1.3-5).

e. Proclaiming the return of Jesus, the urgency of the hour, and the reality that soon every knee will bow and every tongue confess that Jesus is Lord to the glory of God the Father (Matt. 25.1-13; Phil. 2.10-11; 2 Tim. 4.1, Titus 2.12-13).

The Church Is One Community Where the Sacraments Are Rightly Administered

IV. A Community of Worship

A. The Church recognizes that worship is the primary end of all creation.

1. The worshiper adores, praises, and gives thanks to God for his character and actions, ascribing to him the worth and glory due his Person. This worship is directed to:

a. The Father Almighty who is the Maker of all things visible and invisible.

A Theology of the Church (continued)

b. The Son who by his incarnation, death, and resurrection accomplished salvation and who is now glorified at the Father's right hand.

c. The Spirit who is the Lord and Giver of Life.

2. Worship is the primary purpose of the material heavens and earth, and all life therein (Pss. 148-150; Luke 19.37-40; Rom. 11.36; Rev. 4.11; 15.3-4).

3. Worship is the central activity of the angelic hosts who honor God in his presence (Isa. 6; Rev. 5).

4. Worship is the chief vocation of the "community of saints," all true Christians, living and dead, who seek to glorify God in all things (Ps. 29.2; Rom. 12.1-2; 1 Cor. 10.31; Col. 3.17).

B. The Church offers acceptable worship to God. This means:

1. The worshipers have renounced all false gods or belief systems that lay claim to their allegiance and have covenanted to serve and worship the one true God (Exod. 34.14; 1 Thess. 1.9-10).

2. The worshipers worship:

a. In Spirit - as regenerated people who, through saving faith in Jesus Christ, are filled with the Holy Spirit and under his direction.

b. In Truth - understanding God as he is revealed in Scripture and worshiping in accordance with the teaching of the Word.

c. In Holiness - Living lives that demonstrate their genuine commitment to serve the Living God.

C. The Church worships as a royal priesthood, wholeheartedly offering up sacrifices of praise to God and employing all its creative resources to worship him with excellence.

1. The Christian Church is a people who worship, not a place of worship.

A Theology of the Church (continued)

2. The entire congregation ministers to the Lord, each one contributing a song, a word, a testimony, a prayer, etc. according to their gifts and capacities (1 Cor. 14.26).

3. The Church worships with the full range of human emotion, intellect, and creativity:

   a. Physical expression- raising of hands, dancing, kneeling, bowing, etc.

   b. Intellectual engagement- striving to understand God's nature and works.

   c. Artistic expression- through music and the other creative arts.

   d. Celebratory expression- the Church plays in the presence of God (Prov. 8.30-31) experiencing "Sabbath rest" through festivals, celebrations, and praise.

4. The Church worships liturgically by together reenacting the story of God and his people.

   a. The Church proclaims and embodies the drama of God's redemptive action in its ritual, tradition, and order of worship.

   b. The Church, like the covenant people Israel, orders its life around the celebration of the Lord's Supper and Baptism which reenact the story of God's salvation (Deut. 16.3; Matt. 28.19; Rom. 6.4; 1 Cor. 11.23-26).

   c. The Church remembers the worship and service of saints through the ages, learning from their experiences with the Spirit of God (Deut. 32.7; Pss. 77.10-12; 143.5; Isa. 46.9; Heb. 11).

5. The Church worships in freedom:

   a. Constantly experiencing new forms and expressions of worship which honor God and allow his people to delight in him afresh (Pss. 33.3; 40.3; 96.1; 149.1; Isa. 42.9-10; Luke 5.38; Rev. 5.9).

A Theology of the Church (continued)

b. Being led by the Spirit so that its worship is responsive to God himself (2 Cor. 3.6; Gal. 5.25; Phil. 3.3).

c. Expressing the unchanging nature of God in forms that are conducive to the particular cultures and personalities of the worshipers (Acts 15).

6. The Church worships in right order, making sure that each act of worship edifies the body, and stands in accordance with the Word of God (1 Cor. 14.12, 33, 40; Gal. 5.13-15, 22-25; Eph. 4.29; Phil. 4.8).

D. The Church's worship leads to wholeness:

1. Health and blessing attend the worshiping community (Exod. 23.25; Ps. 147.1-3).

2. The community takes on the character of the One who is worshiped (Exod. 29.37; Ps. 27.4; Jer. 2.5; 10.8; Matt. 6.21; Col. 3.1-4; 1 John 3.2).

V. A Community of Covenant

A. The Church is the gathering of those who participate in the New Covenant. This New Covenant:

1. Is mediated by Jesus Christ, the Great High Priest, and is purchased and sealed by his blood (Matt. 26.28; 1 Tim. 2.5; Heb. 8.6; 4.14-16).

2. Is initiated and participated in only through the electing grace of God (Rom. 8.29-30; 2 Tim. 1.9; Titus 1.1; 1 Pet. 1.1).

3. Is a covenant of peace (*Shalom*) which gives access to God (Ezek. 34.23-31; Rom. 5.1-2; Eph. 2.17-18; Heb. 7.2-3).

4. Is uniquely celebrated and experienced in the Lord's Supper and Baptism (Mark 14.22-25; 1 Cor. 10.16; Col. 2.12; 1 Pet. 3.21).

A Theology of the Church (continued)

5. By faith, both imputes and imparts righteousness to the participants so that God's laws are put in the hearts and written on their minds (Jer. 31.33; Rom. 1.17; 2 Cor. 5.21; Gal. 3.21-22; Phil. 1.11; 3.9; Heb. 10.15-17; 12.10-11; 1 Pet. 2.24).

B. The Covenant enables us to understand and experience Christian sanctification:

1. Righteousness: right relationships with God and others (Exod. 20.1-17; Mic. 6.8; Mark 12.29-31; James 2.8).
2. Truth: right beliefs about God and others (Ps. 86.11; Isa. 45.19; John 8.31-32, 17.17; 1 Pet. 1.22).
3. Holiness: right actions toward God and others (Lev. 11.45; 20.8; Eccles. 12.13; Matt. 7.12; 2 Cor. 7.1; Col. 3.12; 2 Pet. 3.11).

C. The purpose of the New Covenant is to enable the Church to be like Christ Jesus:

1. Jesus is the new pattern for humanity:
   a. The second Adam (Rom. 5.12-17; 1 Cor. 15.45-49).
   b. The likeness into which the Church is fashioned (Rom. 8.29; 1 John 3.2).
   c. His life, character, and teaching are the standard for faith and practice (John 13.17; 20.21; 2 John 6, 9, 1 Cor. 11.1).
2. This covenant is made possible by the sacrifice of Christ himself (Matt. 26.27-29; Heb. 8-10).
3. The apostolic ministry of the new covenant is meant to conform believers to the image of Christ (2 Cor. 3; Eph. 4.12-13).

A Theology of the Church (continued)

D. The Covenant binds us to those who have gone before.

1. It recognizes that the Church is one (Eph. 4.4-5).

2. It reminds us that we are surrounded by a cloud of witnesses who have participated in the same covenant (Heb. 12.1).

3. It reminds us that we are part of a sacred chain:

God-Christ-Apostles-Church.

4. It reminds us that we share the same:

a. Spiritual parentage (John 1.13; 3.5-6; 2 Cor. 1.2; Gal. 4.6; 1 John 3.9).

b. Family likeness (Eph. 3.15; Heb. 2.11).

c. Lord, faith and baptism (Eph. 4.5).

d. Indwelling Spirit (John 14.17; Rom. 8.9; 2 Cor. 1.22).

e. Calling and mission (Eph. 4.1; Heb. 3.1; 2 Pet. 1.10).

f. Hope and destiny (Gal. 5.5; Eph. 1.18; Eph. 4.4; Col. 1.5).

5. Causes us to understand that since we share the same covenant, administered by the same Lord, under the leadership of the same Spirit with those Christians who have come before us, we must necessarily reflect upon the creeds, the councils, and the actions of the Church throughout history in order to understand the apostolic tradition and the ongoing work of the Holy Spirit (1 Cor. 11.16).

VI. A Community of Presence

A. "Where Jesus Christ is, there is the Church" - Ignatius of Antioch (Matt. 18.20).

A Theology of the Church (continued)

B. The Church is the dwelling place of God (Eph. 2.19-21):

1. His nation
2. His household
3. His temple

C. The Church congregates in eager anticipation of God's presence (Eph. 2.22).

1. The Church now comes into the presence of God at every gathering:
   a. Like the covenant people in the Old Testament, the Church gathers in the presence of God (Exod. 18.12; 34.34; Deut. 14.23; 15.20; Ps. 132.7; Heb. 12.18-24).
   b. The gathered Church makes manifest the reality of the Kingdom of God by being in the presence of the King (1 Cor. 14.25).
2. The Church anticipates the future gathering of the people of God when the fullness of God's presence will be with them all (Ezek. 48.35; 2 Cor. 4.14; 1 Thess. 3.13; Rev. 21.13).

D. The Church is absolutely dependent on the presence of the Spirit of Christ.

1. Without the presence of the Holy Spirit there is no Church (Acts 2.38; Rom. 8.9; 1 Cor. 12.13; Gal. 3.3; Eph. 2.22; 4.4; Phil. 3.3).
2. The Holy Spirit creates, directs, empowers, and teaches congregations of believers (John 14.16-17, 26; Acts 1.8; 2.17; 13.1; Rom. 15.13, 19; 2 Cor. 3.18).
3. The Holy Spirit gives gifts to the Church so that it can accomplish its mission, bringing honor and glory to God (Rom. 12.4-8; 1 Cor. 12.1-31; Heb. 2.4).
4. The Holy Spirit binds the Church together as the family of God and the body of Christ (2 Cor. 13.14; Eph. 4.3).

A Theology of the Church (continued)

E. The Church is a Kingdom of priests which stands in God's presence (1 Pet. 2.5, 9):

1. Ministering before the Lord (Ps. 43.4; Ps. 134.1-2).
2. Placing God's blessing on his people (Num. 6.22-27; 2 Cor. 13.14).
3. Bringing people before the attention of God (1 Thess. 1.3; 2 Tim. 1.3).
4. Offering themselves and the fruit of their ministry to God (Isa. 66.20, Rom. 12.1; 15.16).

F. The Church lives in God's presence through prayer.

1. Prayer as access to the Holy of Holies (Rev. 5.8).
2. Prayer as communion with God (Ps. 5.3; Rom. 8.26-27).
3. Prayer as intercession.
   a. For the world (1 Tim. 2.1-2).
   b. For the saints (Eph. 6.18-20, 1 Thess. 5.25).
4. Prayer as thanksgiving (Phil. 4.6; Col. 1.3).
5. Prayer as the warfare of the Kingdom.
   a. Binding and loosing (Matt. 16.19).
   b. Engaging the principalities and powers (Eph. 6.12,18).

The Church Is a Holy Community Where Discipline Is Rightly Ordered

VII. A Community of Reconciliation

A. The Church is a community that is reconciled to God: all reconciliation is ultimately dependent on God's reconciling actions toward humanity.

A Theology of the Church (continued)

1. God's desire to reconcile is evidenced by sending his prophets and in the last days by his Son (Heb. 1.1-2).

2. The incarnation, the life, the death, and the resurrection of Jesus are the ultimate acts of reconciliation from God toward humanity (Rom. 5.8).

3. The Gospel is now a message of reconciliation, made possible by Christ's death, that God offers to humanity (2 Cor. 5.16-20).

B. The Church is a community of individuals and peoples that are reconciled to each other by their common identity as one body.

1. By his death Christ united his people who are born of the same seed (1 John 3.9), reconciled as fellow citizens and members of a new humanity (Eph. 2.11-22).

2. The Church community treats all members of God's household with love and justice in spite of differences in race, class, gender, and culture because they are organically united by their participation in the body of Christ (Gal. 3.26-29; Col. 3.11).

C. The Church is a community that is concerned for reconciliation among all peoples.

1. The Church functions an ambassador that invites all people to be reconciled to God (2 Cor. 5.19-20). This task of mission lays the foundation for all the reconciling activities of the Church.

2. The Church promotes reconciliation with and between all people.

   a. Because the Church is commanded to love its enemies (Matt. 5.44-48).

   b. Because the Church is an incarnational community which seeks, like Christ, to identify with those alienated from itself.

A Theology of the Church (continued)

c. Because the Church embodies and works for the vision of the Kingdom of God in which peoples, nations, and nature itself will be completely reconciled and at peace (Isa. 11.1-9; Mic. 4.2-4; Matt. 4.17; Acts 28.31).

d. Because the Church recognizes the eternal plan of God to reconcile all things in heaven and on earth under one head, the Lord Jesus Christ, in order that the Kingdom may be handed over to God the Father who will be all in all (Eph. 1.10; Rom. 11.36; 1 Cor. 15.27-28; Rev. 11.15, 21.1-17).

D. The Church is a community of friendship: friendship is a key part of reconciliation and spiritual development.

1. Spiritual maturity results in friendship with God (Exod. 33.11; James 2.23).
2. Spiritual discipleship results in friendship with Christ (John 15.13-15).
3. Spiritual unity is expressed in friendship with the saints (Rom. 16.5, 9, 12; 2 Cor. 7.1; Phil. 2.12; Col. 4.14; 1 Pet. 2.11; 1 John 2.7; 3 John 1.14).

VIII. A Community of Suffering

A. The Church community suffers because it exists in the world as "sheep among wolves" (Luke 10.3).

1. Hated by those who reject Christ (John 15.18-20).
2. Persecuted by the world system (Matt. 5.10; 2 Cor. 4.9; 2 Tim. 3.12).
3. It is uniquely the community of the poor, the hungry, the weeping, the hated, the excluded, the insulted, and the rejected (Matt. 5.20-22).
4. It is founded on the example and experience of Christ and the apostles (Isa. 53.3; Luke 9.22; Luke 24.46; Acts 5.41; 2 Tim. 1.8; 1 Thess. 2.2).

A Theology of the Church (continued)

B. The Church community imitates Christ in his suffering.

1. Because it purifies from sin (1 Pet. 4.1-2).
2. Because it teaches obedience (Heb. 5.8).
3. Because it allows them to know Christ more fully (Phil. 3.10).
4. Because those who share in Christ's suffering will also share in his comfort and glory (Rom. 8.17-18; 2 Cor. 1.5; 1 Pet. 5.1).

C. The Church community suffers because it identifies with those who suffer.

1. The body of Christ suffers whenever one of its members suffers (1 Cor. 12.26).
2. The body of Christ suffers because it voluntarily identifies itself with the despised, the rejected, the oppressed, and the unlovely (Prov. 29.7; Luke 7.34; Luke 15.1-2).

D. The cross of Christ is both the instrument of salvation and the pattern for Christian life. The cross embodies the values of the Church community.

1. The cross of Christ is the most fundamental Christian symbol. It serves as a constant reminder that the Church is a community of suffering.
2. The basic requirement of discipleship is a willingness to take up the cross daily and follow Jesus (Mark 8.34; Luke 9.23; Luke 14.27).

IX. A Community of Works

A. "Works of Service" are the hallmark of Christian congregations as they do justice, love mercy, and walk humbly with God.

1. The leadership of the Church is charged with preparing God's people for "works of service" (Eph. 4.12).
2. These good works are central to the new purpose and identity which is given us during the new birth. "For we are his workmanship, created in

A Theology of the Church (continued)

Christ Jesus for good works, which God prepared beforehand, that we should walk in them." (Eph. 2.10).

3. These works of service reveal God's character to the world and lead people to give him praise (Matt. 5.16; 2 Cor. 9.13).

B. Servanthood characterizes the Christian's approach to relationships, resources, and ministry.

1. The Church community serves based on the example of Christ who came "not to be served but to serve" (Matt. 20.25-28; Luke 22.27; Phil. 2.7).

2. The Church community serves based on the command of Christ and the apostles (Mark 10.42-45; Gal. 5.13; 1 Pet. 4.10).

3. The Church community serves, first of all, "the least of these" according to the mandates of Christ's teaching (Matt. 18.2-5; Matt. 25. 34-46; Luke 4.18-19).

C. Generosity and hospitality are the twin signs of kingdom service.

1. Generosity results in the giving of one's self and one's good for the sake of announcing and obeying Christ and his kingdom reign.

2. Hospitality results in treating the stranger, the foreigner, the prisoner, and the enemy as one of your very own people (Heb. 13.2).

3. These signs are the true fruit of repentance (Luke 3.7-14; Luke 19.8-10; James 1.27)

D. Stewardship is the foundational truth which governs the way the Church uses resources in order to do "Works of Service."

1. Our resources (time, money, authority, health, position, etc.) belong not to ourselves but to God.

A Theology of the Church (continued)

a. We answer to God for our management of the things entrusted to us personally and corporately (Matt. 25.14-30).

b. Money should be managed in such as way that treasures are laid up in heaven (Matt. 6.19-21; Luke 12.32-34; Luke 16.1-15; 1 Tim. 6.17-19).

c. Seeking first the Kingdom of God is the standard by which our stewardship is measured and the basis upon which more will be entrusted (Matt. 6.33).

2. Proper stewardship should contribute to equality and mutual sharing (2 Cor. 8.13-15).

3. Greed is indicative of dishonest stewardship and a repudiation of God as the owner and giver of all things (Luke 12.15; Luke 16.13; Eph. 5.5; Col. 3.5; 1 Pet. 5.2).

E. Justice is a key goal of the Church as it serves God and others.

1. Doing justice is an essential part of fulfilling our service to God (Deut. 16.20; 27.19; Pss. 33.5; 106.3; Prov. 28.5; Mic. 6.8; Matt. 23.23).

2. Justice characterizes the righteous servant but is absent from the hypocrite and the unrighteous (Prov. 29.7; Isa. 1.17; 58.1-14; Matt. 12.18-20; Luke 11.42).

APPENDIX 24

Translating the Story of God

Rev. Dr. Don L. Davis

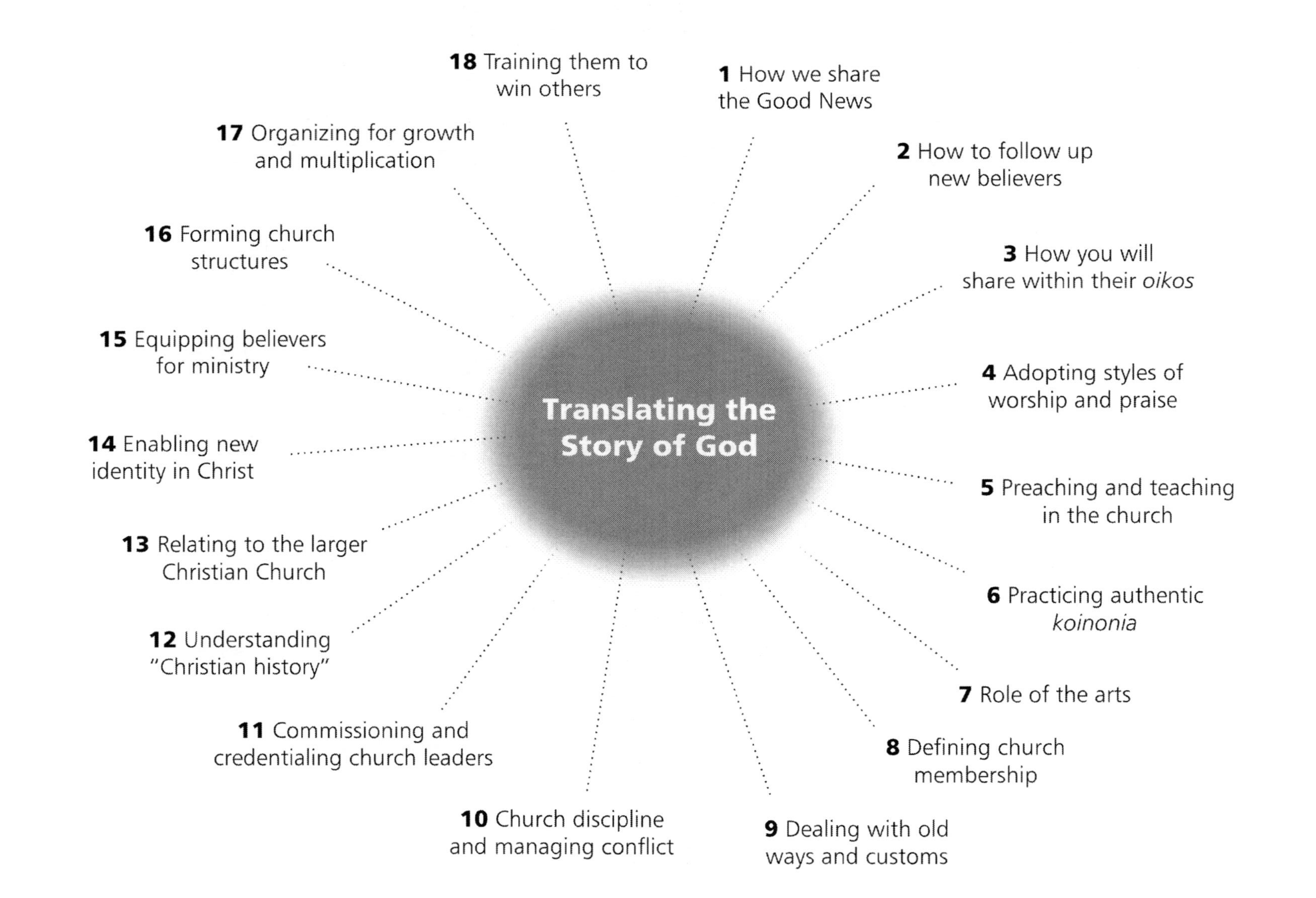

APPENDIX 25

Jesus and the Poor

Don L. Davis

Thesis: The heart of Jesus' ministry of the Kingdom was the transformation and renewal of the those on the underside of life, the poor. He demonstrated his personal heart vision in how he inaugurated his ministry, authenticated his ministry, defined the heart and soul of ministry, identifying himself directly with the poor.

I. Jesus Inaugurated His Ministry with an Outreach to the Poor.

A. The inaugural sermon at Nazareth, Luke 4.16-21

Luke 4.16-21 (ESV) - And he came to Nazareth, where he had been brought up. And as was his custom, he went to the synagogue on the Sabbath day, and he stood up to read. [17] And the scroll of the prophet Isaiah was given to him. He unrolled the scroll and found the place where it was written, [18] "The Spirit of the Lord is upon me, because he has anointed me to proclaim good news to the poor. He has sent me to proclaim liberty to the captives and recovering of sight to the blind, to set at liberty those who are oppressed, [19] to proclaim the year of the Lord's favor." [20] And he rolled up the scroll and gave it back to the attendant and sat down. And the eyes of all in the synagogue were fixed on him. [21] And he began to say to them, "Today this Scripture has been fulfilled in your hearing."

B. The meaning of this inauguration

1. The object of his attention: his choice of texts
2. The object of his calling: his Spirit anointing

Jesus and the Poor (continued)

3. The objects of his love:

   a. Good news to the poor

   b. Release to the captives

   c. Recovery of sight to the blind

   d. Letting the oppressed go free

4. The object of his ministry: the Year of the Lord's favor

C. *Ministry to the poor as the cornerstone of his inaugural ministry*

II. Jesus Authenticated His Ministry by His Actions toward the Poor.

A. John's query regarding Jesus' authenticity, Luke 7.18-23

Luke 7.18-23 (ESV) - The disciples of John reported all these things to him. And John, [19] calling two of his disciples to him, sent them to the Lord, saying, "Are you the one who is to come, or shall we look for another?" [20] And when the men had come to him, they said, "John the Baptist has sent us to you, saying, 'Are you the one who is to come, or shall we look for another?'" [21] In that hour he healed many people of diseases and plagues and evil spirits, and on many who were blind he bestowed sight. [22] And he answered them, "Go and tell John what you have seen and heard: the BLIND RECEIVE THEIR SIGHT, the lame walk, lepers are cleansed, and the deaf hear, the dead are raised up, the POOR HAVE GOOD NEWS PREACHED TO THEM. [23] And blessed is the one who is not offended by me."

B. Will the real Messiah please stand up?

1. The question of John, 19-20

2. The actions of Jesus, 21 (the show-side of "show-and-tell")

Jesus and the Poor (continued)

3. The explanation of his identity, 22-23

   a. Go and tell John what you have seen and heard.

   b. Blind seeing, lame walking, lepers cleansed, deaf hearing, dead being raising, the poor hearing the Gospel

C. *Ministry to the poor is undeniable proof of the Messiah's identity.*

III. Jesus Verified Salvation in Relation to One's Treatment of the Poor.

A. The story of Zaccheus, Luke 19.1-9

Luke 19.1-9 (ESV) - He entered Jericho and was passing through. [2] And there was a man named Zacchaeus. He was a chief tax collector and was rich. [3] And he was seeking to see who Jesus was, but on account of the crowd he could not, because he was small of stature. [4] So he ran on ahead and climbed up into a sycamore tree to see him, for he was about to pass that way. [5] And when Jesus came to the place, he looked up and said to him, "Zacchaeus, hurry and come down, for I must stay at your house today." [6] So he hurried and came down and received him joyfully. [7] And when they saw it, they all grumbled, "He has gone in to be the guest of a man who is a sinner." [8] And Zacchaeus stood and said to the Lord, "Behold, Lord, the half of my goods I give to the poor. And if I have defrauded anyone of anything, I restore it fourfold." [9] And Jesus said to him, "Today salvation has come to this house, since he also is a son of Abraham."

1. The palpitations of Zaccheus

2. The salutation of Zaccheus (to Jesus)

3. The declaration of Zaccheus

   a. Half of all I own I give to the poor.

   b. I restore those wrongly treated by me four-fold.

Jesus and the Poor (continued)

4. The salvation of Zaccheus, vv.9-10

B. Plucking Grain on the Sabbath, Matt.12.1-8

Matt. 12.1-8 (ESV) - At that time Jesus went through the grainfields on the Sabbath. His disciples were hungry, and they began to pluck heads of grain and to eat. [2] But when the Pharisees saw it, they said to him, "Look, your disciples are doing what is not lawful to do on the Sabbath." [3] He said to them, "Have you not read what David did when he was hungry, and those who were with him: [4] how he entered the house of God and ate the bread of the Presence, which it was not lawful for him to eat nor for those who were with him, but only for the priests? [5] Or have you not read in the Law how on the Sabbath the priests in the temple profane the Sabbath and are guiltless? [6] I tell you, something greater than the temple is here. [7] And if you had known what this means, 'I DESIRE MERCY, AND NOT SACRIFICE,' you would not have condemned the guiltless. [8] For the Son of Man is lord of the Sabbath."

1. Disciples snacking on corn on the Sabbath
2. The Pharisees disputation: "Look, your disciples are doing what is not lawful to do on the sabbath."
3. Jesus' retort: "I desire mercy and not sacrifice."
   a. Mercy to the poor and broken, not ritual faithfulness
   b. Compassion for the broken, not religious discipline

C. *Ministry to the poor is the litmus test of authentic salvation.*

IV. Jesus Identifies Himself Unreservedly with the Poor.

A. Those who cannot repay you, Luke 14.11-15

Jesus and the Poor (continued)

Luke 14.11-14 (ESV) - "For everyone who exalts himself will be humbled, and he who humbles himself will be exalted." [12] He said also to the man who had invited him, "When you give a dinner or a banquet, do not invite your friends or your brothers or your relatives or rich neighbors, lest they also invite you in return and you be repaid. [13] But when you give a feast, invite the poor, the crippled, the lame, the blind, [14] and you will be blessed, because they cannot repay you. You will be repaid at the resurrection of the just."

B. The Judgment Seat of the King, Matt. 25.31-45

Matt. 25.34-40 (ESV) - Then the King will say to those on his right, "Come, you who are blessed by my Father, inherit the kingdom prepared for you from the foundation of the world. [35] For I was hungry and you gave me food, I was thirsty and you gave me drink, I was a stranger and you welcomed me, [36] I was naked and you clothed me, I was sick and you visited me, I was in prison and you came to me." [37] Then the righteous will answer him, saying, "Lord, when did we see you hungry and feed you, or thirsty and give you drink? [38] And when did we see you a stranger and welcome you, or naked and clothe you? [39] And when did we see you sick or in prison and visit you?" [40] And the King will answer them, "Truly, I say to you, as you did it to one of the least of these my brothers, you did it to me."

1. Two sets of people: sheep and goats
2. Two responses: one blessed and embraced, one judged and rejected
3. Two destinies: the sheep in the Kingdom inherited, prepared from the foundation of the world, the goats in the eternal fire prepared for the devil and his angels
4. Two reactions: one was hospitable, charitable, generous; the other apathetic, heartless, negligent

Jesus and the Poor (continued)

5. The same group of people: the hungry, the thirsty, the stranger, the naked, the sick, the prisoner

6. *The same standard: in the way you treated or mistreated these people, those on the underside of life, so you responded to me.*

C. Jesus made it appear as those who were least deserving but repentant would become heirs of the Kingdom.

Matt. 21.31 (ESV) - "Which of the two did the will of his father?" They said, "The first." Jesus said to them, "Truly, I say to you, the tax collectors and the prostitutes go into the kingdom of God before you."

Mark 2.15-17 (ESV) - And as he reclined at table in his house, many tax collectors and sinners were reclining with Jesus and his disciples, for there were many who followed him. [16] And the scribes of the Pharisees, when they saw that he was eating with sinners and tax collectors, said to his disciples, "Why does he eat with tax collectors and sinners?" [17] And when Jesus heard it, he said to them, "Those who are well have no need of a physician, but those who are sick. I came not to call the righteous, but sinners."

D. Ministry to the poor is ministry to the Lord Jesus - his identification with them is complete.

Conclusion: The heart and soul of Jesus' ministry was directed toward the transformation and liberation of those who were most vulnerable, most forgotten, most neglected. As disciples, may we demonstrate the same.

APPENDIX 26

Ethics of the New Testament: Living in the Upside-Down Kingdom of God

True Myth and Biblical Fairy Tale

Dr. Don L. Davis

The Principle of Reversal

The Principle Expressed	Scripture
The poor shall become rich, and the rich shall become poor	Luke 6.20-26
The law breaker and the undeserving are saved	Matt. 21.31-32
Those who humble themselves shall be exalted	1 Pet. 5.5-6
Those who exalt themselves shall be brought low	Luke 18.14
The blind shall be given sight	John 9.39
Those claiming to see shall be made blind	John 9.40-41
We become free by being Christ's slave	Rom. 12.1-2
God has chosen what is foolish in the world to shame the wise	1 Cor. 1.27
God has chosen what is weak in the world to shame the strong	1 Cor. 1.27
God has chosen the low and despised to bring to nothing things that are	1 Cor. 1.28
We gain the next world by losing this one	1 Tim. 6.7
Love this life and you'll lose it; hate this life, and you'll keep the next	John 12.25
You become the greatest by being the servant of all	Matt. 10.42-45
Store up treasures here, you forfeit heaven's reward	Matt. 6.19
Store up treasures above, you gain Heaven's wealth	Matt. 6.20
Accept your own death to yourself in order to live fully	John 12.24
Release all earthly reputation to gain Heaven's favor	Phil. 3.3-7
The first shall be last, and the last shall become first	Mark 9.35
The grace of Jesus is perfected in your weakness, not your strength	2 Cor. 12.9
God's highest sacrifice is contrition and brokenness	Ps. 51.17
It is better to give to others than to receive from them	Acts 20.35
Give away all you have in order to receive God's best	Luke 6.38

APPENDIX 27

Empowering People for Freedom, Wholeness, and Justice

Theological and Ethical Foundations for World Impact's Development Ministries

Don Davis and Terry Cornett

A Theology of Development

Prologue

Love of God and love of neighbor have been pivotal themes of both Old and New Testament theology from their inception. From the time of the early Church forward, there has been a concern to demonstrate God's love and character to the world in word and deed, through faith and works, by both evangelistic proclamation and acts of justice and mercy.

Starting with its forerunners in Puritan, Pietistic, Moravian, and Wesleyan reform and revival movements, and extending into the modern Protestant missions movement, evangelical missionaries have combined a strong emphasis on evangelism and the establishment of churches with a serious attempt to engage in action that would foster justice and righteousness, especially on behalf of the poor and oppressed.

Evangelical reformers and missionaries have started schools and hospitals aimed at being accessible to the least advantaged segments of society, formed orphanages and worked for the reform of child labor laws, established businesses and cooperative ventures among the poor, supported legislation to abolish slavery and to ensure the protection of human rights, worked to upgrade the status of women in society, and mediated conflicts between warring groups and nations.[1]

Although Christians generally agree that evangelism and social action are important responsibilities of the Church, there is considerable variation in both the terms that are used to designate these responsibilities, and the way in which they are defined and placed in relation to one another. As a missions agency which is engaged in both of these activities, it is important to establish our definition of terms and a statement of the theological relationship which exists between these two tasks.

[1] See Paul E. Pierson's article, "Missions and Community Development: A Historical Perspective," (Elliston 1989, 1-22) for an introduction to the history of development work in evangelical missions and Donald W. Dayton's book "Discovering an Evangelical Heritage" (Dayton, 1988) for a helpful look at evangelical reform movements.

Empowering People for Freedom, Wholeness, and Justice (continued)

1. The Kingdom of God as the Basis of Evangelism, Church Planting and Development

1.1 The Kingdom of God as the Basis for Mission

"Missiology is more and more coming to see the Kingdom of God as the hub around which all of mission work revolves" (Verkuyl 1978, 203). Evangelism, church-planting and development work are not based on a few isolated "proof-texts," but are an abiding response to the theme of the Kingdom which is woven throughout the scriptural record. The Kingdom of God embodies the essence of what God's mission (*Missio Dei*) in the world is and provides a basis for seeing how our own activities are intended to fit into God's overall plan.[2]

[2] See George Eldon Ladd (1974, 45-134), for an introduction to a biblical theology of the Kingdom.

1.2 The Kingdom as Restoration

The Scriptures assert what human experience everywhere reveals; something has gone dramatically wrong with the world. The Bible teaches that the basis of this problem is humanity's rejection of God's rulership. The Genesis account of the Fall shows humanity repudiating God's right to give direction and boundaries to their decisions. From that time forward, evil filled the void left by the absence of God's loving rule. The world ceased to function correctly; death replaced life; disease replaced health; enmity replaced friendship; domination replaced cooperation; and scarcity replaced abundance. All human relationships with God and with each other were poisoned by the inner desire of each individual and social group to replace God's authority with their own rule.

In a response of grace to this situation, God decided not to reject and destroy the world, but to redeem it. He set in motion a plan to liberate the world from its bondage to evil powers, and to restore all things to perfection under his Kingly rule. Throughout the Scriptures this plan of reclamation is described as the "*Kingdom of God*," and insight into its nature and means of coming are progressively revealed.

Johannes Verkuyl summarizes the message of the Kingdom in this fashion:

> *The heart of the message of the Old and New Testament is that God . . . is actively engaged in the reestablishment of His liberating dominion over the cosmos and all of humankind. In seeking out Israel, He sought all of us and our entire world, and in Jesus Christ He laid the foundation of the Kingdom. Jesus Christ the Messiah "promised to the fathers," is the* ***auto basileia***[3]*: in Him the Kingdom has both come, and is coming in an absolutely unique way and with exceptional clarity. In His preaching Jesus divulges the riches, the* ***thesaurus*** *of that Kingdom: reconciliation,*

[3] That is, the One who in his own person fully embodies the rule of God.

Empowering People for Freedom, Wholeness, and Justice (continued)

the forgiveness of sins, victory over demonic powers. Standing within the tradition of the Mosaic law, He expounds the core message of . . . the prophets; He accomplishes the reconciliation of the world to God; He opens the way to the present and future Kingdom which demands decisions of us in all aspects of life (Verkuyl 1993, 72).

1.3 Responsibilities for Those Who Seek God's Kingdom

The implications of the Kingdom of God for mission can be delineated in three central truths. A kingdom-centered theology and missiology will be concerned for:

- Evangelizing so that people are converted to Christ as Lord.
- Creating churches where people are discipled and bear fruit.
- Helping the Church live out its commitment to bring freedom, wholeness, and justice in the world.

Thus:

A truly Kingdom-centered theology . . . can never neglect the call for the conversion of persons among all peoples and religious communities. To everyone of whatever religious persuasion the message must be repeated: "The Kingdom of God is at hand; repent, and believe in the Gospel." . . . Kingdom-centered theology entails a call to recognition of the lordship of the King and new orientation to the constitution of His Kingdom. In the absence of this aspect, proclamation of the good news of the Gospel is impossible. A theology and missiology informed by the biblical notion of the rule of Christ will never fail to identify personal conversion as one of the inclusive goals of God's Kingdom . . .

The Church . . . is raised up by God among all nations to share in the salvation and suffering service of the Kingdom . . . The Church constitutes the firstling, the early harvest of the Kingdom. Thus, although not limited to the Church, the Kingdom is unthinkable without the Church. Conversely, growth and expansion of the Church should not be viewed as ends but rather as means to be used in the service of the Kingdom. . . . The keys of the Kingdom have been given to the Church. It does not fulfill its mandate by relinquishing those keys but rather by using them to open up the avenues of approach to the Kingdom for all peoples and all population groups at every level of human society . . .

Empowering People for Freedom, Wholeness, and Justice (continued)

> *Finally, the gospel of the Kingdom addresses itself to all immediate human need, both physical and mental. It aims to right what is wrong on earth. It enjoins engagement in the struggle for racial, social, cultural, economic, and political justice. . . . The good news of the Kingdom has to do with all of these things. For this reason missiology must bend its efforts to the erection of a multiplicity of visible signs of God's Kingdom throughout the length and breadth of this planet (Verkuyl 1993, 72-73).*

Evangelism, church planting and development spring from a common theological base: a desire to live out the implications of the Kingdom of God which has broken into this present age in the person of Jesus Christ, the King of kings. This Kingdom is both *already* and *not yet*. It is currently *forcefully advancing* and *spreading like yeast through dough*, but also awaiting the return of Christ *when every knee will bow* and there will be a *new heaven and a new earth*. Our evangelism and our development work acknowledge God's kingly rule, now, during a time when the world, as a whole, does not. We announce the good news of the in-breaking Kingdom of peace and justice, call people to repentance and salvation through faith in its King, hope in its inevitable complete triumph, and live out obedience to its commands and values in the present moment.

2. Kingdom Work

Since evangelism/church planting and development work are intimately related, those who engage in them often find that their roles and projects overlap. While this is both normal and good, a clear beginning definition of each role may help to minimize the confusion which can sometimes result from this process.

2.1 Missionaries

Missionaries are called to pioneer new outreaches that focus on the evangelization of peoples in unreached (or under-reached) areas, social classes, or cultural groups.

Therefore, we assert that:

> *Missionaries cross class and cultural barriers to evangelize and disciple unreached groups so that reproducing churches are formed among them and placed at the service of God's kingdom rule.*

Empowering People for Freedom, Wholeness, and Justice (continued)

2.2 Development Workers

Development workers are called to confront conditions and structures in the world that do not submit themselves to the rule of God.

Therefore, we assert that:

> *Development workers enable individuals, churches and communities to experience movement toward the freedom, wholeness, and justice of the Kingdom of God.*

2.3 The Common Link

Both missionaries and Christian development workers are united in their common commitment to further God's kingdom rule in all areas of life.

Missionary activity is centered around the proclamation of "good news" that calls people into the Kingdom of God through an experience of salvation and regeneration. It focuses on bringing unreached peoples, cultures, and subcultures into the community of the redeemed (i.e., "bringing the world into the Church"). All of this is done with an eye toward creating churches which can disciple their members to acknowledge God's rulership and live out the values of his Kingdom in their individual and corporate life.

Missionary activity also encompasses development that seeks to call every area of life into conformity with God's kingdom rule. It evaluates every concrete life-situation in light of the Lord's Prayer ("thy Kingdom come, thy will be done, on earth as it is in heaven") and engages in deeds of compassion, love, and justice that demonstrate the nature of God's divine plan for all peoples. It focuses on bringing God's rule to bear on every human relationship and structure (i.e., "bringing the Church into the world").

3. Theological Relationship between Evangelism and Development

3.1 A Partnership Relationship

Missionary evangelism and church-planting and Christian development work are partners in the process of proclaiming, demonstrating, and extending the rule of the King. Both are responses to the fact that God has announced his desire to reconcile the world to himself through the gift of his Son. Although each is a legitimate response to God's plan for the world, neither is a sufficient response in and of itself.

Empowering People for Freedom, Wholeness, and Justice (continued)

Both word and deed are necessary components of the Church's announcement of, and faithfulness to, the Kingdom of God.

3.2 Interdependence and Interconnectedness

The relationship between Missions and Development is not a simple one. Their interconnectedness has many facets.

- *They are connected by a common goal.*

  Neither missionaries nor development workers are satisfied until God's reconciliation with man and man's reconciliation with man is completely realized. We believe that this makes both missions and development work Christocentric in orientation, since it is "in Christ" that God is reconciling the world to himself. Christ is the King. It is his sacrificial, reconciling death that provides the objective basis for reconciliation between humanity and God, and within human relationships and structures. It is his kingly authority and presence that allows the Kingdom to break into this present age destroying the works of darkness and creating authentic communities gathered under God's rule.

- *They retain a degree of independence from each other.*

  Evangelism and church-planting can sometimes be done without any immediate focus on development work. Conversely, development work can be sometimes be done without accompanying church-planting activity. Because both are authentic responses to God's activity in the world, they can, when appropriate, operate independently from each other. While each is a legitimate activity in its own right, it will obviously be healthier and more normal to find them occurring together.

- *They need each other for lasting effectiveness.*

  Without evangelism, there are no changed lives, no reconcilers who understand God's plan for man and society, and who undertake change in the power of the Spirit. Without development, the churches established by mission become withdrawn, and do not function as "salt and light" within their local and national communities. Missionary efforts are undermined when the existing church does not make visible in its life the effects of God's

Empowering People for Freedom, Wholeness, and Justice (continued)

kingdom rule. The integration of the two is aptly expressed in Ephesians 2:8-10 which states, "For by grace you have been saved through faith. And this is not your own doing; it is the gift of God, [9] not a result of works, so that no one may boast. [10] For we are his workmanship, created in Christ Jesus for good works, which God prepared beforehand, that we should walk in them."

These facets may be summarized as "a threefold relationship between evangelism and social activity. First, Christian social activity [development] is a *consequence* of evangelism, since it is the evangelized who engage in it. Second it is a *bridge* to evangelism, since it expresses God's love and so both overcomes prejudice and opens closed doors. Third, it is a *partner* of evangelism, so that they are 'like two blades of a pair of scissors or the two wings of a bird'" (Stott 1995, 52).

3.3 The Need for Specialization

Modern missions have seen the rise of both mission and development agencies. This occurs as organizations specialize in one component of the overall task God has given. This recognition of the need for specialization arose early on in the life of the Church.

J. Chongham Cho comments:

> *In Acts 6 . . . a distinction between evangelism and social action was made. This was not a division in essence but for the sake of practical efficacy of the church's mission and as the solution to a problem which arose in the church. This is a necessary deduction from the nature of the church as Christ's body. Although we should resist polarization between evangelism and social action, we should not resist specialization (Cho 1985, 229).*

As a missions agency, our primary focus is evangelism and discipleship which results in the planting of indigenous churches. The fact that evangelism, church-planting and development are interconnected means that missions agencies, especially those who focus on the poor and oppressed, will engage in some form of development work. However, the mission agency must be careful to structure its development work so that it encourages the central task of evangelism and church-planting rather than detracts from it.[4] We should engage in development work which fosters the formation, health, growth, and reproducibility of indigenous churches among the poor.

[4] See Appendix A for a variety of perspectives on how improperly implemented development work can adversely affect missionary work.

Empowering People for Freedom, Wholeness, and Justice (continued)

Specialization allows organizations to maximize the training and resources that can be committed to a specific part of the overall task of mission. The development agency may engage in many good and necessary projects that have no immediate connection to evangelism and the planting and nurturing of emerging churches. The missions agency appreciates the many development agencies that engage in this type of work. Although the mission agency will want to network with them (and pray that God will vastly increase their number and effectiveness), the mission agency itself will focus on development projects that assist the task of evangelism, discipleship, and the establishment of indigenous churches. Without this commitment to specialization, the mission agency will lose its ability to accomplish its part of the larger task.

4. Development Work within Our Mission Agency

4.1 Statement of Purpose

While we recognize the legitimacy of engaging in development work for its own sake as a direct godly response to human need, we believe that we are called to specialize in development work that specifically supports and contributes to the task of evangelism, discipleship and church-planting. In light of this, we affirm the following statement.

The aim of World Impact's development ministries is to support the evangelism, discipleship, and church-planting goals of World Impact by:

- *Demonstrating the Love of Christ*

  Many oppressed people have little basis for understanding God's love for them and the essential justice and compassion of his character. Development work can provide a living witness to the love of Christ and his concern for justice and peace in urban neighborhoods. Holistic ministry can come alongside the verbal proclamation of the Gospel, verifying its credibility and enriching the depth of understanding among its hearers. Development work can function pre-evangelistically to prepare people to genuinely listen to the claims of Christ and his message of salvation.

- *Empowering Emerging Churches*

  Emerging urban churches often have few physical resources with which to face the enormous needs of the city. Development work can partner with the pastors of planted-churches, giving access to resources and programs

Empowering People for Freedom, Wholeness, and Justice (continued)

that can meet immediate needs within their congregation, encourage leadership development, and help their congregations engage in effective holistic outreach to their community.

- *Modeling the Implications of the Gospel*

  We cannot hope to reproduce churches committed to engage in a task they have never seen lived out in practice. We engage in development work because we expect newly planted churches to do likewise. We want to provide a living example that the Gospel will necessarily move from belief to action, from word to deed.

4.2 An Important Reminder

One cautionary note is in order. We cannot, through our own efforts, bring the Kingdom of God. As Paul Hiebert reminds us, "Our paradigms are flawed if we begin missions with human activity. Mission is not primarily what we do. It is what God does" (Hiebert 1993, 158). Evangelism, church-planting and development work all function, first and foremost, at the disposal of the Spirit of God. Knowing what should be done, and how we should do it, is never primarily determined through strategic diagrams or well-thought-out organizational approaches. Our first duty is to be faithful to the King, to listen to his instructions, and to respond to his initiatives.

An Ethic of Development

5. Introduction

We have stated that:

> *Development workers enable individuals, churches and communities to experience movement toward the freedom, wholeness, and justice of the Kingdom of God.*

The process by which we move toward this goal, and the decisions we make to achieve these ends must be guided by an ethic which is consistent with God's standard for human relationships.

Ethics has to do with human conduct and character. It is the systematic study of the principles and methods for distinguishing right from wrong and good from bad. A Christian ethic of development helps us make decisions about development issues in

Empowering People for Freedom, Wholeness, and Justice (continued)

light of biblical revelation and theology. It enables us to think and act clearly so that we can discern what is right to do and how it should be done.

Ethics is concerned that our theology be applied to our behaviors and attitudes. It is not content to simply understand the truth. Instead, it continually seeks to help us discover how to apply the truth (and attempts to motivate us to do so). True ethical behavior means that ethical principles are understood, internalized, and applied to the situation through the development of specific strategies and practices. In an organization, true ethical behavior also requires that strategies and practices undergo regular testing, evaluation and refinement. This ensures that the organization is accomplishing in practice what it affirms in principle.

Finally, it should be noted that our experiences always confront us with paradoxes, anomalies and competing priorities. An ethic of development does not attempt to condense life into a neatly packaged system. Rather, it provides principles that will help us to clarify what is most important in the particular situation that are facing. Each ethical decision must involve discussion about how the various principles outlined below interrelate and about which are the most significant values for a given decision. Only in dialogue and in prayer can the correct decision be discerned.

The ethical principles of the Kingdom of God can be expressed in the values of freedom, wholeness, and justice. These values are the root and the fruit of doing development from a kingdom perspective.

6. World Impact's Development Work is Committed to Freedom

Freedom is the ability to exercise our God-given capacity to make choices that express love. Therefore, development should engender freedom by helping individuals:

- Gain dignity and respect.
- Be empowered to make wise choices.
- Take responsibility for themselves and others.

This process involves helping individuals *understand* and *achieve* what they need to live freely in community as biblically responsible, self-directing, maturing servants of God's Kingdom. It implies the development of relationships characterized neither by dependence nor independence, but by loving *interdependence* that results in partnership, mutuality, and increased freedom.

Empowering People for Freedom, Wholeness, and Justice (continued)

6.1 Development affirms human beings as precious and unique in the sight of God, and believes that they have been granted unique capacities and potentials by God.

Explanation

As beings made in the image of God, every person regardless of station or place, is worthy of dignity and respect. People are to be cherished, nurtured, and provided for according to their intrinsic value and preciousness to God. Biblically based development will never exploit people for the sake of economic purposes or treat people as instruments, but instead will value them as ends-in-themselves, to be loved and respected for their worth before God.

Implications

- *People are to be given priority in every dimension of development.*

  Development should contribute to the potential for self-sufficiency, should enhance the quality of life, and should encourage good stewardship among those participating in the programs.

- *Mutual respect is foundational to authentic development.*

  For the poor, life in the urban community is full of inconvenience, difficulty, and shame. The needy daily experience the indignities of being poor in an affluent society. Oftentimes they are accused of moral laxity, subjected to stifling bureaucracies, and pre-judged as causing their own poverty through incompetence or lack of motivation. Development is sensitive to these messages which are given to the needy in our society. It recognizes that the poor are the objects of God's compassion and good news, chosen to be rich in faith and heirs to the Kingdom of God (James 2.5). Development seeks to demonstrate God's righteous cherishing of the poor through its specific actions and relationships.

  Aid not founded on genuine respect can easily humiliate the poor. Therefore, assistance offered to those in need must affirm their dignity and self-respect. Anything that diminishes the worth and significance of the poor in the development process is sinful and injurious to the well-being of all, both those offering the aid and those receiving it.

Empowering People for Freedom, Wholeness, and Justice (continued)

- *The workplace should operate as a caring community.*

  While an impersonal atmosphere characterizes many business environments, Christian development strives to create a relational framework for trainees and employees. Development workers and those participating in the development project must develop habit patterns of caring for each other beyond the constraints of the project at hand.

6.2 Development should empower people to take full responsibility for their own lives and to care for the needs of others.

Explanation

Development emerges from the conviction that all work is honorable. God has mandated that human beings earn their living with integrity and excellence. This mandate for individual work is grounded in God's initial command given to humankind at creation, and continues on and is reaffirmed in the teachings of the apostles. While God demands that his people be generous and hospitable to the needy and the stranger (2 Cor. 9), God likewise commands all to work honestly with their own hands (1 Thess. 4), and further charges that those who refuse to work ought to correspondingly be denied benevolent aid, that is, "if anyone will not work, neither let him eat," (cf. 2 Thess. 3.10).

Development rejects the notion that the creation of wealth is intrinsically evil. Such a view is simplistic and fails to grapple with the biblical notion of Christian stewardship. Development aims to create abundance, but never for the sake of selfish gain or lustful greed. Rather, development takes seriously the biblical requirement that we work, not merely to meet our own needs, but so that from the abundance God has provided we may use our goods and resources to meet the needs of others, especially those who are our brothers and sisters in the body of Christ (cf. Eph. 4; 2 Cor. 8; Gal. 6). The biblical standard is that those who stole before they entered the Kingdom are to steal no more, but to work honorably in quietness and integrity, in order that they may have sufficient resources to meet their own needs, and have sufficient wealth to care for others. Development not only seeks to honor the needy by ensuring they can participate in the basic human right to work, it also challenges them to trust God to supply their needs through honorable labor that allows them to be providers for themselves and others.

Empowering People for Freedom, Wholeness, and Justice (continued)

Implications

- *Nothing can excuse a worker, leader, or professional from the perils and potentials of personal responsibility.*

  Christian workers are not exempt from the vices of laziness, slothfulness, mismanagement, and greed, and they will not be spared from the consequences of such habits and conduct.

- *It is a primary aim of development to increase the maturity of everyone involved in the process.*

  It is assumed that the maturing individual will be increasingly characterized by vision (establishing and owning life-long purposes, aspirations and priorities), responsibility (acting on those purposes, aspirations and priorities with motivation, perseverance and integrity), and wisdom (increasing in skill, understanding and the ability to discern and do what is right for themselves and others).

  Maturing individuals should move from dependence toward autonomy, from passivity toward activity, from small abilities to large abilities, from narrow interests to broad interests, from egocentricity to altruism, from ignorance toward enlightenment, from self-rejection toward self-acceptance, from compartmentability toward integration, from imitation toward originality and from a need for rigidity toward a tolerance for ambiguity (Klopfenstein 1993, 95-96).

- *Decisions are best handled at the closest point to those affected.*

  National policies and procedures exist to:

  » Provide a framework for effective decision making.

  » Express the values and purposes that are corporately shared.

  » Ensure equity between peoples and projects at many different sites.

  » Provide accountability which safeguards integrity.

  Responsible decision making within a community assumes that there are mature individuals with a commitment to these common purposes and that open communication exists between the people involved. When these elements are present, most decision making should be done by the people who are responsible to implement the decisions. All decisions must take into consideration the local context and the unique people, relationships, and project conditions that are present.

- *Wages should be fair.*

  When development work involves employment, the employee should be compensated equitably in relation to their contribution toward the success or profitability of the project.

- *Training programs should include teaching on the importance of stewardship and giving.*

  The need for people to give to God, to others and to their community should be made explicit in the development process. Each person's self-identity as a contributor should be reinforced and the intrinsic connection between receiving and giving (Luke 6.38) should be established.

6.3 Development work must discourage the inclination toward dependency.

Explanation

Development emphasizes that each person should be trained and equipped to achieve their potential to be self-sustaining and self-directing. Creating or nurturing dependency undercuts the deep human need to be a co-creator with God in using our gifts to honor him, and finding our significance and place in the world. Dependency can occur from either end of the people-helping relationship; the developer can create a sense of his or her own indispensability which leads to dependency, or the trainee can easily refuse to progress and grow on to interdependence and depth. Dependency pollutes the process of authentic development by creating unhealthy relationships which damage the trainee's initiative and self-motivation.

Implications

- *Trainees must be required to demonstrated initiative.*

  The basic rule of thumb is "Don't do for people what they can do for themselves-even if it means that the project (or training) will go slowly" (Hoke and Voorhies 1989, 224). When too much is done for the people who

Empowering People for Freedom, Wholeness, and Justice (continued)

are being assisted, the developer has taken from the trainees the opportunity to learn from their mistakes. Dependency, even when resulting from a spirit of benevolence and sympathy, inevitably stunts the growth of those who are so affected.

- *Development should avoid the extremes of authoritarian paternalism, on the one hand, and non-directive laissez-faire(ism) on the other.*

  Developers, by definition, are leaders, and cannot avoid their responsibility to mentor, train, teach, and provide direction to those they serve. Maintaining complete decision-making control, however, does not foster interdependent relationships. While close accountability is essential in the earliest stages of training, development workers must recognize the need to modify strategies and involvement based on the competency and ongoing progress of the learners.[5]

- *Projects should help trainees gain control of their own destiny.*

  Projects must be regularly evaluated to insure that they are not keeping people dependent on long-term employment by WIS. Projects which equip people to gain employment with existing businesses or start businesses of their own are the goal.

[5] *For a discussion of the Hersey-Blanchard training model that tailors leadership style to the competencies and attitudes of the trainee see **Leadership Research** (Klopfenstein, 1995)*

7. World Impact's Development Work Is Committed to Wholeness.

Wholeness (*Shalom*) is the personal and communal experience of peace, abundance, goodness, soundness, well-being, and belonging. Wholeness is founded on *righteousness* (right relationships with God and man), *truth* (right beliefs about God and man), and *holiness* (right actions before God and man). *Shalom* is a gift of God and a sign of his Kingdom's presence.

7.1 Development should create an environment where cooperative relationships can flourish.

Explanation

Development that leads to wholeness acknowledges that human activity takes place in community. The web of relationships that occurs in the work environment (e.g. trainer to trainee, co-worker to co-worker,etc.), must reflect our values of Christian community.

Empowering People for Freedom, Wholeness, and Justice (continued)

Implications

- *People are not means to an end.*

  Development seeks, first of all, to develop people. This will necessarily involve equipping them (and holding them accountable to) accomplishing tasks. However, it is the maturing of the person, not the completion of the task that is always the primary end of development work.

- *All people in the development process should work for each other as if they are working for Christ himself.*

  Colossians 3.23-24 reminds us that our work is ultimately directed toward and rewarded by Christ. Development projects must operationalize this principle. This suggests that our work must be done with excellence, integrity, diligence, meekness, love and whatever other virtues are necessary for proper service to God.

- *Relational dynamics must be taken seriously.*

  A development project which produces an excellent product and equips people with marketable skills, but which is characterized by disharmony or disunity among its employees has not achieved its goal. The developer must seek to develop genuine community within the workplace.

*7.2 **Development activities should demonstrate the truth of the Gospel.***

Explanation

1 John 3:18 exhorts us to love not merely with words or tongue, "but with actions and in truth." The love of Christ is given not to "souls" but to whole persons. Development activities should minister unashamedly to the whole person and should serve as evangelism by example. Development work functions as a sign of the Kingdom by enabling people, families, and\or communities to experience the love and care of Christ. This suggests that development workers must know Christ intimately and be able to communicate his love to others.

Implications

- *Development projects may emphasize mental, physical, social, or economic development.*

Empowering People for Freedom, Wholeness, and Justice (continued)

All aspects of human need are of concern to the development worker. As the development worker's love for people takes shape in concrete actions, it should be their intent that people "may see your good deeds and praise your Father in heaven." (Matt. 5.16).

- *Development workers should be maturing disciples of Christ who are actively engaged in ongoing spiritual growth.*

  Who we are is more important than what we do. Only as development workers are actively seeking to live in Christ's love and listen to his Spirit, will they effectively communicate his love to those they work with.

- *Development workers must receive care for their own physical, mental, emotional, and spiritual health and development.*

  Development workers face unique pressures in dealing with human need. They often feel particular stress from standing in between, and identifying with, both the interests of the particular people they serve and the organization they represent (See Hiebert 1989, 83). Physical, emotional or spiritual burn-out is an ever present possibility. Therefore, it is important that development workers give adequate time and attention to maintaining their own health so that they can continue to effectively minister to the needs of others.

- *Development workers need to be specifically equipped in evangelism and an understanding of missions.*

  Christian development workers usually understand that development and evangelism should work in partnership, but are often undertrained in evangelism (See Hoke and Voorhies 1989). Development workers also need to receive general training in missions and management in addition to being trained for their specific task of development (See Pickett and Hawthorne 1992, D218-19) since many of their daily tasks require an understanding of these disciplines.

7.3 Development activities should be above reproach.

Explanation

Wholeness and holiness are inseparable concepts. The way in which development work is conducted will have a profound impact on its ability to effect transformation. For development work to contribute to the wholeness, soundness, and well-being of people it must take special care to sustain integrity in word and deed.

Implications

- *Development projects should maintain high ethical standards.*

  Lack of adequate funds or personnel and the pressures of immediate human need can tempt us to "cut corners" in the way we develop and administrate projects. This temptation must be resisted. Our product cannot be artificially separated from our process. Development projects must serve as a witness to the government, society at large, and the people they train through adherence to high ethical standards of business conduct.

- *Development projects must work within the framework of our 501(c)(3) non-profit status.*

  State and Federal laws limit the ability of non-profits to create situations where individuals directly receive wealth and resources from the corporation. (This prevents individuals inside and outside of the organization from abusing the non-profit status for personal gain). As programs are created to empower people and share resources, the development workers must make sure that they are structured in such a way that they fall within the legal guidelines.

- *Appeals to donors must not motivate by guilt, overstate the need, promise unrealistic results, or demean the dignity of aid recipients.*

  Compressing the complexity of human need and relationships into an appeal to donors is a difficult and complicated task. It is, however, necessary and important work. Development workers in the field should take personal responsibility for relaying needs and vision in an accurate manner to those involved in publishing printed materials about a project.

Empowering People for Freedom, Wholeness, and Justice (continued)

8. World Impact's Development Work Is Committed to Justice

Justice results from a recognition that all things belong to God and should be shared in accordance with his liberality and impartiality. Biblical justice is concerned both with equitable treatment and with the restoration of right relationship. It abhors oppression, prejudice and inequality because it understands that these separate people from each other and from God. Development which is based on justice is an important step toward repairing damaged relationships between individuals, classes and cultures which may harbor suspicion and ill-will toward one another. Development work seeks to engender right actions which lead to right relationships.

8.1 Development is rooted in a biblical understanding of God as Creator and Ruler of the universe which demands that all things be reconciled in him.

Explanation

God has delegated to humanity the responsibility to be stewards of his world. This understanding manifests itself in concern for three broad categories of relationship: relations with God, relations with others, and relations with the environment (See Elliston 1989, *Transformation*, 176). Although these relationships were broken by the entrance of sin in the world, God's kingdom rule now demands their restoration.

Development recognizes that until the fullness of the Kingdom of Christ is manifested, there will inevitably be poverty, exploitation, and misery caused by sin's perversion of these three areas of relationship. This realization, neither paralyzes nor discourages authentic Christian development. While understanding the nature of moral evil in the world, authentic development seeks to demonstrate models of justice and reconciliation which reflect the justice of Christ's Kingdom.

Implications

- *Development intends to move people toward right relationship with God.*

  Authentic reconciliation between people is based on their mutual reconciliation with God. Although "common grace" and the "image of God" provide a ground for some degree of reconciliation between all people, it is ultimately in right relationship with God through Christ that the most profound and lasting form of reconciliation can occur. Therefore, development work is eager to assist in preparing people for hearing the Gospel by witnessing to its truth and living out its implications.

- *Reconciliation between individuals, classes, and cultures is a key value.*

  Development will inevitably involve new ways of power-sharing, using resources, making decisions, enforcing policy, and relating to others. There is a need to innovate rather than simply imitate existing models. It is extremely important that the viewpoints of peoples from different classes and cultures be represented in the planning of any development project.

- *Development projects must not be wasteful of resources or harmful to the physical environment.*

  God's command to humankind is to recognize his ownership, and neither exploit nor destroy his earth, but to tend and care for it. Stewardship involves using the earth's resources to glorify him and meet the needs of our neighbors while keeping in mind our responsibility to future generations. Development must be sustainable, i.e., it must not simply consume resources but cultivate them as well.

8.2 Development recognizes the systemic and institutional foundations of producing wealth and experiencing poverty.

Explanation

The Bible delineates various moral vices that can lead to poverty in the lives of individuals (e.g., laziness, sloth, neglect of responsibility, cf. Prov. 6; Prov. 24, etc.), However, it is also clear that poverty can be caused by large scale societal and economic factors that create conditions of need, oppression, and want (cf. Isa. 1; Isa. 54, Amos 4, 5, etc.). Even a cursory reading of Scripture reveals that throughout biblical history the prophets condemned certain practices of business, politics, law, industry, and even religion that contributed to the imbalances among various groups within society, and led to the oppression of the poor. Development seeks to be prophetic by affirming that God is committed to the poor and the needy, and will not tolerate their oppression indefinitely. Development is not naive. It does not attribute all poverty in society to individual moral vice. On the contrary, struggling against injustice demands that people recognize the ever-present possibility of demonic influence in human structures (1 John 5.19).

Empowering People for Freedom, Wholeness, and Justice (continued)

Implications

- *Spiritual warfare is a key component of the development process.*

  Ephesians 6.12 reminds us that "we do not wrestle against flesh and blood, but against the rulers, against the authorities, against the cosmic powers over this present darkness, against the spiritual forces of evil in the heavenly places." Development work that does not intentionally and regularly set aside time for prayer and other spiritual disciplines is unlikely to effect lasting change. Development workers should have a plan for spiritual warfare that is as significant a focus as the plan for the development work itself.

  Development workers should also realize that their projects will experience spiritual attack. The accumulation of money or power within a project can be entry points for the perversion of that project despite its best intentions. Relationships between development project leaders, or between development workers and those they are training, can be twisted through the stress of conflict, jealousy, miscommunication, and cultural differences. Both personal relationships and institutional programs need to be protected from spiritual forces that would corrupt or destroy them. This requires an ongoing commitment to spiritual warfare, and to personal and corporate holiness.[6]

- *Development work should challenge unjust practices.*

  Development workers must prepare people to speak out against unjust practices in ways which demonstrate both the love and justice of God. While the non-profit organization is not itself a forum for political advocacy, it is responsible to train people to value justice and to make decisions in a moral context. In the marketplace, workers will be confronted by individual and systemic injustices and should be trained to respond to them in a manner which honors Christ and the values of his Kingdom.

- *The role of the Church in development must not be neglected.*

  Ephesians 2.14 records that it is "Christ himself" who is our peace and who has "destroyed the barrier, the dividing wall of hostility" between Jew and Gentiles. Reconciliation is rooted in the person and work of Christ and thus

*[6] See Thomas McAlpine, **Facing the Powers** (McAlpine, 1991) for a helpful discussion of ways in which Reformed, Anabaptist, Charismatic, and Social Science perspectives share both differing perspectives and common ground in understanding and confronting spiritual powers.*

Empowering People for Freedom, Wholeness, and Justice (continued)

the importance of Christ's body, the Church, cannot be overlooked. Missionary development projects should both flow out of and result in dynamic churches.

8.3 Development does not seek to guarantee equality of outcome, but equality of opportunity.

Explanation

Development concentrates on providing an environment in which people can learn the importance and disciplines of work, gain skills which enhance the value of their work, and apply the disciplines and skills they acquire. However, no human endeavor is exempt from the moral force of our ability to choose, i.e., to decide whether or not to fully use the gifts, opportunities, and potentials we have been given. Because of variations of motivation, effort and preparation, differences in incomes are inevitable, and ought to be expected. Development programs should both teach and reward initiative.

Implications

- *Each trainee plays a critical role in their own success.*

  While the developers can offer a vast amount of expertise and aid in creating wealth for the trainees, many of the most important attributes necessary for prolonged success are controlled by the trainees. Without the requisite vision, energy, and commitment to do the work for long enough time so profits can be seen, success will not occur. These qualities arise from the drive and conviction of the trainees, not merely from the availability of the developers. Because of this, development cannot guarantee the success of all those involved in the project.

- *Faithful stewardship should lead to increased responsibility.*

  All development projects should have a plan for rewarding faithfulness, skill development, and diligence. Justice demands that increased effort lead to increased reward.

Empowering People for Freedom, Wholeness, and Justice (continued)

8.4 Development workers should respect cultural differences and strive to create a training style that is culturally conducive to those being empowered.

Explanation

Every human culture is "a blueprint that gives the individuals of a society a way of explaining and coping with life. It teaches people how to think, act and respond appropriately in any given situation. It allows people to work together based on a common understanding of reality. It organizes ways of thinking and acting into forms that can be passed on to others" (Cornett 1991, 2). Culture shapes every form of human activity from the observable behaviors (language, dress, food, etc.) to the internal thoughts and attitudes (thinking styles, definitions of beauty and worth, etc.). Understanding how a culture perceives reality, what it values, and how it functions is fundamental information for the development worker.

Although all human cultures are affected by sinful perspectives, attitudes and behaviors which must be confronted by the Gospel, human cultures themselves are celebrated by the Scriptures. The apostles confirmed that becoming a Christian did not entail having to change one's original culture (Acts 15). The vision of God's Kingdom from Old Testament (Micah 4) to New (Rev. 7.9) involves people from every nation, language and ethnicity. Missionaries from Paul onward have contextualized the Gospel, putting eternal truth in forms that could be understood and practiced by people of diverse cultures (See Cornett 1991, 6-9). Development workers, likewise, must respect cultural differences and seek to contextualize their instruction and resources (See Elliston, Hoke and Voorhies 1989).

Development workers have a unique interest in empowering groups that have been marginalized, oppressed or neglected by the larger society. This will frequently involve working with groups or individuals that are distinct from the dominant culture. Development work will effectively empower immigrants, unassimilated people groups, or people who have been victimized by race or class discrimination, only if it understands and respects the cultural distinctives of these groups.

Finally, development workers must prepare people to live and work in a pluralistic society. Learning how to successfully relate to customers and co-workers from other cultures has become a key component of job training. Although development work must start with the cultural context of those being assisted, it must also enable those workers to respect other cultures and to successfully work in the larger society.

Empowering People for Freedom, Wholeness, and Justice (continued)

Implications

- *Development workers should understand the culture(s) and sub-culture(s) of the people they work with.*

  Development workers should, first of all, gain a basic understanding of the nature of human culture and of strategies for developing effective cross-cultural training relationships.[7] They should gain the fundamental skills necessary for working in the cross-cultural environment (language acquisition, etc.). It is highly desirable for the development worker to have a mentor either from the culture or who is an experienced observer of the culture to assist in the training process.

- *The work environment should be functionally appropriate and aesthetically pleasing when viewed from the perspective of the culture(s) that work or do business there.*

  All human cultures desire environments that combine functionality with beauty. There is significant variation, however, in how beauty and functionality are defined, prioritized and applied from one culture to another. The physical environment in which the development project occurs should take cultural concerns into account.

- *Development workers should be sensitive to how conflict is handled by the culture of the people they work among.*

  Conflict is an inevitable part of working together. It can be a healthy opportunity for growth if handled correctly. Cultural differences, however, can sabotage the process of conflict management. The development worker must take cultural attitudes toward directness/indirectness, shame/guilt, individualism/collectivism, etc. seriously and adapt their conflict management style to reflect those concerns. They must also take seriously their responsibility to prepare people from sub-cultures to work within the dominant culture.

- *Development workers should be sensitive to roles or work that is considered degrading by the culture.*

  Although all honest work carries dignity before God, cultural perceptions of role and status have tremendous power to shape attitudes. Whenever possible, work should be chosen that is not repugnant to the culture. If this

*[7] Basic resources for gaining an understanding of culture include **The Missionary and Culture** (Cornett 1991), **Beyond Culture** (Hall 1976), **Christianity Confronts Culture** (Mayers 1974), **Ministering Cross-Culturally** (Lingenfelter and Mayers 1986) and **Cross-Cultural Conflicts: Building Relationships for Effective Ministry** (Elmer 1993).*

Empowering People for Freedom, Wholeness, and Justice (continued)

is not possible, careful preparation and training should be done to ensure that each person understands the necessity and dignity of the work involved. In some cases it may be necessary to challenge the cultural value system (see Miller, 1989) but this should be done sensitively and with adequate preparation and involvement of the trainees.

- *Developers should prepare trainees for situations that they are likely to encounter in the workplace.*

  People from event-oriented cultures, for example, need to understand the time-oriented culture that defines American business practices. Helping workers learn skills and disciplines for success in the larger society is an important part of the training process.

8.5 The goal of development is to glorify God through excellence and service, not merely to make a profit.

Explanation

In the ethics of the corporate world, the highest indicator of success is usually the profitability of the business. However, development work that is informed by kingdom values involves a broader vision. Development seeks to emphasize the importance of people-nurturing and training and the production of a quality product that meets human need.

Since producing quality Christian and professional leadership models is a high aim of our development efforts, we must unashamedly emphasize both external profits as well as internal gains. On the one hand, a business, if it is to survive, must be profitable and able to stand on its on. On the other hand, we must strive to produce men and women who are spiritually mature as well as professionally oriented and technically competent. The creation of wealth is not an end in itself; it is a by-product of engaging in business with an eye toward excellence, in the name of Christ.

Empowering People for Freedom, Wholeness, and Justice (continued)

Implications

- *No skill will be taught or product produced simply because it is valued by society or likely to produce a profit.*

  All skills and products must be consistent with the aims of justice, peace and wholeness that characterize the kingdom rule of Christ. Skills and modes of production that degrade human dignity and products that promote injustice, inequity, or human misery are not to be considered fitting for development regardless of their acceptance by the society at large.

- *The aim of development work must not only be to help people obtain and generate resources but also to help them commit to using those resources on behalf of the Kingdom of God.*

  Helping people to obtain education, skills or wealth is ultimately unproductive if these things are not placed at God's service and the service of others. Good development projects will offer people the opportunity to serve God not only with the profits from their labor but through the work itself. Developers must teach and model that work is an opportunity for service to God (Col. 3.23-24).

9. The Need for Application

Each of the points listed above has a section titled "Explanation" and a section titled "Implications." However, for the paper to be complete one more step is necessary. Every implication must be accompanied by a series of *applications*. These applications should be created by development workers in the field, and structured for the unique needs of the local situation.

In creating these applications, the following guidelines should be followed:

- Each local ministry should thoroughly review the "Implications" sections and decide on specific steps which will enable them to apply these principles to their particular development project.
- These steps should be developed in a way that involves the people most affected by each development project.
- Once finalized, the application steps should be committed to writing.
- These applications should be regularly taught and reviewed.

Empowering People for Freedom, Wholeness, and Justice (continued)

- These applications should be included in each regularly scheduled evaluation done by the project.
- Following each scheduled evaluation, there should be a revising and updating of these applications based on what has been learned in experience.

Appendix A

Selected Quotes on the Role of Development Work within the Mission Agency

Christian social transformation differs from secular relief and development in that it serves in an integrated, symbiotic relationship with other ministries of the Church, including evangelism and church planting (Elliston 1989, 172).

My experience with scores of ministries among the poor has taught me that economic projects, when used as entrees into communities, do not facilitate church planting or growth. . . . the two goals—relief and church planting—are different. They are both Christian, and at times compatible. But many times they do not support each other well at all. . . . It appears that where workers enter a community with a priority to proclaim, many deeds of mercy, acts of justice and signs of power will occur. From these the church will be established. But when workers enter with a priority of dealing with economic need, they may assist the people economically very well, but they rarely establish as church. There is a time for both, and there are life callings to do both, but they must be distinguished (Grigg 1992, 163-64).

Avoid institutions if possible at the beachhead stage (community development programs unrelated to church planting, schools, clinics, etc.); they will come later. In Honduras we developed community development work but it grew out of the churches, not vice versa. We taught obedience to the great commandment of loving our neighbor in a practical way. A poverty program can aid church planting if the two are integrated by the Holy Spirit. But churches dependant on charitable institutions are almost always dominated by the foreign missionary and seldom reproduce (Patterson 1992, D-80).

Empowering People for Freedom, Wholeness, and Justice (continued)

All too often native pastors and churches have become preoccupied with ministries that attract Western dollars (such as orphan work) while neglecting more basic pastoral care and evangelism. Even development work, if not wisely administered, can hinder church growth (Ott 1993, 289).

There is a very real danger of recruiting missionary-evangelists primarily on the basis of their abilities and expertise. "Whatever your special interest is, we can use it in our mission"— this is an all-too-common approach to recruitment. As a result, many workers become frustrated when their special ability is not fully utilized; they react by simply "doing their thing" and contributing only indirectly to the task of planting growing churches. Consequently, the so-called secondary or supporting ministries have a way of becoming primary and actually eclipsing the central task! (Hesselgrave 1980, 112).

It is unfortunate that Christian service and witness often seem to be competing concerns in Christian outreach when, in fact, both are biblical and complementary. . . . One reason for this tension is that service enterprises such as hospitals and educational institutions have a way of preempting finances and energies so that evangelism and witness tend to get crowded out (Hesselgrave 1980 p. 328).

Since we believe in the unity of the Bible, we must say that 'The Great Commission is not an isolated command, (but) a natural outflow of the character of God. . . The missionary purpose and thrust of God. . .' Thus, we should not take the Great Commandment and the Great Commission as though they are mutually exclusive. We should take the Great Commandment—to love others—and the Great Commission—to preach—together, integrated in the mission of Jesus Christ, for it is the same Lord, who commanded and commissioned the same disciples and his followers. Therefore, as Di Gangi says, 'to communicate the gospel effectively we must obey the great commandment as well as the great commission' (Cho 1985, 229).

Empowering People for Freedom, Wholeness, and Justice (continued)

Works Cited

Cho, J. Chongham. "The Mission of the Church." See Nicholls, 1985.

Cornett, Terry G., ed. "The Missionary and Culture." *World Impact Ministry Resources*. Los Angeles: World Impact Mission Studies Training Paper, 1991.

Dayton, Donald W. *Discovering an Evangelical Heritage*. 1976. Peabody, MA: Hendrickson, 1988.

Elliston, Edgar J., ed. *Christian Relief and Development: Developing Workers for Effective Ministry*. Dallas: Word Publishing, 1989.

------. "Christian Social Transformation Distinctives." See Elliston, 1989.

Elliston, Edgar J., Stephen J. Hoke, and Samuel Voorhies. "Issues in Contextualizing Christian Leadership." See Elliston, 1989.

Grigg, Viv. "Church of the Poor." *Discipling the City*. 2nd ed. Ed. Roger S. Greenway. Grand Rapids: Baker Book House, 1992.

Hall, Edward T. *Beyond Culture*. Garden City, NY: Anchor Books, 1976.

Hesselgrave, David. *Planting Churches Cross-Culturally: A Guide for Home and Foreign Missions*. Grand Rapids: Baker Book House, 1980.

Hiebert, Paul G. "Evangelism, Church, and Kingdom." See Van Engen, et. al., 1993.

------. "Anthropological Insights for Whole Ministries." See Elliston, 1989.

Hoke, Stephen J. and Samuel J. Voorhies. "Training Relief and Development Workers in the Two-Thirds World." See Elliston, 1989.

Klopfenstein, David E. and Dorothy A. Klopfenstein. "Leadership Research." CityGates. 1 (1995): 21-26.

Klopfenstein, David, Dotty Klopfenstein and Bud Williams. *Come Yourselves Apart: Christian Leadership in the Temporary Community*. Azusa, CA: Holysm Publishing, 1993.

Ladd, George Eldon. *A Theology of the New Testament*. Grand Rapids: Wm. B. Eerdmans, 1974.

Empowering People for Freedom, Wholeness, and Justice (continued)

McAlpine, Thomas H. *Facing the Powers: What are the Options?* Monrovia, CA: MARC-World Vision, 1991.

Miller, Darrow L. "The Development Ethic: Hope for a Culture of Poverty." See Elliston, 1989.

Nicholls, Bruce J., ed. *In Word and Deed: Evangelism and Social Responsibility.* Grand Rapids: Wm. B. Eerdmans, 1985.

Ott, Craig. "Let the Buyer Beware." *Evangelical Missions Quarterly*, 29 (1993): 286-291.

Patterson, George. "The Spontaneous Multiplication of Churches." See Winter and Hawthorne, 1992.

Pickett, Robert C. and Steven C. Hawthorne. "Helping Others Help Themselves: Christian Community Development." See Winter and Hawthorne, 1992.

Stott, John. "Twenty Years After Lausanne: Some Personal Reflections." *International Bulletin of Missionary Research.* 19 (1995): 50-55.

Van Engen, Charles, et. al., eds. *The Good News of the Kingdom: Mission Theology for the Third Millennium.* Maryknoll: Orbis Books, 1993.

Verkuyl, Johannes. *Contemporary Missiology: An Introduction.* Grand Rapids: Wm. B. Eerdmans, 1978.

------. "The Biblical Notion of Kingdom: Test of Validity for Theology of Religion." See Van Engen, et. al., 1993.

Winter, Ralph D. and Steven C. Hawthorne, eds. *Perspectives on the World Christian Movement: A Reader.* Rev. ed. Pasadena: William Carey Library, 1992.

APPENDIX 28

Understanding Leadership as Representation

The Six Stages of Formal Proxy

Don L. Davis

Luke 10.1 (ESV) After this the Lord appointed seventy-two others and sent them on ahead of him, two by two, into every town and place where he himself was about to go. . .

Luke 10.16 (ESV) "The one who hears you hears me, and the one who rejects you rejects me,and the one who rejects me rejects him who sent me."

John 20.21 (ESV) Jesus said to them again, "Peace be with you. As the Father has sent me, even so I am sending you."

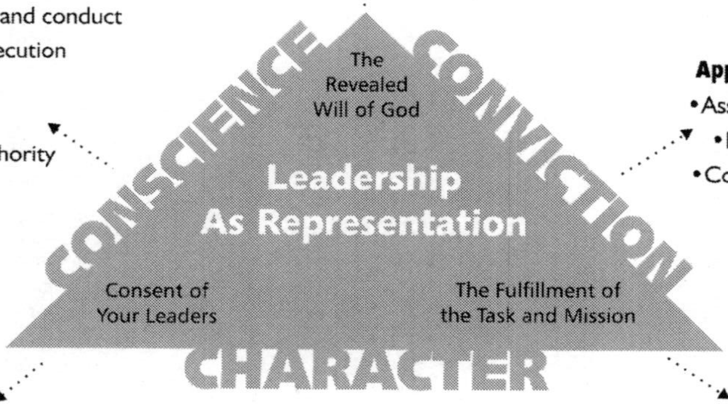

Leadership As Representation

Conscience — Conviction — Character

The Revealed Will of God

Consent of Your Leaders

The Fulfillment of the Task and Mission

Commissioning (1)

Formal Selection and Call to Represent

- Chosen to be an emissary, envoy, or proxy
- Confirmed by appropriate other who recognize the call
- Is recognized to be a member of a faithful community
- Calling out of a group to a particular role of representation
- Calling to a particular task or mission
- Delegation of position or responsibility

Equipping (2)

Appropriate Resourcing and Training to Fulfill the Call

- Assignment to a supervisor, superior, mentor, or instructor
- Disciplined instruction of principles underlying the call
- Constant drill, practice, and exposure to appropriate skills
- Recognition of gifts and strengths
- Expert coaching and ongoing feedback

Entrustment (3)

Corresponding Authorization and Empowerment to Act

- Delegation of authority to act and speak on commissioner's behalf
- Scope and limits of representative power provided
- Formal deputization (right to enforce and represent)
- Permission given to be an emissary (to stand in stead of)
- Release to fulfill the commission and task received

Mission (4)

Faithful and Disciplined Engagement of the Task

- Subordination of one's will to accomplish the assignment
- Obedience: carrying out the orders of those who sent you
- Fulfilling the task that was given to you
- Freely acting within one's delegated authority to fulfill the task
- Maintaining loyalty to those who sent you
- Using all means available to do one's duty, whatever the cost
- Full recognition of one's answerability to the one(s) who commissioned

Reckoning (5)

Official Evaluation and Review of One's Execution

- Reporting back to sending authority for critical review
- Formal comprehensive assessment of one's execution and results
- Judgment of one's loyalties and faithfulness
- Sensitive analysis of what we accomplished
- Readiness to ensure that our activities and efforts produce results

Reward (6)

Public Recognition and Continuing Response

- Formal publishing of assessment's results
- Acknowledgment and recognition of behavior and conduct
- Corresponding reward or rebuke for execution
- Review made basis for possible reassignment or recommissioning
- Assigning new projects with greater authority

APPENDIX 29

Five Views of the Relationship between Christ and Culture

*Based on **Christ and Culture** by H. Richard Niebuhr, New York: Harper and Row, 1951*

Christ against Culture	Christ and Culture in Paradox	Christ the Transformer of Culture	Christ above Culture	The Christ of Culture
Opposition	*Tension*	*Conversion*	*Cooperation*	*Acceptance*
Therefore come out from them and be separate, says the Lord. Touch no unclean thing, and I will receive you. - 2 Cor. 6.17 (cf. 1 John 2.15)	Give to Caesar what is Caesar's, and to God what is God's. - Matt. 22.21 (cf. 1 Pet. 2.13-17)	In putting everything under him, God left nothing that is not subject to him. Yet at present we do not see everything subject to him. - Heb. 2.8 (cf. Col. 1.16-18)	Indeed, when Gentiles, who do not have the law, do by nature things required by the law, they are a law for themselves. - Rom 2.14 (cf. Rom. 13.1, 5-6)	Every good and perfect gift is from above, coming down from the Father of the heavenly lights, who does no change like shifting shadows. - James 1.17 (cf. Phil. 4.8)
Culture is radically affected by sin and constantly opposes the will of God. Separation and opposition are the natural responses of the Christian community which is itself an alternative culture.	Culture is radically affected by sin but does have a role to play. It is necessary to delineate between spheres: Culture as law (restrains wickedness), Christianity as grace (gives righteousness). Both are an important part of life but the two cannot be confused or merged.	Culture is radically affected by sin but can be redeemed to play a positive role in restoring righteousness. Christians should work to have their culture acknowledge Christ's lordship and be changed by it.	Culture is a product of human reason and is part of a God-given way to discover truth. Although culture can discern real truth, sin limits its capacities which must be aided by revelation. Seeks to use culture as a first step toward the understanding of God and his revelation.	Culture is God's gift to help man overcome his bondage to nature and fear and advance in knowledge and goodness. Human culture is what allows us to conserve the truth humanity has learned. Jesus' moral teaching moves human culture upward to a new level.
Tertullian Menno Simons Anabaptists	Martin Luther Lutherans	St. Augustine John Calvin Reformed	Thomas Aquinas Roman Catholic	Peter Abelard Immanual Kant Liberal Protestant

APPENDIX 30

The Picture and the Drama

Image and Story in the Recovery of Biblical Myth

Don L. Davis

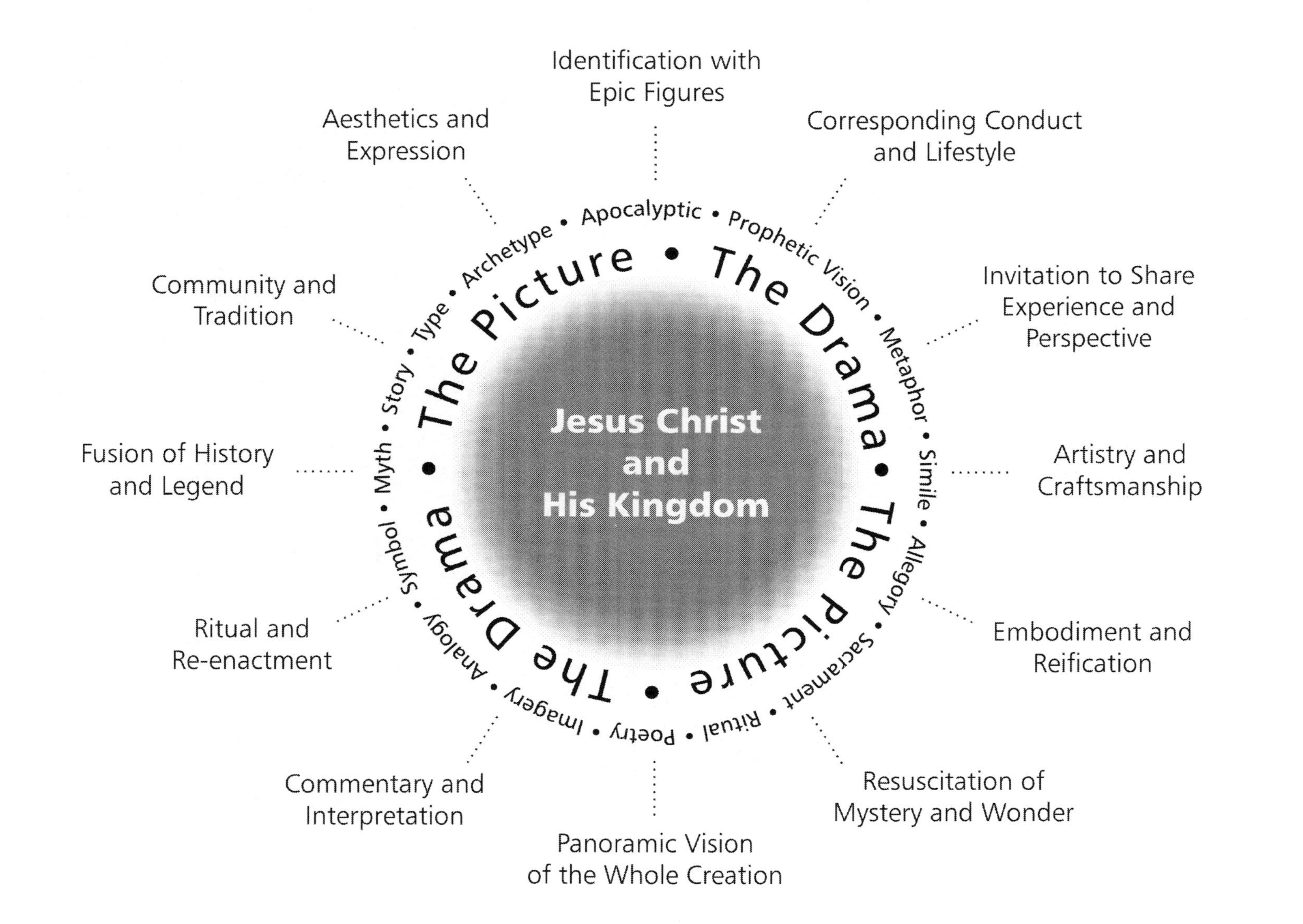

APPENDIX 31

Fit to Represent

Multiplying Disciples of the Kingdom of God

Rev. Dr. Don L. Davis • Luke 10.16 (ESV) - The one who hears you hears me, and the one who rejects you rejects me, and the one who rejects me rejects him who sent me.

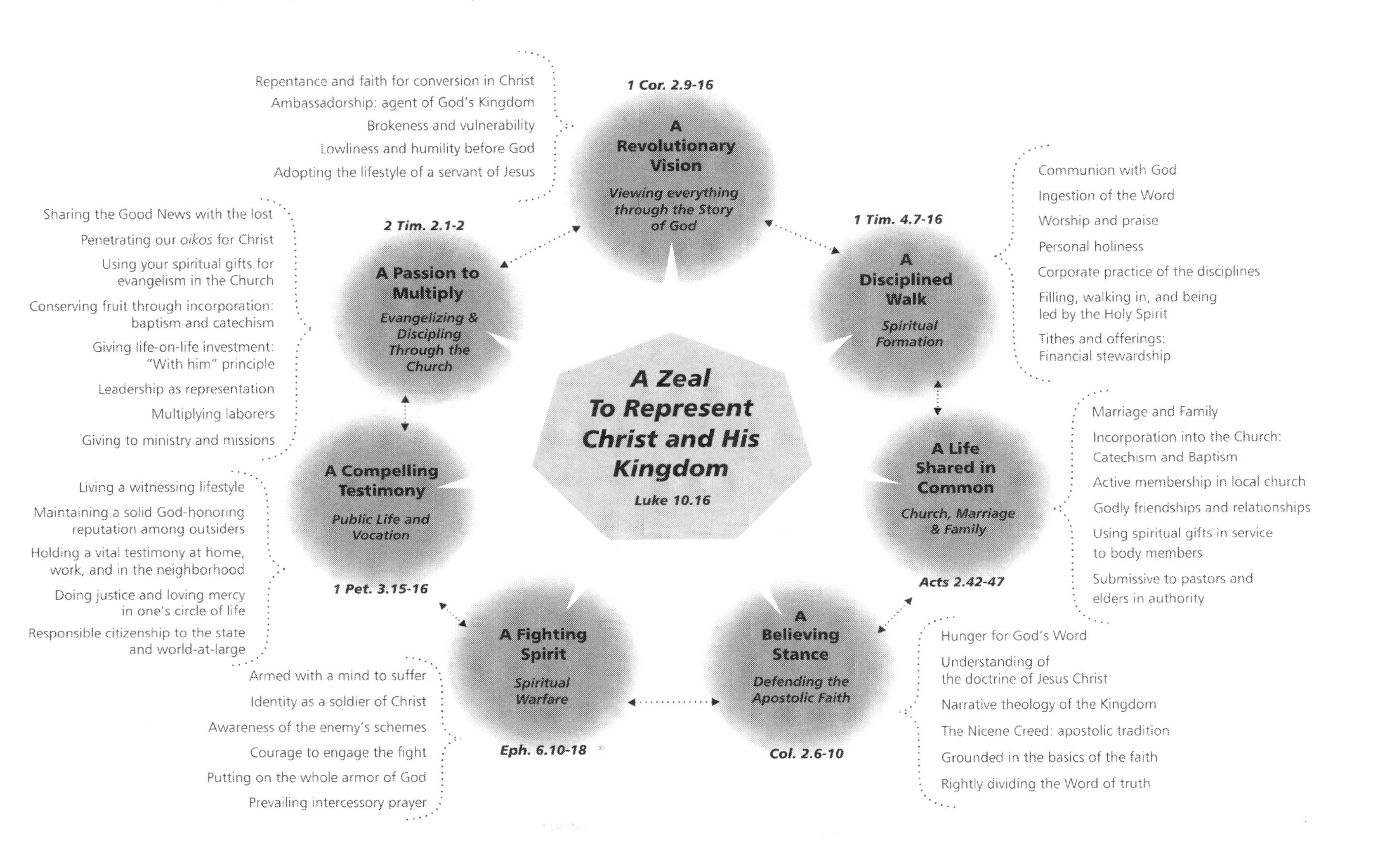

APPENDIX 32

Our Declaration of Dependence: Freedom in Christ

Rev. Dr. Don. L. Davis, January 11, 2003

It is important to teach morality within the realm of freedom (i.e., Gal. 5.1, "It is for freedom Christ has set you free"), and always in the context of using your freedom in the framework of bringing God glory and advancing Christ's Kingdom. I emphasize the "6-8-10" principles of 1 Corinthians, and apply them to all moral issues.

1. 1 Cor. 6.9-11, Christianity is about transformation in Christ; no amount of excuses will get a person into the Kingdom.
2. 1 Cor. 6.12a, We are free in Christ, but not everything one does is edifying or helpful.
3. 1 Cor. 6.12b, We are free in Christ, but anything that is addictive and exercising control over you is counter to Christ and his Kingdom.
4. 1 Cor. 8.7-13, We are free in Christ, but we ought never to flaunt our freedom, especially in the face of Christians whose conscience would be marred and who would stumble if they saw us doing something they found offensive.
5. 1 Cor. 10.23, We are free in Christ; all things are lawful for us, but neither is everything helpful, nor does doing everything build oneself up.
6. 1 Cor. 10.24, We are free in Christ, and ought to use our freedom to love our brothers and sisters in Christ, and nurture them for other's well being (cf. Gal. 5.13).
7. 1 Cor. 10.31, We are free in Christ, and are given that freedom in order that we might glorify God in all that we do, whether we eat or drink, or anything else.
8. 1 Cor. 10.32-33, We are free in Christ, and ought to use our freedom in order to do what we can to give no offense to people in the world or the Church, but do what we do in order to influence them to know and love Christ, i.e., that they might be saved.

This focus on freedom, in my mind, places all things that we say to adults or teens in context. Often, the way in which many new Christians are discipled is through a

Our Declaration of Dependence - Freedom in Christ (continued)

rigorous taxonomy (listing) of different vices and moral ills, and this can at times give them the sense that Christianity is an anti-act religion (a religion of simply not doing things), and/or a faith overly concerned with not sinning. Actually, the moral focus in Christianity is on freedom, a freedom won at a high price, a freedom to love God and advance the Kingdom, a freedom to live a surrendered life before the Lord. The moral responsibility of urban Christians is to live free in Jesus Christ, to live free unto God's glory, and to not use their freedom from the law as a license for sin.

The core of the teaching, then, is to focus on the freedom won for us through Christ's death and resurrection, and our union with him. We are now set free from the law, the principle of sin and death, the condemnation and guilt of our own sin, and the conviction of the law on us. We serve God now out of gratitude and thankfulness, and the moral impulse is living free in Christ. Yet, we do not use our freedom to be wiseguys or knuckle-heads, but to glorify God and love others. This is the context in which we address the thorny issues of homosexuality, abortion, and other social ills. Those who engage in such acts feign freedom, but, lacking a knowledge of God in Christ, they are merely following their own internal predispositions, which are not informed either by God's moral will or his love.

Freedom in Christ is a banner call to live holy and joyously as urban disciples. This freedom will enable them to see how creative they can be as Christians in the midst of so-called "free" living which only leads to bondage, shame, and remorse.

APPENDIX 33

Representin'

Jesus as God's Chosen Representative

Rev. Dr. Don L. Davis

Jesus Fulfills The Duties Of Being an Emissary

1. Receiving an *Assignment*, **John 10.17-18**
2. Resourced with an *Entrustment*, **John 3.34; Luke. 4.18**
3. Launched into *Engagement*, **John 5.30**
4. Answered with an *Assessment*, **Matthew 3.16-17**
5. New assignment after *Assessment*, **Philippians 2.9-11**

The Temptation of Jesus Christ
Challenge to and Contention with God's Rep

Mark 1.12-13 (ESV)
The Spirit immediately drove him out into the wilderness. **[13]** *And he was in the wilderness forty days, being tempted by Satan.* And he was with the wild animals, and the angels were ministering to him.

To represent another

Is to be selected to stand in the place of another, and thereby fulfill the assigned duties, exercise the rights and serve as deputy for, as well as to speak and act with another's authority on behalf of their interests and reputation.

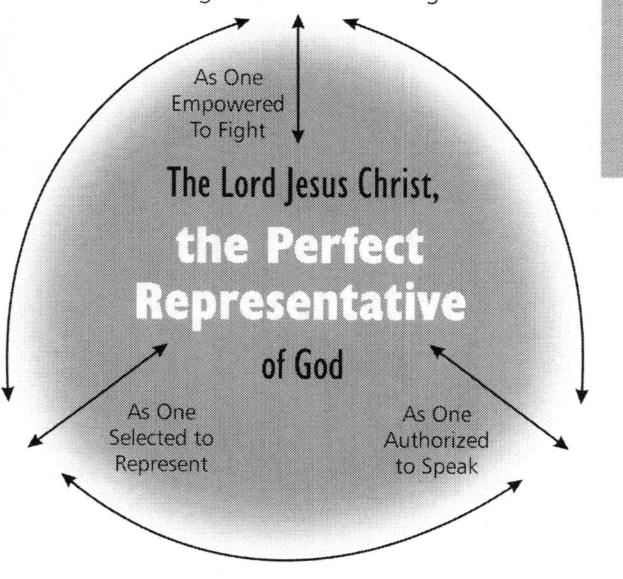

The Baptism of Jesus Christ
Commissioning and Confirmation of God's Rep

Mark 1.9-11 (ESV) *In those days Jesus came from Nazareth of Galilee and was baptized by John in the Jordan.* **[10]** And when he came up out of the water, immediately he saw the heavens opening and the Spirit descending on him like a dove. **[11]** And a voice came from heaven, "You are my beloved Son; with you I am well pleased."

The Public Preaching Ministry of Jesus Christ
Communication and Conveyance by God's Rep

Mark 1.14-15 (ESV) Now after John was arrested, Jesus came into Galilee, proclaiming the gospel of God, **[15]** and saying, "The time is fulfilled, and the kingdom of God is at hand; repent and believe in the gospel."

APPENDIX 34

Picking Up on Different Wavelengths

Integrated vs. Fragmented Mindsets and Lifestyles

Dr. Don L. Davis

A Fragmented Mindset and Lifestyle	An Integrated Lifestyle and Mindset
Sees things primarily in relation to one's own needs	Sees all things as one and whole
Sees something other than God as a substitute point of reference and coordination for meaning and truth	Sees God in Christ as the ultimate point of reference and coordination for all meaning and truth
Seeks God's blessing upon one's own personal enhancement	Aligns personal goals with God's ultimate plan and purposes
Understands the purpose of life to experience the greatest level of personal fulfillment and enhancement possible	Understands the purpose of life to make the maximum contribution possible to God's purpose in the world
Only relates to others in connection to their effect upon and place within one's individual personal space	Deeply identifies with all people and things as an integral part of God's great plan for his own glory
Defines theology as seeking to express someone's perspective on some religious idea or concept	Defines theology as seeking to comprehend God's ultimate designs and plans for himself in Jesus Christ
Applications are rooted in seeking right responses to particular issues and situations	Applications are byproducts of understanding what God is doing for himself in the world
Focuses on the style of analysis (to discern the processes and make-up of things)	Focuses on the style of synthesis (to discern the connection and unity of all things)
Seeks to understand biblical revelation primarily from the standpoint of one's private life ("God's plan for my life")	Seeks to understand biblical revelation primarily from the standpoint of God's plan for whole ("God's plan for the ages")
Governed by pressing concerns to ensure one's own security and significance in one's chosen endeavors ("My personal life plan")	Decision making is governed by commitment to participate as co-workers with God in the overall vision ("God's working in the world")
Coordinates itself around personal need as a working paradigm and project	Connects and correlates itself around God's vision and plan as a working paradigm
Sees mission and ministry as the expression of one's personal giftedness and burden, bringing personal satisfaction and security	Sees mission and ministry as the present, practical expression of one's identity vis-a-vis the panoramic vision of God
Relates knowledge, opportunity, and activity to the goals of personal enhancement and fulfillment	Relates knowledge, opportunity, and activity to a single, integrated vision and purpose
All of life is perceived to revolve around the personal identity and needs of the individual	All of life is perceived to revolve around a single theme: the revelation of God in Jesus of Nazareth

Picking Up on Different Wavelengths (continued)

Scriptures on the Validity of Seeing All Things as Unified and Whole

Ps. 27.4 (ESV) - One thing have I asked of the Lord, that will I seek after: that I may dwell in the house of the Lord all the days of my life, to gaze upon the beauty of the Lord and to inquire in his temple.

Luke 10.39-42 (ESV) - And she had a sister called Mary, who sat at the Lord's feet and listened to his teaching. [40] But Martha was distracted with much serving. And she went up to him and said, "Lord, do you not care that my sister has left me to serve alone? Tell her then to help me." [41] But the Lord answered her, "Martha, Martha, you are anxious and troubled about many things, [42] but one thing is necessary. Mary has chosen the good portion, which will not be taken away from her."

Phil. 3.13-14 (ESV) - Brothers, I do not consider that I have made it my own. But one thing I do: forgetting what lies behind and straining forward to what lies ahead [14] I press on toward the goal for the prize of the upward call of God in Christ Jesus.

Ps. 73.25 (ESV) - Whom have I in heaven but you? And there is nothing on earth that I desire besides you.

Mark 8.36 (ESV) - For what does it profit a man to gain the whole world and forfeit his life?

Luke 18.22 (ESV) - When Jesus heard this, he said to him, "One thing you still lack. Sell all that you have and distribute to the poor, and you will have treasure in heaven; and come, follow me."

John 17.3 (ESV) - And this is eternal life, that they know you the only true God, and Jesus Christ whom you have sent.

1 Cor. 13.3 (ESV) - If I give away all I have, and if I deliver up my body to be burned, but have not love, I gain nothing.

Gal. 5.6 (ESV) - For in Christ Jesus neither circumcision nor uncircumcision counts for anything, but only faith working through love.

Picking Up on Different Wavelengths (continued)

Col. 2.8-10 (ESV) - See to it that no one takes you captive by philosophy and empty deceit, according to human tradition, according to the elemental spirits of the world, and not according to Christ. [9] For in him the whole fullness of deity dwells bodily, [10] and you have been filled in him, who is the head of all rule and authority.

1 John 5.11-12 (ESV) - And this is the testimony, that God gave us eternal life, and this life is in his Son. [12] Whoever has the Son has life; whoever does not have the Son of God does not have life.

Ps. 16.5 (ESV) - The Lord is my chosen portion and my cup; you hold my lot.

Ps. 16.11 (ESV) - You make known to me the path of life; in your presence there is fullness of joy; at your right hand are pleasures forevermore.

Ps. 17.15 (ESV) - As for me, I shall behold your face in righteousness; when I awake, I shall be satisfied with your likeness.

Eph. 1.9-10 (ESV) - making known to us the mystery of his will, according to his purpose, which he set forth in Christ [10] as a plan for the fullness of time, to unite all things in him, things in heaven and things on earth.

John 15.5 (ESV) - I am the vine; you are the branches. Whoever abides in me and I in him, he it is that bears much fruit, for apart from me you can do nothing.

Ps. 42.1 (ESV) - As a deer pants for flowing streams, so pants my soul for you, O God.

Hab. 3.17-18 (ESV) - Though the fig tree should not blossom, nor fruit be on the vines, the produce of the olive fail and the fields yield no food, the flock be cut off from the fold and there be no herd in the stalls, [18] yet I will rejoice in the Lord; I will take joy in the God of my salvation.

Matt. 10.37 (ESV) - Whoever loves father or mother more than me is not worthy of me, and whoever loves son or daughter more than me is not worthy of me.

Ps. 37.4 (ESV) - Delight yourself in the Lord, and he will give you the desires of your heart.

Ps. 63.3 (ESV) - Because your steadfast love is better than life, my lips will praise you.

Picking Up on Different Wavelengths (continued)

Ps. 89.6 (ESV) - For who in the skies can be compared to the Lord? Who among the heavenly beings is like the Lord

Phil. 3.8 (ESV) - Indeed, I count everything as loss because of the surpassing worth of knowing Christ Jesus my Lord. For his sake I have suffered the loss of all things and count them as rubbish, in order that I may gain Christ

1 John 3.2 (ESV) - Beloved, we are God's children now, and what we will be has not yet appeared; but we know that when he appears we shall be like him, because we shall see him as he is.

Rev. 21.3 (ESV) - And I heard a loud voice from the throne saying, "Behold, the dwelling place of God is with man. He will dwell with them, and they will be his people, and God himself will be with them as their God.

Rev. 21.22-23 (ESV) - And I saw no temple in the city, for its temple is the Lord God the Almighty and the Lamb. [23] And the city has no need of sun or moon to shine on it, for the glory of God gives it light, and its lamp is the Lamb.

Ps. 115.3 (ESV) - Our God is in the heavens; he does all that he pleases.

Jer. 32.17 (ESV) - Ah, Lord God! It is you who has made the heavens and the earth by your great power and by your outstretched arm! Nothing is too hard for you.

Dan. 4.35 (ESV) - all the inhabitants of the earth are accounted as nothing, and he does according to his will among the host of heaven and among the inhabitants of the earth; and none can stay his hand or say to him, "What have you done?"

Eph. 3.20-21 (ESV) - Now to him who is able to do far more abundantly than all that we ask or think, according to the power at work within us, [21] to him be glory in the Church and in Christ Jesus throughout all generations, forever and ever. Amen.

APPENDIX 35

In Christ

Rev. Dr. Don L. Davis

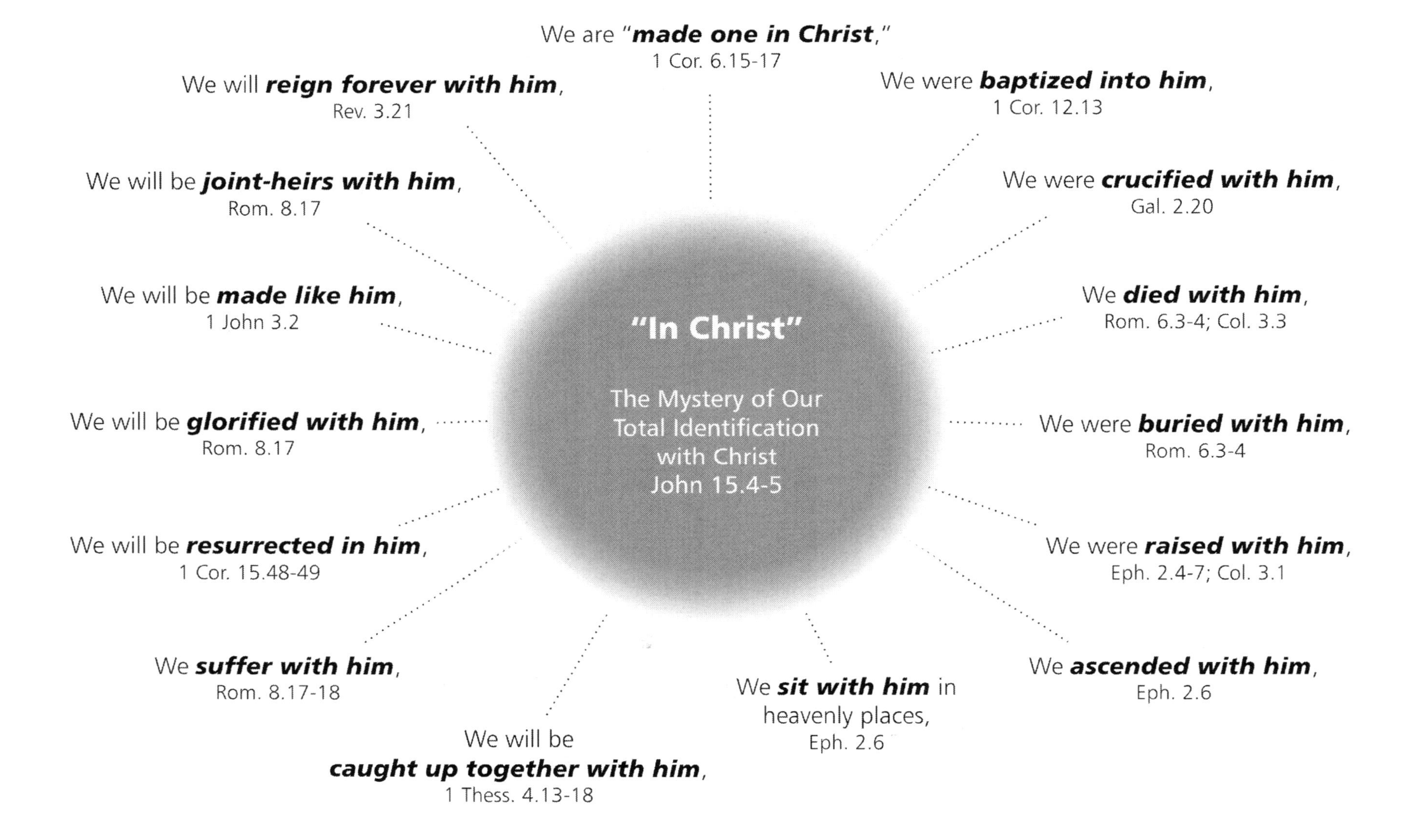

APPENDIX 36

Union with Christ: The Christocentric Paradigm

Christianity as Union with, Allegiance to, and Devotion to Jesus of Nazareth

Representative Texts

Rom. 6.4-5 (ESV) - We were buried therefore with him by baptism into death, in order that, just as Christ was raised from the dead by the glory of the Father, we too might walk in newness of life. [5] For if we have been united with him in a death like his, we shall certainly be united with him in a resurrection like his.

Col. 2.6-7 (ESV) - Therefore, as you received Christ Jesus the Lord, so walk in him, [7] rooted and built up in him and established in the faith, just as you were taught, abounding in thanksgiving.

John 14.6 (ESV) - Jesus said to him, "I am the way, and the truth, and the life. No one comes to the Father except through me."

Gal. 2.20 (ESV) - It is no longer I who live, but Christ who lives in me. And the life I now live in the flesh I live by faith in the Son of God, who loved me and gave himself for me.

Eph. 2.4-7 (ESV) - But God, being rich in mercy, because of the great love with which he loved us, [5] even when we were dead in our trespasses, made us alive together with Christ - by grace you have been saved - [6] and raised us up with him and seated us with him in the heavenly places in Christ Jesus, [7] so that in the coming ages he might show the immeasurable riches of his grace in kindness toward us in Christ Jesus.

Rom. 8.16-17 (ESV) - The Spirit himself bears witness with our spirit that we are children of God, [17] and if children, then heirs - heirs of God and fellow heirs with Christ, provided we suffer with him in order that we may also be glorified with him.

Eph. 5.2 (ESV) - And walk in love, as Christ loved us and gave himself up for us, a fragrant offering and sacrifice to God.

John 15.4-5 (ESV) - Abide in me, and I in you. As the branch cannot bear fruit by itself, unless it abides in the vine, neither can you, unless you abide in me. [5] I

Union with Christ: The Christocentric Paradigm (continued)

am the vine; you are the branches. Whoever abides in me and I in him, he it is that bears much fruit, for apart from me you can do nothing.

Col. 3.17 (ESV) - And whatever you do, in word or deed, do everything in the name of the Lord Jesus, giving thanks to God the Father through him.

1 John 2.6 (ESV) - whoever says he abides in him ought to walk in the same way in which he walked.

Gal. 5.24 (ESV) - And those who belong to Christ Jesus have crucified the flesh with its passions and desires.

Rom. 8.29 (ESV) - For those whom he foreknew he also predestined to be conformed to the image of his Son, in order that he might be the firstborn among many brothers.

Rom. 13.14 (ESV) - But put on the Lord Jesus Christ, and make no provision for the flesh, to gratify its desires.

1 Cor. 15.49 (ESV) - Just as we have borne the image of the man of dust, we shall also bear the image of the man of heaven.

2 Cor. 3.18 (ESV) - And we all, with unveiled face, beholding the glory of the Lord, are being transformed into the same image from one degree of glory to another. For this comes from the Lord who is the Spirit.

Phil. 3.7-8 (ESV) - But whatever gain I had, I counted as loss for the sake of Christ. [8] Indeed, I count everything as loss because of the surpassing worth of knowing Christ Jesus my Lord. For his sake I have suffered the loss of all things and count them as rubbish, in order that I may gain Christ.

Phil. 3.20-21 (ESV) - But our citizenship is in heaven, and from it we await a Savior, the Lord Jesus Christ, [21] who will transform our lowly body to be like his glorious body, by the power that enables him even to subject all things to himself.

1 John 3.2 (ESV) - Beloved, we are God's children now, and what we will be has not yet appeared; but we know that when he appears we shall be like him, because we shall see him as he is.

John 17.16 (ESV) - They are not of the world, just as I am not of the world.

Union with Christ: The Christocentric Paradigm (continued)

Col. 1.15-18 (ESV) - He is the image of the invisible God, the firstborn of all creation. [16] For by him all things were created, in heaven and on earth, visible and invisible, whether thrones or dominions or rulers or authorities - all things were created through him and for him. [17] And he is before all things, and in him all things hold together. [18] And he is the head of the body, the church. He is the beginning, the firstborn from the dead, that in everything he might be preeminent.

Heb. 2.14-15 (ESV) - Since therefore the children share in flesh and blood, he himself likewise partook of the same things, that through death he might destroy the one who has the power of death, that is, the devil, [15] and deliver all those who through fear of death were subject to lifelong slavery.

Rev. 1.5-6 (ESV) - and from Jesus Christ the faithful witness, the firstborn of the dead, and the ruler of kings on earth. To him who loves us and has freed us from our sins by his blood [6] and made us a kingdom, priests to his God and Father, to him be glory and dominion forever and ever. Amen.

2 Tim. 2.11-13 (ESV) - The saying is trustworthy, for: If we have died with him, we will also live with him; [12] if we endure, we will also reign with him; if we deny him, he also will deny us; [13] if we are faithless, he remains faithful—for he cannot deny himself.

Rev. 3.21 (ESV) - The one who conquers, I will grant him to sit with me on my throne, as I also conquered and sat down with my Father on his throne.

APPENDIX 37

Faithfully Re-Presenting Jesus of Nazareth

Don L. Davis

Eph. 4.17-19 (ESV) - Now this I say and testify in the Lord, that you must no longer walk as the Gentiles do, in the futility of their minds. [18] They are darkened in their understanding, alienated from the life of God because of the ignorance that is in them, due to their hardness of heart. [19] They have become callous and have given themselves up to sensuality, greedy to practice every kind of impurity.

Eph. 4.20-23 (ESV) - But that is not the way you learned Christ! - [21] assuming that you have heard about him and were taught in him, as the truth is in Jesus, [22] to put off your old self, which belongs to your former manner of life and is corrupt through deceitful desires, [23] and to be renewed in the spirit of your minds.

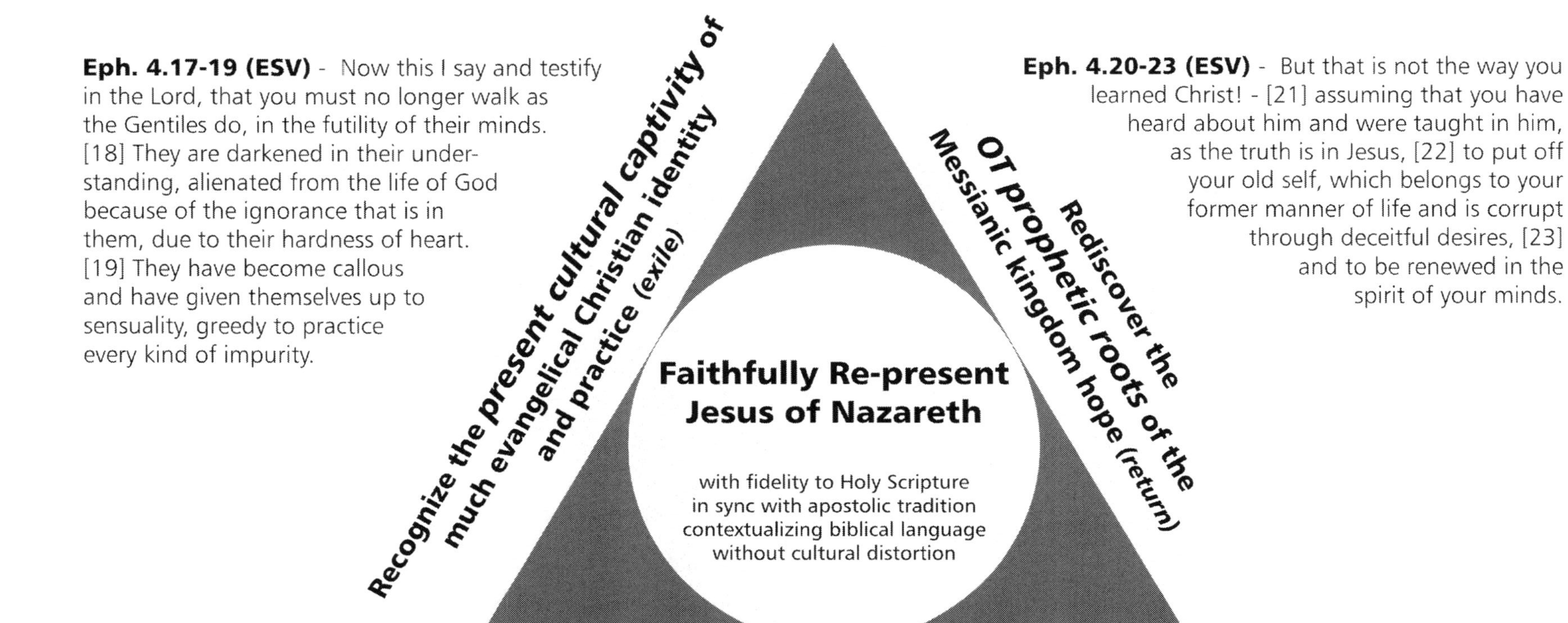

Eph. 4.24-25 (ESV) - and to put on the new self, created after the likeness of God in true righteousness and holiness. [25] Therefore, having put away falsehood, let each one of you speak the truth with his neighbor, for we are members one of another.

APPENDIX 38

From Deep Ignorance to Credible Witness

Rev. Dr. Don L. Davis

8

Witness - Ability to give witness and teach

2 Tim. 2.2
Matt. 28.18-20
1 John 1.1-4
Prov. 20.6
2 Cor. 5.18-21

And the things you have heard me say in the presence of many witnesses entrust to reliable men who will also be qualified to teach others. - 2 Tim. 2.2

7

Lifestyle - Consistent appropriation and habitual practice based on beliefs

Heb. 5.11-6.2
Eph. 4.11-16
2 Pet. 3.18
1 Tim. 4.7-10

And Jesus increased in wisdom and in stature, and in favor with God and man. - Luke 2.52

6

Demonstration - Expressing conviction in corresponding conduct, speech, and behavior

James 2.14-26
2 Cor. 4.13
2 Pet. 1.5-9
1 Thess. 1.3-10

Nevertheless, at your word I will let down the net. - Luke 5.5

5

Conviction - Committing oneself to think, speak, and act in light of information

Heb. 2.3-4
Heb. 11.1, 6
Heb. 3.15-19
Heb. 4.2-6

Do you believe this? - John 11.26

4

Discernment - Understanding the meaning and implications of information

John 16.13
Eph. 1.15-18
Col. 1.9-10
Isa. 6.10; 29.10

Do you understand what you are reading? - Acts 8.30

3

Knowledge - Ability to recall and recite information

2 Tim. 3.16-17
1 Cor. 2.9-16
1 John 2.20-27
John 14.26

For what does the Scripture say? - Rom. 4.3

2

Interest - Responding to ideas or information with both curiosity and openness

Ps. 42.1-2
Acts 9.4-5
John 12.21
1 Sam. 3.4-10

We will hear you again on this matter. - Acts 17.32

1

Awareness - General exposure to ideas and information

Mark 7.6-8
Acts 19.1-7
John 5.39-40
Matt. 7.21-23

At that time, Herod the tetrarch heard about the fame of Jesus. - Matt. 14.1

0

Ignorance - Unfamiliarity with information due to naivete, indifference, or hardness

Eph. 4.17-19
Ps. 2.1-3
Rom. 1.21; 2.19
1 John 2.11

Who is the Lord that I should heed his voice? - Exod. 5.2

APPENDIX 39

Your Kingdom Come: "The Story of God's Glory"

Living Under His Reign and Doing Missions in an Unchurched World

Rev. Dr. Don L. Davis

I. The Significance of Story, the Importance of Myth, and the Kingdom of God

A. Human beings operate according to their interpretive frameworks: human beings exist as "walking worldviews."

1. Every human existence is basically a "story-ordered world."

2. Myth-making as a primary act of human beings

3. The role of culture: enabling us to compose our realities from scratch

B. Integrating the details: story and the need to live purposefully

1. Purposeful mindset: relating all details to the whole

2. Provisional mindset: relating to details as wholes

C. The problem of a reductionistic faith

1. Reductionism–substituting a comprehensive religious vision of Christian faith for an alternative, smaller, usually culturally-oriented substitute notion, activity, relationship, or element

2. Rationalism–spending the majority of time using modern scientific proofs and arguments to underwrite faith in Jesus, reducing Christian faith to holding of particular, contextualized doctrinal positions over against other contrary views

3. Moralism–reducing the Christian vision to personal and communal decency and ethics, e.g., living well in a nuclear family context, holding certain views on selected socially controversial moral issues

D. Elements of a comprehensive biblical worldview

1. The recovery of "Christian myth"

2. *The Picture and the Drama*: From Before to Beyond Time

Your Kingdom Come: "The Story of God's Glory" (continued)

3. Living in the upside-down Kingdom of God: the *Principle of Reversal*

4. Philosophical big picture: the *Presence of the Future*

E. Components of a guiding worldview (Arthur Holmes)

1. It has a *wholistic* goal. (Where did we come from and where are we going?)

2. It is a *perspectival* approach. (From what vantage point do we see things?)

3. It is an *exploratory* process. (How do we continue to understand our lives?)

4. It is *pluralistic*. (What other views are suggested by our collective vision?)

5. It has *action outcomes*. (What ought we to do in light of our mythic vision?)

F. The wonder of story

1. The centrality of human experience

2. The richness of human affections

3. The use of sanctified imagination

4. The power of concrete image, action, and symbol

5. The immediacy of heightened reality

6. The enjoyment of artistic craftsmanship

G. Key propositions of story theology

William J. Bausch lists ten propositions related to story theology that help us understand the significance and importance of the study of stories and the understanding of Bible and theology. (William J. Bausch, *Storytelling and Faith*. Mystic, Connecticut: Twenty-Third Publications, 1984.)

1. Stories introduce us to *sacramental presences*.

2. Stories are always more important than *facts*.

Your Kingdom Come: "The Story of God's Glory" (continued)

3. Stories remain *normative (authoritative)* for the Christian community of faith.

4. *Christian traditions* evolve and define themselves through and around stories.

5. The stories of God precede, produce, and empower the *community of God's people.*

6. Community story implies *censure, rebuke, and accountability.*

7. Stories produce *theology.*

8. Stories produce *many theologies.*

9. Stories produce *ritual and sacrament.*

10. Stories are *history.*

H. The importance of the biblical framework of the Kingdom

1. Kingdom teaching is the ultimate point of reference.

2. Teaching on the kingdom story was the heart of Jesus' teaching.

3. The kingdom story is the central focus of biblical theology.

4. The kingdom story is final criterion for judging truth and value.

5. The kingdom story provides an indispensable key to understanding human history.

6. The kingdom story is the basic biblical concept that enables us to coordinate and fulfill our destinies under God's reign today, where we live and work.

II. *Tua Da Gloriam:* "The Story of God's Glory"

Ps. 115.1-3 - Not to us, O Lord, not to us, but to your name give glory, for the sake of your steadfast love and your faithfulness! [2] Why should the nations say, "Where is their God?" [3] Our God is in the heavens; he does all that he pleases.

Your Kingdom Come: "The Story of God's Glory" (continued)

From Before to Beyond Time (Adapted from Suzanne de Dietrich, *God's Unfolding Purpose*. Philadelphia: Westminster Press, 1976.)

A. *Before Time* (Eternity Past), Ps. 90.1-3

1. The eternal triune God, Ps. 102.24-27

2. God's eternal purpose, 2 Tim. 1.9; Isa. 14.26-27

   a. To glorify his name in creation, Prov. 16.4; Ps. 135.6; Isa. 48.11

   b. To display his perfections in the universe, Ps. 19.1

   c. To draw out a people for himself, Isa. 43.7, 21

3. The mystery of iniquity: the rebellion of the Dawn of the Morning (*Lucifer*), Isa. 14.12-20; Ezek. 28.13-17

4. The principalities and powers, Col. 2.15

B. *The Beginning of Time* (The Creation), Gen. 1-2

1. The creative Word of the triune God, Gen. 1.3; Pss. 33.6, 9; 148.1-5

2. The creation of humanity: the Imago Dei, Gen. 1.26-27

C. *The Tragedy of Time* (the Fall and the Curse), Gen. 3

1. The Fall and the Curse, Gen. 3.1-9

2. The *protoevangelium*: the promised Seed; Gen. 3.15

3. The end of Eden and the reign of death, Gen. 3.22-24

4. First signs of grace; Gen. 3.15, 21

D. *The Unfolding of Time* (God's plan revealed through the people Israel)

1. The Abrahamic promise and the covenant of Yahweh (Patriarchs); Gen. 12.1-3; 15; 17; 18.18; 28.4

2. The Exodus and the covenant at Sinai, Exodus

3. The conquest of the inhabitants and the Promised Land, Joshua through 2 Chronicles

Your Kingdom Come: "The Story of God's Glory" (continued)

4. The city, the temple, and the throne, Ps. 48.1-3; 2 Chron. 7.14; 2 Sam. 7.8ff.

    a. The role of the prophet, *to declare the word of the Lord*, Deut. 18.15

    b. The role of the priest, *to represent God and the people*, Heb. 5.1

    c. The role of the king, *to rule with righteousness and justice in God's stead*, Ps. 72

5. The Captivity and the Exile, Daniel, Ezekiel, Lamentations

6. The return of the remnant, Ezra, Nehemiah

E. *The Fullness of Time* (Incarnation of the Messiah Yeshua [Christ Jesus]), Gal. 4.4-6

1. The Word becomes flesh, John 1.14-18; 1 John 1.1-4

2. The testimony of John the Baptist, Matt. 3.1-3

3. The Kingdom has come in the person of Jesus of Nazareth, Mark 1.14-15; Luke 10.9-11; 10.11; 17.20-21

    a. Revealed in his person, John 1.18

    b. Exhibited in his works, John 5.36; 3.2; 9.30-33; 10.37-38; Acts 2.22; 10.38-39

    c. Interpreted in his testimony, Matt. 5-7

4. The secret of the Kingdom revealed, Mark 1.14-15

    a. The Kingdom is already present, Matt. 12.25-29

    b. The Kingdom is not yet consummated, Matt. 25.31-46

5. The passion and death of the crucified King, Matt. 26.36-46; Mark 14.32-42; Luke 22.39-46; John 18.1ff.

    a. To destroy the devil's work: *Christus Victor*, 1 John 3.8; Gen. 3.15; Col. 2.15; Rom. 16.20; Heb. 2.14-15

    b. To make atonement for sin: *Christus Victum*, 1 John 2.1-2; Rom. 5.8-9; 1 John 4.9-10; 1 John 3.16

Your Kingdom Come: "The Story of God's Glory" (continued)

c. To reveal the Father's heart, John 3.16; Titus 2.11-15

6. *Christus Victor*: the resurrection of the glorious Lord of life, Matt. 28.1-15; Mark 16.1-11; Luke 24.1-12

F. *The Last Times* (the descent and age of the Holy Spirit)

1. The *arrabon* of God: the Spirit as Pledge and Sign of the Kingdom's presence, Eph. 1.13-14; 4.30; Acts 2.1-47

2. "This is that:" Peter, Pentecost, and the presence of the future

   a. The Church as foretaste and agent of the Kingdom of God, Phil. 2.14-16; 2 Cor. 5.20

   b. The present reign of Messiah Jesus, 1 Cor. 15.24-28; Acts 2.34; Eph. 1.20-23; Heb. 1.13

   c. The ushering in of God's kingdom community "in-between the times"; Rom. 14.7

3. The Church of Messiah Jesus: sojourners in the Already and the Not Yet Kingdom

   a. The Great Confession: Jesus is Lord, Phil. 2.9-11

   b. The Great Commission: go and make disciples among all nations, Matt. 28.18-20; Acts 1.8

   c. The Great Commandment: love God and people, Matt. 22.37-39

4. The Announcement of the Mystery: Gentiles as fellow-heirs of Promise, Rom. 16.25-27; Col. 1.26-28; Eph. 3.3-11

   a. Jesus as the Last Adam, the head of a new human race, 1 Cor. 15.45-49

   b. God drawing out of the world a new humanity, Eph. 2.12-22

5. In-between the times: tokens of *Age of Sabbath and of Jubilee*, Acts 2.17ff., cf. Joel 2; Amos 9; Ezek. 36.25-27

G. *The Fulfillment of Time* (The *Parousia* of Christ), 1 Thess. 4.13-17

1. Completion of world mission: the evangelization of the world's *ethnoi*, Matt. 24.14; Mark 16.15-16; Rom. 10.18

2. The apostasy of the Church, 1 Tim. 4.1-3; 2 Tim. 4.3; 2 Thess. 2.3-12

3. The Great Tribulation, Matt. 24.21ff; Luke 21.24

4. The *Parousia*: the Second Coming of Jesus, 1 Thess. 4.13-17; 1 Cor. 15.50-58; Luke 21.25-27; Dan. 7.13

5. The reign of Jesus Christ on earth, Rev. 20.1-4

6. The Great White Throne and Lake of Fire, Rev. 20.11-15

7. "For he must reign": the final placement of all enemies under Christ's feet, 1 Cor. 15.24-28

H. *Beyond Time* (Eternity Future)

1. The creation of the new heavens and earth, Rev. 21.1; Isa. 65.17-19; 66.22; 2 Pet. 3.13

2. The descent of the New Jerusalem: the abode of God comes to earth, Rev. 21.2-4

3. The times of refreshing: the glorious freedom of the children of God, Rom. 8.18-23

4. The Lord Christ gives over the Kingdom to God the Father, 1 Cor. 15.24-28

5. The Age to Come: the triune God as all-in-all – Zech. 14.9; 2.10; Jer. 23.6; Matt. 1.23; Ps. 72.8-11; Mic. 4.1-3

III. Implications of the *Drama of All Time*

A. God's sovereign purpose underwrites all human history.

1. Whatever he pleases, he does, Ps. 135.6.

2. God's counsels and plans stand forever, to all generations, Ps. 33.11; Ps. 115.3.

Your Kingdom Come: "The Story of God's Glory" (continued)

3. God declares the end of all things from the beginning, Isa. 46.10.
4. Nothing and no one can withstand the plan of God for salvation and redemption, Dan. 4.35.

B. God is the central character in the unfolding of the divine drama, Eph. 1.9-11.

C. Missions is the *recovery of that which was lost* at the beginning of time.

1. God's sovereign rule, Mark 1.14-15
2. Satan's infernal rebellion, Gen. 3.15 with Col. 2.15; 1 John 3.8
3. Humankind's tragic fall, Gen. 3.1-8 cf. Rom. 5.5-8

D. Making disciples among all nations is *fulfilling our role in the script of Almighty God!*

Christ's death for our sins — His payment of the penalty declared against us — was His legal victory whereby He erased Satan's legal claim to the human race. But Christ also won dynamic victory. That is, when He was justified and made alive, adjudged and declared righteous in the Supreme Court of the universe, Satan, the arch foe of God and man, was completely disarmed and dethroned. Christ burst forth triumphantly from that age-old prison of the dead. Paul says that He "spoiled principalities and powers" and "made a show of them openly, triumphing over them in it." (Colossians 2.15).

~ Paul Billheimer. *Destined for the Throne*. Minneapolis: Bethany House Publishers, 1996. p. 87.

IV. "Thy Kingdom Come": Living Under God's Reign

A. The distinctiveness of Jesus' gospel: "The Kingdom is at hand," Mark 1.14-15.

B. Jesus and the inauguration of the Age to Come into this present age

1. The coming of John the Baptist, Matt. 11.2-6
2. The inauguration of Jesus's ministry, Luke 4.16-21
3. The confrontation of Jesus with demonic forces, Luke 10.18ff.; 11.20
4. The teaching of Jesus and his claim of absolute authority on earth, Mark 2.1-12; Matt. 21.27; 28.18

C. "The Kingdom has come and the strong man is bound": Matt. 12.28, 29

1. The Kingdom of God "has come" – *pleroo*
2. The meaning of the Greek verb: "to fulfill, to complete, to be fulfilled, as in prophecy"
3. The invasion, entrance, manifestation of God's kingly power

Your Kingdom Come: "The Story of God's Glory" (continued)

4. Jesus as the binder of the strong man: Matt. 12.25-30 (ESV) - Knowing their thoughts, he said to them, "Every kingdom divided against itself is laid waste, and no city or house divided against itself will stand. [26] And if Satan casts out Satan, he is divided against himself. How then will his kingdom stand? [27] And if I cast out demons by Beelzebul, by whom do your sons cast them out? Therefore they will be your judges. [28] But if it is by the Spirit of God that I cast out demons, then the kingdom of God has come upon you. [29] Or how can someone enter a strong man's house and plunder his goods, unless he first binds the strong man? Then indeed he may plunder his house. [30] Whoever is not with me is against me, and whoever does not gather with me scatters."

D. Two manifestations of the Kingdom of God: The Already/Not Yet Kingdom (Oscar Cullman, *Christ and Time*; George Ladd, *The Gospel of the Kingdom*)

1. The *first advent*: the rebellious prince bound and his house looted and God's reign has come

2. The *second advent*: the rebellious prince destroyed and his rule confounded with the full manifestation of God's kingly power in a recreated heaven and earth

Jesus' message was the Kingdom of God. It was the center and circumference of all He taught and did. . . . The Kingdom of God is the master-conception, the master-plan, the master purpose, the master-will that gathers everything up into itself and gives it redemption, coherence, purpose, goal.
~ E. Stanley Jones

V. The Christo-centric Order: Messiah Yeshua of Nazareth as Centerpiece in Both God's Revelation and Rule

A. Messiah's *mission*: to destroy the works of the devil, 1 John 3.8

B. Messiah's *birth*: the invasion of God into Satan's dominion, Luke 1.31-33

C. Messiah's *message*: the Kingdom's proclamation and inauguration, Mark 1.14-15

D. Messiah's *teaching*: kingdom ethics, Matt. 5-7

E. Messiah's *miracles*: his kingly authority and power, Mark 2.8-12

F. Messiah's *exorcisms*: his defeat of the devil and his angels, Luke 11.14-20

G. Messiah's *life and deeds*: the majesty of the Kingdom, John 1.14-18

Your Kingdom Come: "The Story of God's Glory" (continued)

H. Messiah's *resurrection*: the victory and vindication of the King, Rom.1.1-4

I. Messiah's *commission*: the call to proclaim his Kingdom worldwide, Matt 28.18-20

J. Messiah's *ascension*: his coronation, Heb. 1.2-4

K. Messiah's *Spirit*: the *arrabon* (surety, pledge) of the Kingdom, 2 Cor. 1.20

L. Messiah's *Church*: the foretaste and agent of the Kingdom, 2 Cor. 5.18-21

M. Messiah's *session in heaven*: the generalship of God's forces, 1 Cor. 15.24-28

N. Messiah's *Parousia (coming)*: the final consummation of the Kingdom, Rev. 19

VI. The Kingdom of God as Present and Offered in the Midst of the Church

A. The *Shekinah* has reappeared in our midst as his temple, Eph. 2.19-22.

B. The people (*ecclesia*) of the living God congregate here: Christ's own from every kindred, people, nation, tribe, status, and culture, 1 Pet. 2.8-9.

C. God's *Sabbath* is enjoyed and celebrated here, freedom, wholeness, and the justice of God, Heb. 4.3-10.

D. The *Year of Jubilee* has come: forgiveness, renewal, and restitution, Col. 1.13; Matt. 6.33; Eph. 1.3; 2 Pet. 1.3-4.

E. The Spirit (*arrabon*) indwells us: God lives here and walks among us here, 2 Cor. 1.20.

F. We taste the powers of the Age to Come: Satan is bound in our midst, the Curse has been broken here, deliverance is experienced in Jesus' name, Gal. 3.10-14.

G. We experience the *shalom* of God's eternal Kingdom: the freedom, wholeness, and justice of the new order are present here, Rom. 5.1; Eph. 2.13-22.

H. We herald the good news of God's reign (*evanggelion*): we invite all to join us as we journey to the full manifestation of the Age to Come, Mark 1.14-15.

Your Kingdom Come: "The Story of God's Glory" (continued)

I. Here we cry *Maranantha*!: our lives are structured by the living hope of God's future and the consummation, Rev. 22.17-21.

When Christ took his seat in the heavens, He proved conclusively that Satan's devastation was complete, that he was utterly undone. Hell was thrown into total bankruptcy. Satan was not only stripped of his legal authority and dominion, but by an infinitely superior force he was stripped of his weapons also. But this is not all. When Jesus burst forth from that dark prison and "ascended up on high," all believers were raised and seated together with Him "But God . . . brought us to life with Christ. . . . And in union with Christ Jesus he raised us up and enthroned us with him in the heavenly realms" (Ephesians 2.4-6 NEB).

~ Paul Billheimer. *Destined for the Throne*. Minneapolis: Bethany House Publishers, 1996. p. 87.

VII. The Already/Not Yet Kingdom (See *A Schematic for a Theology of the Kingdom and the Church* and *Living in the Already and the Not Yet Kingdom* appendices)

A. Through the Incarnation and the Passion of Christ, Satan was bound.

1. Jesus has triumphed over the devil, 1 John 3.8.
2. Jesus is crowned as Lord of all, Heb. 1.4; Phil. 2.5-11.
3. Satan is now judged, Luke 10.17-21.
4. Satan's power has been severely curtailed, James 4.8.
5. His authority has been broken, 1 Pet. 5.8.
6. His minions are being routed, Col. 2.15.
7. His system is fading away, 1 John 2.15-17.
8. Those he enslaved are being set free, Col. 13-14.
9. His eventual doom has been secured, Rom. 16.20.

B. Although Satan has been defeated, he is still lethal and awaits his own utter destruction.

1. "Bound, but with a long rope," 2 Cor. 10.3-5; Eph. 2.2
2. "A roaring lion, but sick, hungry, and mad," 1 Pet. 5.8
3. Satan continues to be God's active enemy of the Kingdom
4. Blinds the minds of those who do not believe, 2 Cor. 4.4
5. Functions through deception, lying, and accusation, John 8.44
6. Animates the affairs of nations, 1 John 5.19
7. Distracts human beings from their proper ends, cf. Gen. 3.1.ff.

Your Kingdom Come: "The Story of God's Glory" (continued)

8. Oppresses human beings through harassment, slander, fear, accusation, and death, Heb. 2.14-15

9. Resists and persecutes God's people, Eph. 6.10-18

C. Satan's final doom is certain and future.

1. He has been both spoiled and utterly humiliated in the Cross, Col. 2.15.

2. His final demise will come by Christ at the end of the age, Rev. 20.

3. Missions is the announcement and demonstration of the defeat of Satan through Christ.

a. The ministry of reconciliation, 2 Cor. 5.18-21

b. The ministry of disciple-making, Matt. 28.18-20

VIII. The Call to Adventure: Embracing the Story of God as Your Story

A. God's call to salvation and ministry involves participation by faith in the kingdom promise of God.

1. Salvation by grace through faith, Eph. 2.8-10

2. Repentance: metanoia and conversion, Acts 2.38

3. Regeneration by the Holy Spirit of God, John 3.3-8; Titus 3.5

4. Affirm our need for a biblical framework, a disciplined study of the Kingdom of God

Have I experienced the freedom, wholeness, and justice of the Kingdom that I am preaching to others?

B. God's call to salvation and ministry involves demonstration of the life of the Kingdom in one's personal life and faith.

1. As a faithful servant and steward of God's mysteries, 1 Cor. 4.1-2

2. As a godly Christian in one's character, personal life, and family responsibilities, 1 Tim. 3; 1 Pet. 5.1-3; Titus 1

3. As a beloved brother or sister in the midst of the assembly, 2 Cor. 8.22

Your Kingdom Come: "The Story of God's Glory" (continued)

4. As a compelling testimony in the presence of unbelievers and outsiders, Col. 4.5; Matt. 5.14-16

Do I demonstrate in my own personal and family life, and my walk in the body and with my neighbors and associates a compelling testimony of what it means to be Christ's disciple where I live?

C. God's call to salvation and ministry involves separation of one's life and goods to testify and demonstrate the freedom, wholeness, and justice of the Kingdom of God.

1. A willingness to become all things to all men in order to save some, 1 Cor. 9.22-27

2. A readiness to suffer and even die in order for Christ's reign to be proclaimed and extended, Acts 20.24-32

3. A commitment to make oneself unconditionally available to Christ in order to be used to testify solemnly of the grace and gospel as the Spirit leads, John 12.24; Acts 1.8; Matt. 28.18-20

4. Celebrate our Father's gracious intent and action to defeat our mortal enemy, the devil

Have I made myself unconditionally available to Jesus Christ to be used as his bondservant and instrument whenever and wherever he may lead in order for the kingdom message to be proclaimed and demonstrated?

D. God's call to salvation and ministry involves preparation to steward God's mysteries of the Kingdom, the Sacred Scriptures, and the Apostolic doctrine.

1. To rightly divide the Word of truth as God's workman, 2 Tim. 2.15

2. To hear and obey the sacred Scriptures which equip for every good work, 2 Tim. 3.16

3. To defend and guard the apostolic testimony regarding Christ and his Kingdom, 2 Tim. 1.14 with Gal. 1.8-9 and 1 Cor. 15.1-4

Have I spent the requisite time in the Word and in training to be equipped even as I equip others for the work of the ministry?

Your Kingdom Come: "The Story of God's Glory" (continued)

E. God's call to salvation and ministry involves proclamation of the message of the Kingdom through preaching, teaching, and discipling in order that others may enter and make disciples of the Kingdom.

1. To preach the good news of the Kingdom with those who do not know God, its inauguration in the Son of God and its enjoyment and demonstration in the Church, Acts 2.1-18

2. To teach and disciple the faithful in the words of Jesus so that they may be his disciples and mature as members of his body, John 8.31-32; 1 Pet. 2.2; 2 Tim. 3.16-17

3. To equip those who are members of Christ's body to do the work of the ministry in order that the Church may grow numerically and spiritually, Eph. 4.9-15

4. Offer unending praise and worship to our Lord Jesus, who invaded Satan's dominion and crushed his malicious insurrection in God's universe

5. Resolve to embody, express, and proclaim Christ's present and coming reign until he comes

Am I ready and willing to preach the Word of the Kingdom in and out of season in order that the lost may be saved, the saved may mature, and the mature may multiply the fruit of the Kingdom of God?

The Bottom Line: Are you willing to suffer for the message of the Kingdom regarding Messiah Yeshua? (See *Suffering, the Cost of Discipleship and Servant-Leadership* Appendix)

APPENDIX 40

Spiritual Service Checklist

Rev. Dr. Don L. Davis

1. *Salvation*: Has this person believed the Gospel, confessed Jesus as Lord and Savior, been baptized, and formally joined our church as a member?
2. *Personal integrity*: Are they walking with God, growing in their personal life, and demonstrating love and faithfulness in their family, work, and in the community?
3. *Equipped in the Word*: How equipped is this person in the Word of God to share and teach with others?
4. *Support of our church*: Do they support the church through their presence, pray for the leaders and members, and give financially to its support?
5. *Submission to authority*: Does this person joyfully submit to spiritual authority?
6. *Identification of spiritual gifts*: What gifts, talents, abilities, or special resources does this person have for service, and what is their particular burden for ministry now?
7. *Present availability*: Are they open to be assigned to a task or project where we could use their service to build up the body?
8. *Reputation amongst leaders*: How do the other leaders feel about this person's readiness for a new role of leadership?
9. *Resources needed to accomplish*: If appointed to this role, what particular training, monies, resources, and/or input will they need to accomplish the task?
10. *Formal commissioning*: When and how will we make known to others that we have appointed this person to their task or project?
11. *Timing and reporting*: Also, if we dedicate this person to this role/task, when will they be able to start, and how long ought they serve before we evaluate them.
12. *Evaluate and re-commission*: When will we evaluate the performance of the person, and determine what next steps we ought to take in their leadership role at the church?

APPENDIX 41

The Profile of a 21st-Century Disciple

Rev. Dr. Don L. Davis

1. He/she enjoys an intimate communion with the Lord (John 10.1-6; 15.12-14).

a. Is unconditionally available to Christ as Lord (filled with the Holy Spirit)

b. Hungers to become more and more like Christ in vision, character, and service

c. Solid devotional life of personal worship, meditation, and prayer

d. Lifestyle of praise, worship, and celebration

e. Abiding trust in the leading and provision of God in Christ

f. Glorifies God in the temple of his/her body, mind, and spirit

2. He/she upholds a believing stance grounded upon a biblical vision of Christ and his Kingdom (John 8.31-32).

a. Thorough understanding of the Holy Scriptures (i.e. its themes, history, and key principles)

b. Maintains a Christ-centered world view, seeing life from God's vantage point

c. Grounded in the fundamentals of the faith, able to share and reproduce them

d. Growing ability to rightly divide the Word of truth (i.e. hear, read, study, memorize, and meditate)

e. Increasing competence to contend for the faith against all opposition

3. He/she displays a godly walk through conduct and lifestyle at home, on the job and in the community (John 17.14-23).

a. Walks worthy of the Lord in speech, purity, conduct, faith, and character

b. Fulfills sacrificially various roles as a godly member of his/her own household and family

c. Represents Christ in excellence, service, respect, and single-mindedness on the job

d. Maintains godly reputation with friends, neighbors, and community

The Profile of a 21st-Century Disciple (continued)

4. He/she maintains a faithful membership in the body, expressed in active participation in a local congregation of believers (John 13.34-35).

a. Has been baptized into the faith based on their confession of faith in Jesus Christ

b. Participates actively in corporate worship and celebration of the body in praise, worship, and the Lord's Supper

c. Gathers regularly with other members of the body to build up the church through fellowship, prayer, service, and celebration

d. Uses his/her gifts in ministry by serving with other members of the body

e. Communicates regularly in a building and edifying way with the body

5. He/she implements a compelling strategy to make disciples of Jesus at home and abroad (John 20.21).

a. Prays consistently and fervently that the Lord would raise up laborers in his harvest wherever Christ is not yet known, worshiped, and glorified

b. Gives generously of his/her time and resources toward evangelism and missions as God leads

c. Looks for opportunities to share his/her personal testimony with others in order to win others to Christ

d. Spends time establishing new converts in the faith by incorporating them in the body

e. Asks the Spirit for opportunity to disciple faithful Christians who can become laborers together with him/her in fulfilling the Great Commission

APPENDIX 42

Documenting Your Work

A Guide to Help You Give Credit Where Credit Is Due

The Urban Ministry Institute

Avoiding Plagiarism

Plagiarism is using another person's ideas as if they belonged to you without giving them proper credit. In academic work it is just as wrong to steal a person's ideas as it is to steal a person's property. These ideas may come from the author of a book, an article you have read, or from a fellow student. The way to avoid plagiarism is to carefully use "notes" (textnotes, footnotes, endnotes, etc.) and a "Works Cited" section to help people who read your work know when an idea is one you thought of, and when you are borrowing an idea from another person.

Using Citation References

A citation reference is required in a paper whenever you use ideas or information that came from another person's work.

All citation references involve two parts:

- Notes in the body of your paper placed next to each quotation which came from an outside source.
- A "Works Cited" page at the end of your paper or project which gives information about the sources you have used

Using Notes in Your Paper

There are three basic kinds of notes: parenthetical notes, footnotes, and endnotes. At The Urban Ministry Institute, we recommend that students use parenthetical notes. These notes give the author's last name(s), the date the book was published, and the page number(s) on which you found the information. Example:

> In trying to understand the meaning of Genesis 14.1-24, it is important to recognize that in biblical stories "the place where dialogue is first introduced will be an important moment in revealing the character of the speaker . . ." (Kaiser and Silva 1994, 73). This is certainly true of the character of Melchizedek who speaks words of blessing. This identification of Melchizedek as a positive spiritual influence is reinforced by the fact that he is the King of Salem, since Salem means "safe, at peace" (Wiseman 1996, 1045).

Documenting Your Work (continued)

Creating a Works Cited Page

A "Works Cited" page should be placed at the end of your paper. This page:

- lists every source you quoted in your paper
- is in alphabetical order by author's last name
- includes the date of publication and information about the publisher

The following formatting rules should be followed:

1. Title

The title "Works Cited" should be used and centered on the first line of the page following the top margin.

2. Content

Each reference should list:

- the author's full name (last name first)
- the date of publication
- the title and any special information (Revised edition, 2nd edition, reprint) taken from the cover or title page should be noted
- the city where the publisher is headquartered followed by a colon and the name of the publisher

3. Basic form

- Each piece of information should be separated by a period.
- The second line of a reference (and all following lines) should be indented.
- Book titles should be underlined (or italicized).
- Article titles should be placed in quotes.

Example:

Fee, Gordon D. 1991. *Gospel and Spirit: Issues in New Testament Hermeneutics.* Peabody, MA: Hendrickson Publishers.

Documenting Your Work (continued)

4. Special Forms

A book with multiple authors:

Kaiser, Walter C., and Moisés Silva. 1994. *An Introduction to Biblical Hermeneutics: The Search for Meaning.* Grand Rapids: Zondervan Publishing House.

An edited book:

Greenway, Roger S., ed. 1992. *Discipling the City: A Comprehensive Approach to Urban Mission.* 2nd ed. Grand Rapids: Baker Book House.

A book that is part of a series:

Morris, Leon. 1971. *The Gospel According to John.* Grand Rapids: Wm. B. Eerdmans Publishing Co. The New International Commentary on the New Testament. Gen. ed. F. F. Bruce.

An article in a reference book:

Wiseman, D. J. "Salem." 1982. In *New Bible Dictionary.* Leicester, England - Downers Grove, IL: InterVarsity Press. Eds. I. H. Marshall and others.

(An example of a "Works Cited" page is located on the next page.)

For Further Research

Standard guides to documenting academic work in the areas of philosophy, religion, theology, and ethics include:

Atchert, Walter S., and Joseph Gibaldi. 1985. *The MLA Style Manual.* New York: Modern Language Association.

The Chicago Manual of Style. 1993. 14th ed. Chicago: The University of Chicago Press.

Turabian, Kate L. 1987. *A Manual for Writers of Term Papers, Theses, and Dissertations.* 5th edition. Bonnie Bertwistle Honigsblum, ed. Chicago: The University of Chicago Press.

Documenting Your Work (continued)

Works Cited

Fee, Gordon D. 1991. *Gospel and Spirit: Issues in New Testament Hermeneutics*. Peabody, MA: Hendrickson Publishers.

Greenway, Roger S., ed. 1992. *Discipling the City: A Comprehensive Approach to Urban Mission*. 2nd ed. Grand Rapids: Baker Book House.

Kaiser, Walter C., and Moisés Silva. 1994. *An Introduction to Biblical Hermeneutics: The Search for Meaning*. Grand Rapids: Zondervan Publishing House.

Morris, Leon. 1971. *The Gospel According to John*. Grand Rapids: Wm. B. Eerdmans Publishing Co. *The New International Commentary on the New Testament*. Gen. ed. F. F. Bruce.

Wiseman, D. J. "Salem." 1982. In *New Bible Dictionary*. Leicester, England-Downers Grove, IL: InterVarsity Press. Eds. I. H. Marshall and others.

Mentoring
The Capstone Curriculum

Before the Course Begins

- First, read carefully the Introduction of the Module found on page 5, and browse through the Mentor's Guide in order to gain an understanding of the content that will be covered in the course. The Student's Workbook is identical to your Mentor's Guide. Your guide, however, also contains a section of additional material and resources for each lesson, called *Mentor's Notes*. References to these instructions are indicated by a symbol in the margin: 🕮. The Quizzes, Final Exam, and Answer Keys can all be found on the TUMI Satellite Gateway. (This is available to all approved satellites.)
- Second, you are strongly encouraged to view the teaching on both DVDs prior to the beginning of the course.
- Third, you should read any assigned readings associated with the curriculum, whether textbooks, articles or appendices.
- Fourth, it may be helpful to review the key theological themes associated with the course by using Bible dictionaries, theological dictionaries, and commentaries to refresh your familiarity with major topics covered in the curriculum.
- Fifth, please know that the students *are not tested on the reading assignments*. These are given to help the students get a fuller understanding of what the module is teaching, but it is not required that your students be excellent readers to understand what is being taught. For those of you who are receiving this module in any translation other than English, the required reading might not be available in your language. Please select a book or two that is available in your language - one that you think best represents what is being taught in this module - and assign that to your students instead.
- Finally, begin to think about key questions and areas of ministry training that you would like to explore with students in light of the content that is being covered.

Before Each Lesson

Prior to each lesson, you should once again watch the teaching content that is found on the DVD for that class session, and then create a *Contact* and *Connection* section for this lesson.

Preparing the Contact Section

Review the Mentor's Guide to understand the lesson objectives and gather ideas for possible Contact activities. (Two to three Contacts are provided which you may use, or feel free to create your own, if that is more appropriate.)

Then, create a Contact section that introduces the students to the lesson content and captures their interest. As a rule, Contact methods fall into three general categories.

Attention Focusers capture student attention and introduce them to the lesson topic. Attention focusers can be used by themselves with motivated learners or combined with one of the other methods described below. Examples:

- Singing an opening song related to the lesson theme.
- Showing a cartoon or telling a joke that relates to an issue addressed by the lesson.
- Asking students to stand on the left side of the room if they believe that it is easier to teach people how to be saved from the Gospels and to stand on the right side if they believe it is easier to teach people from the Epistles.

Story-telling methods either have the instructor tell a story that illustrates the importance of the lesson content or ask students to share their experiences (stories) about the topic that will be discussed. Examples:

- In a lesson on the role of the pastor, a Mentor may tell the story of conducting a funeral and share the questions and challenges that were part of the experience.
- In a lesson about evangelism, the Mentor may ask students to describe an experience they have had of sharing the Gospel.

Problem-posing activities raise challenging questions for students to answer and lead them toward the lesson content as a source for answering those questions, or they may ask students to list the unanswered questions that they have about the topic that will be discussed. Examples:

- Presenting case studies from ministry situations that call for a leadership decision and having students discuss what the best response would be.

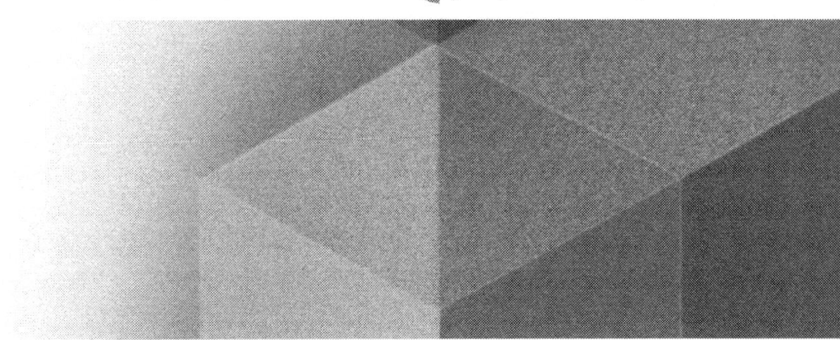

- Problems framed as questions such as "When preaching at a funeral, is it more important for a minister to be truthful or compassionate? Why?"

Regardless of what method is chosen, the key to a successful Contact section is making a transition from the Contact to the Content of the lesson. When planning the Contact section, Mentors should write out a transition statement that builds a bridge from the Contact to the lesson content. For example, if the lesson content was on the truth that the Holy Spirit is a divine Person who is a full member of the Godhead, the Contact activity might be to have students quickly draw a symbol that best represents the Holy Spirit to them. After having them share their drawings and discuss why they chose what they did, the Mentor might make a transition statement along the following lines:

> *Because the Holy Spirit is often represented by symbols like fire or oil in Scripture rather than with a human image like the Father or the Son, it is sometimes difficult to help people understand that the Spirit is a full person within the Godhead who thinks, acts, and speaks as personally as God the Father or Jesus Christ. In this lesson, we want to establish the scriptural basis for understanding that the Spirit is more than just a symbol for "God's power" and think about ways that we can make this plain to people in our congregations.*

This is a helpful transition statement because it directs the students to what they can expect from the lesson content and also prepares them for some of the things that might be discussed in the Connection section that comes later. Although you may adapt your transition statement based on student responses during the Contact section, it is important, during the planning time, to think about what will be said.

Three useful questions for evaluating the Contact section you have created are:

- Is it creative and interesting?
- Does it take into account the needs and interests of this particular group?
- Does it focus people toward the lesson content and arouse their interest in it?

Preparing the Connection Section

Again, review the Mentor's Guide to understand the lesson objectives and gather ideas for possible Connection activities.

Then, create a Connection section that helps students form new associations between truth and their lives (implications) and discuss specific changes in their beliefs, attitudes, or actions that should occur as a result (applications). As you plan, be a little wary of making the Connection section overly specific. Generally this lesson section should come to students as an invitation to discover, rather than as a finished product with all the specific outcomes predetermined.

At the heart of every good Connection section is a question (or series of questions) that asks students how knowing the truth will change their thinking, attitudes, and behaviors. (We have included some Connection questions in order to "prime the pump" of your students, to spur their thinking, and help them generate their own questions arising from their life experience.) Because this is theological and ministry training, the changes we are most concerned with are those associated with the way in which the students train and lead others in their ministry context. Try and focus in on helping students think about this area of application in the questions you develop.

The Connection section can utilize a number of different formats. Students can discuss the implications and applications together in a large Mentor-led group or in small groups with other students (either open discussion or following a pre-written set of questions). Case studies, also, are often good discussion starters. Regardless of the method, in this section both the Mentor and the learning group itself should be seen as a source of wisdom. Since your students are themselves already Christian leaders, there is often a wealth of experience and knowledge that can be drawn on from the students themselves. Students should be encouraged to learn from each other as well as from the Mentor.

Several principles should guide the Connection discussions that you lead:

- First, the primary goal in this section is to bring to the surface the questions that students have. In other words, the questions that occur to students during the lesson take priority over any questions that the Mentor prepares in advance–although the questions raised by an experienced Mentor will

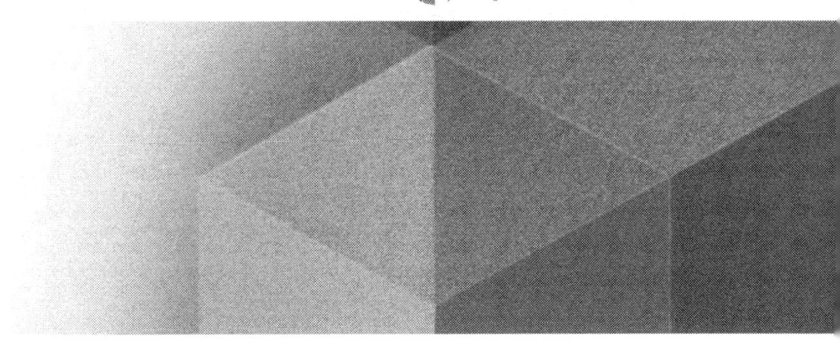

still be a useful learning tool. A corollary to this is to assume that the question raised by one student is very often the unspoken question present among the entire group.

- Second, try and focus the discussion on the concrete and the specific rather than the purely theoretical or hypothetical. This part of the lesson is meant to focus on the actual situations that are being faced by the specific students in your classroom.
- Third, do not be afraid to share the wisdom that you have gained through your own ministry experience. You are a key resource to students and they should expect that you will make lessons you have learned available to them. However, always keep in mind that variables of culture, context, and personality may mean that what has worked for you may not always work for everyone. Make suggestions, but dialogue with students about whether your experience seems workable in their context, and if not, what adaptations might be made to make it so.

Three useful questions for evaluating the Connection section you have created are:

- Have I anticipated in advance what the general areas of implication and application are likely to be for the teaching that is given in the lesson?
- Have I created a way to bring student questions to the surface and give them priority?
- Will this help a student leave the classroom knowing what to do with the truth they have learned?

Finally, because the Ministry Project is the structured application project for the entire course, it will be helpful to set aside part of the Connection section to have students discuss what they might choose for their project and to evaluate progress and/or report to the class following completion of the assignment.

Steps in Leading a Lesson

Opening Activities

- Take attendance.
- Lead the devotion.
- Say or sing the Nicene Creed and pray.
- Administer the quiz.
- Check Scripture memorization assignment.
- Collect any assignments that are due.

Teach the Contact Section

- Use a Contact provided in the Mentor's Guide, or create your own.

Oversee the Content Section

- Present the Content of the lesson using the video teaching.

  Using the Video Segments
  Each lesson has two video teaching segments, each approximately 25 minutes in length. After teaching the Contact section (including the transition statement), play the first video segment for the students. Students can follow this presentation using their Student Workbook which contains a general outline of the material presented and Scripture references and other supplementary materials referenced by the speaker. Once the first segment is viewed, work with the students to confirm that the content was understood.

  Ensuring that the Content is Understood
  Segue
  Using the Mentor's Guide, check for comprehension by asking the questions listed in the "Student Questions and Response" section. Clarify any incomplete understandings that students may demonstrate in their answers.

  Ask students if there are any questions that they have about the content and discuss them together as a class. NOTE - The questions here should focus on

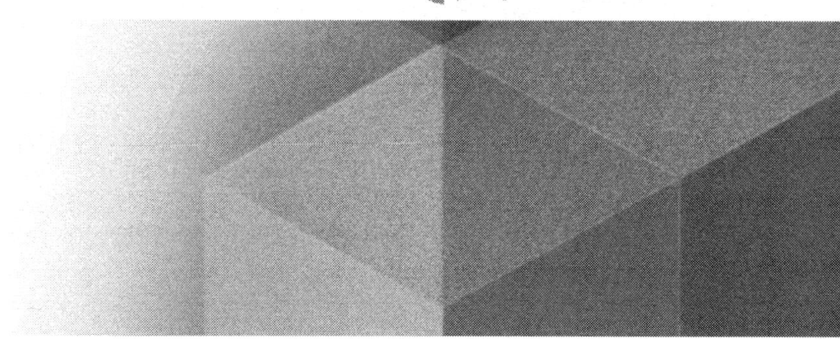

understanding the content itself rather than on how to apply the learning. Application questions will be the focus of the upcoming Connection section.

Take a short class break and then repeat this process with the second video segment.

Teach the Connection Section

- Summary of Key Concepts
- Student Application and Implications
- Case Studies
- Restatement of Lesson's Thesis
- Resources and Bibliographies
- Ministry Connections
- Counseling and Prayer

Remind Students of Upcoming Assignments

- Scripture Memorization
- Assigned Readings
- Other Assignments

Close Lesson

- Close with prayer
- Be available for any individual student's questions or needs following the class

Please see the next page for an actual "Module Lesson Outline."

The quizzes, the final exam, and their answer keys are located at the back of this book.

Module Lesson Outline

Introduction

Lesson Title
Lesson Objectives
Devotion
Nicene Creed and Prayer
Quiz
Scripture Memorization Review
Assignments Due

Contact

Contact (1-3)

Content

Video Segment 1 Outline
Segue 1 (Student Questions and Response)
Video Segment 2 Outline
Segue 2 (Student Questions and Response)

Connection

Summary of Key Concepts
Student Application and Implications
Case Studies
Restatement of Lesson's Thesis
Resources and Bibliographies
Ministry Connections
Counseling and Prayer

Assignments

Scripture Memorization
Reading Assignment
Other Assignments
Looking Forward to the Next Lesson

God's Reign Challenged

1
Page 13
Lesson Introduction

Welcome to the Mentor's Guide for Lesson 1, *God's Reign Challenged.* The overall focus of the Kingdom of God module is to enable your students to grasp the power, wonder, and appeal of the Kingdom of God, and its meaning both for their lives and ministries in the churches they attend and serve. This first lesson is designed to show the students how God's reign was challenged in the rebellion of Satan and the disobedience of the first human pair, and to discuss the effects these acts had upon God's creation. Notice in the objectives that these aims are clearly stated, and you ought to emphasize them throughout the lesson, during the discussions and interaction with the students. The more you can highlight the objectives throughout the class period, the better the chances are that they will understand and grasp the magnitude of these objectives.

2
Page 13
Lesson Objectives

Do not hesitate to discuss these objectives briefly before you enter into the class period. Draw the students attention to the objectives, for in a real sense, this is the heart of your educational aim for the class period in this lesson. Everything discussed and done ought to point back to these objectives. Find ways to highlight these at every turn, to reinforce them and reiterate them as you go.

3
Page 13
Devotion

This devotion focuses on God's absolute confidence in his rule as Almighty God over his creation. In one sense today's lesson is ironic; God is not resisted in any fundamental way that he is frightened, disturbed, or prevented from accomplishing his work. This devotion places emphasis on God's disposition about the resistance; he laughs at those who think that they can oppose his will and reign successfully. Reassure the students of God's dramatic and fundamental power to overcome his enemies, and remind them of his resolve to have his will done in earth as it is being done in heaven.

4
Page 14
Nicene Creed and Prayer

Affirm to your students the Lord's knowledge of the resistance to his will without the slightest sense of panic, fear, or intimidation on his part. As the Sovereign Lord of the Universe, the Lord foresaw such disobedience and has made provision for its

cure in the person of his Son, Jesus Christ, the Lord of all. This prayer speaks of God as the reigning Lord now. Even though men and angels resisted his will, he never relinquished his sovereign rule over all, and is working in the midst of human history to accomplish the reclamation of the universe under his reign.

5
Page 14
Contact

The following contacts relate to the idea of the Bible's claim that the Lord is the Lord of all, which is asserted even in light of horrific and terrible things occurring around us, and throughout human history. In some ways, this is a significant issue in urban ministry, where cities are being destroyed through urban decay, violence, congestion, injustice, and mass neglect. The urban poor especially will be prone to struggle with this issue in theology called "theodicy," that is, the notion of horrible things happening to good people in a universe where God claims to be all-knowing, all-loving, and all powerful. Think through which, if any, of these contacts might touch upon issues about which your students are concerned. Then, discuss briefly the idea, which will lead into the teaching on God as Lord, and his lordship being challenged by Satan and the first human pair, Adam and Eve.

6
Page 15
Summary of Segment 1

This first segment focuses on the Bible's clear declaration that the Lord Almighty, referred to in the Hebrew as *YHWH* (translated as Jehovah, Yahweh) is the sovereign Lord of the Universe. Even though he possesses all might and glory, and even though he was fully aware of the rebellion to come, the Lord allowed the devil and humankind to resist his mighty will. What must be made plain here is that the resistance did not in any way end God's sovereignty over the world, or interfere with his ultimate plan to reign and rule over his creation. Pay close attention to the first portion of the video, which affirms God's inalienable right as Lord to rule and reign over all.

The Bible is replete with statements that the God of the heavens is sovereign, the absolute master of all things, reigning from on high for his own glory. He "has established his throne in the heavens, and his kingdom rules over all" (Ps. 103.19, ESV). He is the God who "rules the kingdom of men and gives it to whom he will" (Dan. 4.17, 25, 34; 5.21; 7.14). David suggests that the God of the Scriptures deserves

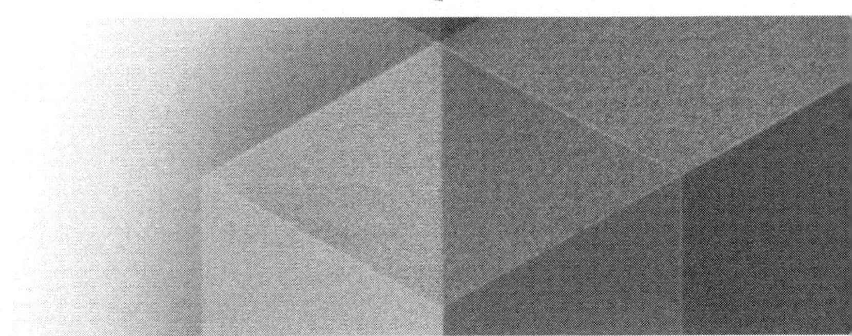

power, glory, majesty, and splendor for what he has created in both heaven and earth (1 Chron. 29.11), which Jesus refers to in his prayer (Matt. 6.13). From the beginning, Scripture says that the sovereign Lord God is the "only Sovereign, the King of kings and Lord of lords" (1 Tim. 6.15; cf. Rev. 19.16).

You should also note as you enter into this first segment that the names of God all denote and express his absolute sovereignty over all that he has made. He is the "God Most High" (*elyon*, Gen. 14.18-20), "God Almighty" (*el sadday*, 17.1; cf. Exod. 6.2), "Sovereign Lord" (*adonay yhwh*, Gen. 15.2; Deut. 3.24, NIV), and "Lord God Almighty" (*kyrios pantokrator*, Rev. 1.8). God is in all things pictured as a Lord, not as one who can be easily resisted or denied.

7
Page 16
Outline Point I

God's self-existence is a critical concept related to his sovereignty. God's rule is anchored in his nature, his very being as the omnipotent, omnipresent, and omniscient Lord of all. See Exodus 6.3 and Psalm 104.24-30 for other texts on his providing for creation, yet not needing it (cf. Ps. 50.7-12).

8
Page 16
Outline Point I-B

God's right to rule also flows from the fact that all things belong to him. As Creator and Maker of all things, God may dispense and dispose within the universe as he sees fit. He is not bound by any outside law or will except his own person, and all things everywhere belong to him alone. This fact regarding the triune God lays the foundation for understanding him as the Lord of all (see Ps. 103.19).

9
Page 16
Outline Point I-C

The story of the Kingdom does not begin with men and women, or even with angels and Lucifer. God's reign begins with his person, almighty and supreme, exalted high above all creation and things. The theology that must be asserted here is one that reflects the grandeur and glory of God as one exalted above all, as one who knows no imperfections, whose excellencies are numberless and beyond degree, who must humble himself to behold the things in heaven and in earth, who has set his glory above the heavens (Ps. 8.1).

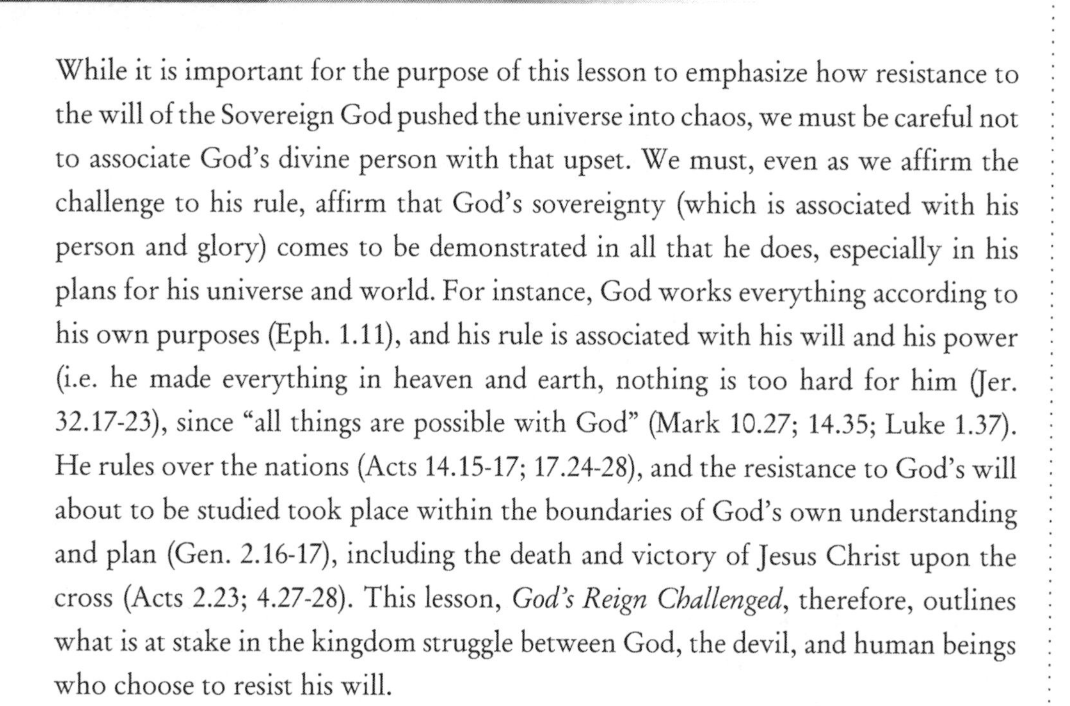

While it is important for the purpose of this lesson to emphasize how resistance to the will of the Sovereign God pushed the universe into chaos, we must be careful not to associate God's divine person with that upset. We must, even as we affirm the challenge to his rule, affirm that God's sovereignty (which is associated with his person and glory) comes to be demonstrated in all that he does, especially in his plans for his universe and world. For instance, God works everything according to his own purposes (Eph. 1.11), and his rule is associated with his will and his power (i.e. he made everything in heaven and earth, nothing is too hard for him (Jer. 32.17-23), since "all things are possible with God" (Mark 10.27; 14.35; Luke 1.37). He rules over the nations (Acts 14.15-17; 17.24-28), and the resistance to God's will about to be studied took place within the boundaries of God's own understanding and plan (Gen. 2.16-17), including the death and victory of Jesus Christ upon the cross (Acts 2.23; 4.27-28). This lesson, *God's Reign Challenged*, therefore, outlines what is at stake in the kingdom struggle between God, the devil, and human beings who choose to resist his will.

10
Page 17
Outline Point II

Note here the consciousness and intentionality of the devil. His intent is to rob God of his place and perfection, to take to himself the glory and praise that is due to God alone. This is the heart of evil, the beginning of rebellion, and the core of the demonic in Scripture, that is, the intent to defy God and take to oneself the glory that only God is due, who will never share his glory and praise with another (cf. Isa. 42.8).

11
Page 21
Conclusion

What is plain from the Genesis story is that God judges the serpent and the first human pair, who demonstrate in their actions the shame and guiltiness for their actions. Conviction, as a state of one's own recognition that one has opposed God's sovereign rule and transgressed his good will, actually is affected through the energy and power of the triune God: it comes from the Father (Heb. 12.5), from the work of the Son (Jude 15; Rev. 3.19), through the actions of the Holy Spirit (John 16.7-11). Today, this kind of inner sense comes through the work of the Word as it is proclaimed by Christian witnesses, especially preachers, who are called to speak and

declare boldly the good news of the Kingdom of God in Christ (Matt. 18.15; John 16.7, 8; Eph. 5.11, 13; 1 Tim. 5.20; 2 Tim. 4.2; Titus 1.9, 13; 2.15). In a real sense, the power of the Word of God in the Law is to convict those who have opposed God's rule by enabling them to see precisely where, when, and how they have turned from God's good word to carry out their own actions (James 2.9). In one sense, this tragic story is played out every single time someone resists the Spirit of God to strive forward in self-sufficiency and self-reliance.

12
Page 21
Student Questions and Response

These questions are designed to ensure that the students understand the critical aims and facts presented in the first video segment. You will have to gauge your time well, especially if your students are intrigued with the concepts, and want to discuss their implications at length. Allow for the proper time to focus in on the main points, in order to still have enough time for a break before the next video segment is started.

13
Page 22
Summary of Segment 2

This video segment concentrates on the threefold result of the Fall in terms of its impact on the world (the *kosmos*), the sin nature of humankind (the *sarx*), and the release of the devil into the universe (the *kakos*). These three concepts are interrelated in the Scriptures, and although in the segment they are discussed separately, it will be necessary for you as Mentor to draw interconnections between them. As the multiple fruit of the single Fall, we ought to expect that these three realities share in the same DNA, in terms of their origins being rooted in the attempt to defy and oppose God's righteous reign in the universe. The more you can help your students understand the interconnections between the world, the flesh, and the devil, the better they will be able to think in terms of the nature of evil in the world, and develop a sophisticated understanding of what is the spiritual origin behind the horrific acts that have taken place in the world since the Fall.

What we ought not do, however, is to create a sense here of dualism, the evil sphere of the earth locked in battle against the righteous sphere of heaven, or of the Church. As you will see, creation is not seen in terms of evil; rather, it is the organized power of darkness which animates and controls the lives of so many

millions who neither know nor believe in the saving grace of Jesus Christ. What the New Testament teaches clearly is that, as a result of the Fall, the arch enemy of God, the devil, lies in control of the power of self-will and evil in our sphere, who as the head of these dark spiritual powers now exercises his will in a limited way as their head, which appear, as one has suggested, "to be organized on a vast scale and with great efficiency" (Eph. 6.12). It is clear that these forces and powers control and enslave the environments and lives of those who do not know God (Eph. 2.1-2; Col. 3.6). Scripture teaches that, in opposition to God, the devil rules a kingdom, one which is in his control (Matt. 4.8), and which opposes the work and standard of the rule of God in Jesus (Luke 11.18).

14
Page 23
Outline Point I

Make certain that the students do not confuse the term "world" with the meaning of "creation." They are not the same, although our English translation of the Bible tends to relate them in a confused way. The term "world," when applied to creation, suggests that sphere which God created by his sovereign power, the universe and all the things, both sentient and non-sentient within it. It has to do with the product of God's creative power. The term "world" (as *kosmos*) relates to the godless and menacing system of evil which is animated by greed, lust, and pride, which defies God's will and reign in every way, which influences the nations and hinders the advancement of God's Kingdom. Make sure that the students do not confuse the term "world" as creation with the term "world" (*kosmos*) as system and structure of godless evil in the world.

15
Page 23
Outline Point I-C

The principalities and powers discussed here have to do with the hierarchy of demons and fallen angels that Jesus overcame through his death on the cross (cf. Col. 2.15). Those powers and angelic hierarchies of resistance which followed the devil in his rebellion against the Lord God have now been defeated through the death, burial, and resurrection of Jesus who made a show of them through his death on the cross.

Many of the passages that refer to principalities and powers allude to human authorities (Rom. 13.1-3; Titus 3.1). Still, a common use of this Pauline phrase of principalities (*archai*) and authorities (*exousiai*) or powers (*dynameis*) makes it plain that he is referring these terms to cosmic, angelic intelligences; most of the time referring to them with the dark forces of demonism (Rom. 8.38; 1 Cor. 15.24; Eph. 1.21; 3.10; 6.12; Col. 1.16; 2.10; 2.15). Other terms used in this vein are dominions (*kyriotetes*, Eph. 1.21; Col. 1.16), thrones (*thronoi*, Col. 1.16), and the rulers (*archontes*) of this age (1 Cor. 2.6). The issue, it appears from Paul's usage, is not to give us an in-depth picture into the hierarchy of wrong or evil, but to establish that the world is subject to these powers, which makes it detestable to God, and aligned for certain judgment.

16
Page 25
Outline Point II

At least four major implications regarding the nature of sin are mentioned briefly here on in the video. The act of personal sin, of the sin nature, of imputed guilt and sin, and the reality of physical and spiritual death are all connected to the notion of sarx presented. What is important for the students to see is the thoroughgoing effect that the Fall had upon the depravity and sinfulness of humankind. The Fall of Adam and Eve had a chilling effect historically on all of humankind, which has now affected every human being. Since all of human progeny were intimately connected to the first human pair, their disobedience and rebellion has tainted the seed of the entire human race, and now, through our own acts of defiance and rebellion, we participate afresh in the Fall through our choices and decisions of sin.

17
Page 27
Outline Point III

In the discussion to come, you as Mentor ought to take note of the significance of this fact in terms of the Fall, and the ongoing struggle and conflict of the Kingdom. In a real sense, the kingdom conflict which underlies the structure of the Bible as revelation and the kingdom story as theology is the struggle between God and Satan, or rather, between Satan and God's Anointed, the Lord Jesus Christ. Jesus was manifested into the world in order to put down and destroy the works of the devil (cf. Gen. 3.15; 1 John 3.8; Heb. 2.14; Col. 1.13, etc.). Make sure that you notice that the speaker suggests that the release of the Evil One into the world represents

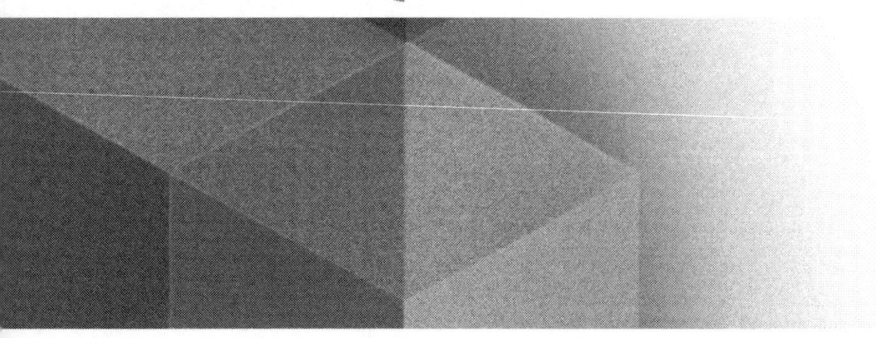

the most devastating result of the Fall, more devastating than any of the other effects, and thus, is at the center of God's attention in restoring his reign in the universe.

18
Page 30
Student Questions and Response

In leading this discussion, make sure that the students are clear on the primary effects that the Fall had upon the world, human beings, and the devil. These effects are at the center of the drama of the Kingdom of God, and represent for the student of Scripture a triad of evil that can enable them to understand the nature of evil in the world, and the unfolding of evil historically, in terms of its influence in human history. Do not hesitate to clearly emphasize the reality of *kakos*, as this is the most significant of all the effects and results of the Fall, and the one which Jesus will refer to more than any other in his earthly ministry in conflict with the rulers of the powers of darkness.

19
Page 31
Summary of Key Concepts

Listed in this section are the fundamental truths written in sentence form which the students should have received from this lesson, that is, from the videos and your guided discussion with them. Make sure that these concepts are clearly defined and carefully considered, for their quiz work and final exam will be taken from these items directly.

20
Page 32
Student Application and Implications

In helping your students think through their own situations, you might want to design some questions or use those provided below as water to "prime the pump" of their interests, so to speak. What is significant here is not the questions written below, but for you, in conversation with your students, to settle on a cadre of issues, concerns, questions, and ideas that flow directly from their experience, and relate to their lives and ministries. Do not hesitate to spend the majority of time on some question that arose from the video, or some concern that is especially relevant in their ministry context right now. The goal of this section is for you to enable them to think critically and theologically in regards to their own lives and ministry contexts. Again, the questions below are provided as guides and primers, and ought

not to be seen as absolute necessities. Pick and choose among them, or come up with your own. The key is relevance now, to their context and to their questions.

21
Page 32
Case Studies

The three case studies provided focus on the juxtaposition of the idea of God being in charge as Lord of all and the reality of pain and destruction in the city and the world. Undoubtedly your students will have witnessed horrible things in their lives, in the lives of the members of their churches, in their families and neighbors, and in their worlds. They must now be able to use these insights to make sense of those evil deeds and terrible things, while at the same time, affirm that God Almighty is still Lord. While God's rule and reign has been resisted, he nevertheless is Lord and King of all, and is working out his will through the Church and through his Spirit. Of course, until Jesus comes in glory, the Lord's prayer will never fully be made true (that is, God's will being done on earth as it is done in heaven). Nevertheless, in the world, where we still endure tribulation and pain (John 16.33), Jesus has overcome the world (John 12.9-11). Helping your students live with the reality of the "already/not yet" Kingdom is a critical part of this Capstone module. Use the case studies to discuss the difficulties of this truth, and help them strive to relate fluidly to this, in light of the trouble and tragedy that exists in the city.

22
Page 34
Resources and Bibliographies

These book excerpts are quite handy in detailing the truth that although God is the Lord of history, due to the Fall, the universe has been exposed to the power of evil, and yet, God in his grace has determined to destroy evil in the person of his Son. This reality of the Fall is merely the first act of the kingdom drama, but it is critical, for it provides a context for your students to understand what is at stake in the struggle for rulership and ownership in the universe. Billheimer's text is especially helpful in this regard.

23
Page 34
Counseling and Prayer

If time is available, spend time together in prayer, thanking God for his sovereignty and power, and his determination to defeat the powers and the forces that have run amok over humankind since the Fall. Praise God for the opportunity we have as men and women of the Church, to represent the reign of God in the city, and ask God for boldness and power to become better vessels of his rule and reign in the places where he has placed us.

24
Page 35
Assignments

Make certain that the students understand the assignment for next week, especially the written piece. This is not difficult; the goal is that they would read the material as best as they can and write a few sentences on what they take them to mean. This is a critical intellectual skill for your students to learn, so make sure that you encourage them in this process. Of course, for those students who might find this difficult, assure them of the intent behind this assignment, and emphasize their understanding of the material being the key, not their writing skills. We want to improve their skills, but not at the expense of their encouragement and edification. Nor, however, do we want to sell them short. Strike to find the midpoint between challenge and encouragement here.

25
Page 35
Looking Forward to the Next Lesson

Keep the students aware of the interconnection of all the kingdom lessons. This first lesson highlights the problem; it is the doormat into the drama of God, listing and focusing upon human and angelic rebellion. Always tie what is being studied to what has gone before, and what is upcoming. The next lesson focuses on God's inauguration of the kingdom rule, and his intent to bring the universe back under his reign. Praise God, in Jesus Christ God has restored himself to the center of the universe, and is gathering out of the world a people who will belong to him forever!

God's Reign Inaugurated

1
Page 39
Lesson Introduction

Welcome to the Mentor's Guide for Lesson 2, *God's Reign Inaugurated.* The goal of this *Kingdom of God* module is to provide your students with a biblical framework to understand what God is doing in human history, and prepare them to be able witnesses of Christ and his Kingdom. This second lesson is designed to show the students how God's reign has been infiltrating the world since the time of the Fall; God has not abandoned his creation, but has covenanted to bring to himself a people who would be his forever, through the salvific work of his Son, Jesus Christ. Adopting the mindset and disposition of a warrior, God covenanted with Abraham to bless all the families of the earth through his line, and thus, God determined to restore his reign to the earth. God renewed the covenant through the patriarchs, his people Israel, through the tribe of Judah and the family of David. Finally, in the fullness of time, Jesus of Nazareth appeared, whose presence represents the realization of the Kingdom on earth. Through his death, burial, resurrection, and ascension, the rule of God has come in power. While the consummation of the Kingdom is still future, at the Second Coming of Christ, the Kingdom of God has come in the person of Jesus. This high theology represents the teaching aims of lesson two, *God's Reign Inaugurated.*

Please notice again in the objectives that these truths are clearly stated. As usual, your responsibility as Mentor is to emphasize these concepts throughout the lesson, especially during the discussions and interaction with the students. The more you can highlight the objectives throughout the class period, the better the chances are that they will understand and grasp the magnitude of these objectives.

2
Page 39
Devotion

The theme of today's lesson is the inauguration of the Kingdom of God, not in terms of a single event, but in the sense of an unfolding vision, with the presence of Jesus Christ representing the culmination of the Kingdom's announcement. In a real sense, God began the announcement of his rule restored to earth with the *proto-evangelium*, the first telling of the Good News in Genesis 3.15. In the announcement that the serpent's head would be crushed by the Seed of the woman, God announced his resolve to bring order and beauty back to the earth, which was marred through the rebellion and disobedience of humankind and the great prince,

the devil. This quiet, confident announcement of the Kingdom of God being "at hand" or "near" suggests that with Jesus' presence in the world, the Kingdom has come.

3
Page 41
Contact

The contacts of this lesson all deal with identifying the beginning and/or start of God's resolve to restore the Kingdom of God to earth. The notion of beginning is key, not only for introducing the Lesson, but will also be critical for the application of the truths in this session. For instance, knowing that God's initiative lies at the heart of all of his salvific work is critical for our own attitude of thanks to God, as well as the confidence that we hold that the work of the Kingdom is in fact God's own work. God is the worker, and we are coworkers with him in his harvest, for "we are God's fellow workers. You are God's field, God's building" (1 Cor. 3.9, ESV). God is the primary actor in the drama of salvation, and our role is to participate with God as co-workers in his vineyard. The heart of this contact is emphasizing the issues of the students, of course, but to do so in light of this central truth.

4
Page 42
Summary of Segment 1

The focus of this first lesson is the working of God in history as a free and sovereign God on behalf of his created universe. God, because of his love and commitment to his universe, committed himself to work to restore his kingdom rule in the earth. This resolve, fueled by his love and grace, is the primary power, motive, and energy in the kingdom drama. In other words, despite the involvement of key characters and nations in God's salvation history, the heart of redemption flows from God's heart, his determination to bring to himself a remnant of people who would live forever in a recreated world where his glory and praise would be central. In understanding segment one of the video, it is critical to have this concept as a backdrop for all of the issues and items covered. This backdrop is critical to the full appreciation of the miracle of salvation, that is, that a sovereign and free God, who had been ignored and rejected, in spite of the disobedience of the first human pair, resolved to bring them back under his reign for his own glory.

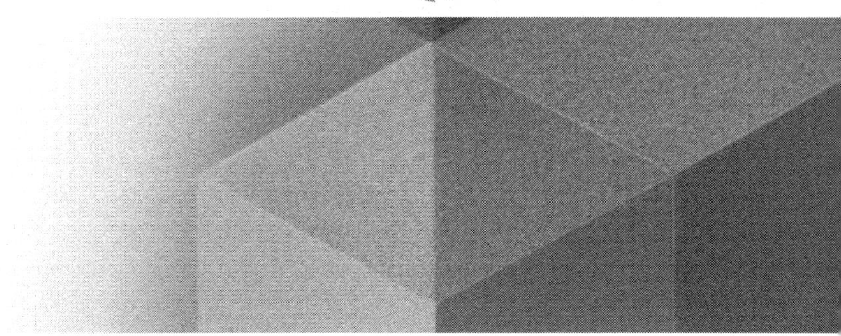

Difficult issues emerge in the discussion of God's freedom and the rebellion of the devil and of Adam and Eve. It is important to emphasize throughout this lesson that the Lord God retained his sovereignty over everything in the universe, over everything he made, even though his reign was challenged by his creation. God never relinquished or surrendered to any other power or force his absolute control of events. Even in the face of direct opposition to his will, nothing can occur without his consent, even if he himself is not the primary cause of every event. Amazingly difficult to understand, this is also true of evil, which functions under limits set by God and exists by his permission. Evil and rebellion cannot go beyond the boundaries which God determines to limit and circumscribe it (Job 1; 1 Cor. 10.13). The rebellion of the devil and the Fall of Adam and Eve must therefore also be seen as allowed by God to be a part of his higher kingdom purpose, and yet, they themselves were held entirely responsible for their decisions and responses in regards to God's will. God cannot, however, be blamed in any way for allowing his creation the freedom to respond or not respond to his will.

5
Page 42
Outline Point I

In one sense it is important to understand that the notion of God as Warrior goes to the heart of the kingdom vision. In fact, there is a kind of sacred nature associated with warfare in the Bible when God's people at God's initiative encounter God's foes in God's power. There are, for example, worship and religious rituals connected to sacred warfare, of which the Lord is the primary Warrior. Some of these items were actually performed before the battle. The soldiers of Israel were required to make preparations to do battle in a war that Yahweh initiated. In some very unusual circumstances, such as in the battle of Jericho, the fighting men were circumcised, which is hardly a smart thing to do before engaging in battle (Josh. 5; cf. Gen. 34)! There is some evidence to show that every act of doing battle in the name of Yahweh was preceded by some kind of worship sacrifice, which shows the fighting to be more than merely a military operation. The Kingdom of God is essentially warfare; God doing battle against those forces which rebelled against his sovereign will, and those who resist his will today (e.g. 1 Sam. 13.1-15).

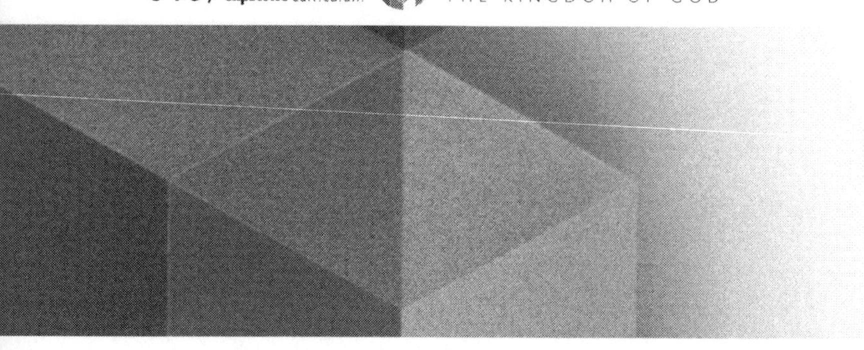

God's resolve to reconstitute his Kingdom in human history is demonstrated in the oft-repeated statement of the Old Testament, occurring in the formula "I will be their God and they shall be My people" (cf. Jer. 11.4; 24.7; 30.22; 32.38; Ezek. 11.20; 14.11; 36.28; 37.23; Zech. 8.8; etc.). These citations reveal that God, through his covenant commitments to Abraham and his people, has made himself available to his creation without reserve to fight his enemies and work through his people as his "peculiar treasure" (*segulla*, Exod. 19.5; Deut. 7.6; 14.2; 26.18; Ps. 135.4; Mal. 3.17). This possession of his people, is for the sake of the nations, which God had determined to offer salvation through Abraham's Seed.

6
Page 45
Outline Point II

What is critical here in understanding God's motive is the connection between his sovereign will and his motive of grace, love, and kindness, or, as the Bible puts it, God's "lovingkindness" or "covenant-love" (*hesed*), a term with which (*berit*) is often associated (cf. Deut. 7.9; 1 Kings 8.23; Dan. 9.4). (One interesting example of this is in 1 Samuel 20.8, where *hesed* is ascribed to Jonathan as he enters into his covenant relationship with David.) Not only is this a clear picture of the resolve of the Lord to redeem and transform the world back to its original government, but it also shows how God functions out of this mighty love, a lovingkindness that animates his actions on behalf of those who need his grace.

"Israel" was the name that the angel gave to Jacob after the all night prayer struggle with the angel at Peniel listed in Genesis 32.28. The name was conferred out of the context of the struggle, because Jacob struggled with God and in a sense prevailed, he was granted the name because "as a prince he had power with God and prevailed." This name, Israel, is the common name given to the descendants of Jacob, who himself was the grandson of Abraham, to whom God made the Promise, the same Promise which was renewed to both Isaac and to Jacob. Therefore, the people of God, the people of the covenant represented by the entire people of the twelve tribes are called "Israelites," the "children of Israel" (Josh. 3.17; 7. 25; Judg. 8.27; Jer. 3.21), and the "house of Israel" (Exod. 16.31; 40.38).

7
Page 47
Outline Point III

What is critical to see is the lineage of Abraham, and the ongoing renewal of God's Promise to Abraham and to his descendants, represented historically by the people

of Israel. In the Old Testament, the name is used in different ways. For instance, upon Saul's death, the ten tribes of the North appropriated the name "Israel" to themselves, as if they themselves represented the entire nation (see 2 Sam. 2.9, 10, 17, 28; 3.10, 17; 19.40-43). As the nation developed, after the split of the kingdom after King Solomon, the rulers and kings of the ten Northern tribes were called the "kings of Israel," while the kings of the two Southern tribes (Benjamin and Judah) were called "kings of Judah." After both the Northern and Southern kingdoms were brought under captivity by Assyria and Babylon respectively, the name "Israel" began to be used again to represent the entire nation as descendants of Abraham.

Looking forward to the time when under the rule of God the people of God of all eras gather under God's rule in the consummated Kingdom, we see that the term "Israel" has been associated with this company, that is, the "True Israel" (Ps. 73.1; Isa. 45.17; 49.3; John 1.47; Rom. 9.6; 11.26).

What must be emphasized here is the historical continuation of God's promise to Abraham's descendants as the people through whom the Messiah, or Seed, would come, the one who would rescue Israel and through her, the nations.

8
Page 49
Student Questions and Response

In these questions you will find the focus is upon mastering the data and the facts associated with the claims made in the first video segment. Concentrate on ensuring that the students understand the answers in light of the lesson aims of the first segment, especially God's commitment as Warrior, and his covenant faithfulness shown through Abraham, Israel, Judah, and David. Make certain that you watch the clock here, covering the questions below and those posed by your students, and watch for any tangents which may lead you from rehearsing the critical facts and main points.

9
Page 50
Summary of Segment 2

This second segment focuses on the realization of the Kingdom's presence in the person of Jesus of Nazareth. In a real sense, Jesus is the King whose person is the ground of his authority. In other words, who Jesus is becomes the basis of his Sovereign Majesty and authority. Jesus of Nazareth performs in his life and ministry

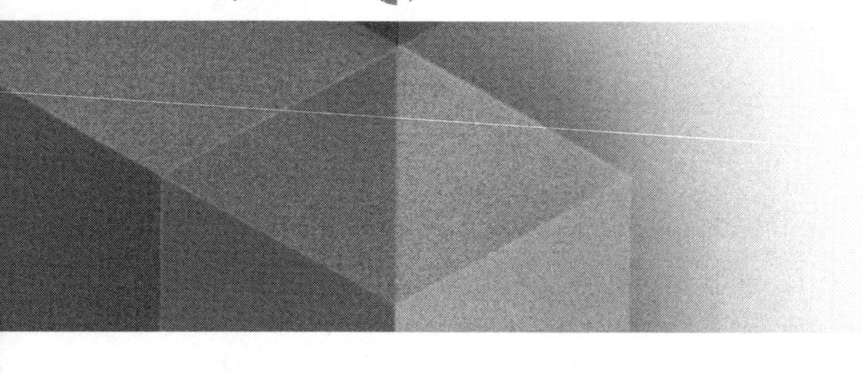

the role of Yahweh's King, calling a people out of the world that would be his peculiar possession (Isa. 55.5; John 10.16, 27). As Lord and King, Jesus has provided to his people his own judgments and standards which ought to regulate the operations and actions of his people in every way they govern themselves (1 Cor. 5.4-5; 12.28; Eph. 4.11-12; Matt. 28.19-20; 18.17-18; 1 Tim. 5.20; Titus 3.10). It is his kingly power and authority by which he protects, supports, and preserves his people in the midst of their tribulations, conflicts, and trials for his name's sake (2 Cor. 12.9-10; Rom. 8.35-39), and through his kingly authority received from his Father, he as Lord defeats, constricts, and marshals his power to limit the influence and effects of his enemies (Acts 12.17; 18.9-10; 1 Cor. 15.25). As the one appointed by God to have all authority in heaven and on earth, he commands and arranges all things to exist for his greater glory and honor, and determines the inherent good in all things (Rom. 8.28; 14.11; Col. 1.18; Matt. 28.19-20). And as Judge, he will one day execute the righteous sentence of the Father upon all those who reject the good news of the Kingdom, and will himself take vengeance on those refusing his reign and disobeying his Gospel (Ps. 2.9; 2 Thess. 1.8).

This basic outline of Jesus as King reveals truths that are complimented by the ideas contained in this video segment. What must be emphasized is that what was merely promise and shadow in the Abrahamic covenant, now in Jesus of Nazareth, has become the reality and the substance. In the person of Jesus Christ, God has made known the glory and power of his Kingdom. Its presence and power are now revealed in the life and deeds of Jesus. In this sense, the presence of Jesus in the world represents a special kind of inauguration of the Kingdom of God, different, more richly presented, and more decisively engaged than any picture of God's rule previously given. Jesus represents a kind of final revelation of God in regards to the kingdom message, its power, and its manifestation (Heb. 1.1-4).

10
Page 51
Outline Point I

Jesus' entrance into the world represents a new level of intensity and focus to the Lord's divine battle to restore his reign in the world. In a real sense, Jesus of Nazareth intensifies the battle of the Kingdom in the world by focusing not so much on human sin and evil, but on the malevolent powers of the Evil One, and the spiritual powers and principalities. Jesus inaugurates the Kingdom with genuine

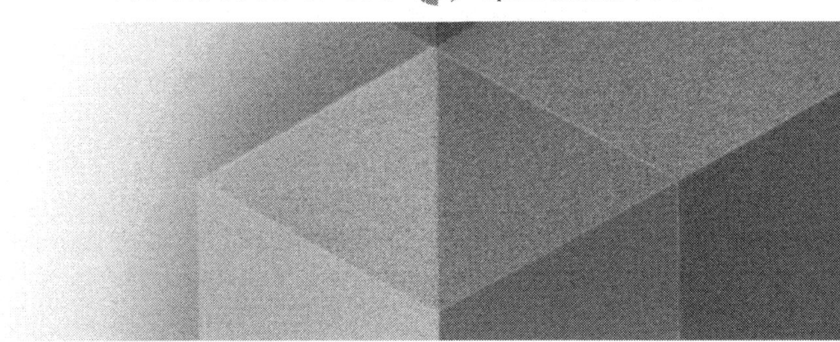

violence against the kingdom of the devil, but he does not fight the battle with spear and sword, but with the weapons of spiritual warfare in the Holy Spirit. For instance, when Peter resorts to the use of the sword in protection of Jesus, he rebukes him and goes to the cross instead, which is the ultimate secret weapon of the Kingdom of God (Matt. 26.50–56).

This notion of Jesus as the supreme Warrior and Christ's death on the cross as the ultimate weapon is described by Paul in Colossians where he speaks of Jesus' death as disarming the powers and authorities (Col. 2.15), and their ultimate defeat through the cross. Jesus' death and ascension are figured as a classic kind of victory celebration, a parade of the great General who brings the spoils and prisoners of war in his mighty Victor's train. This notion can be seen also in Ephesians 4.7-8, with its quotation from Psalm 68, a classic hymn of divine warfare. Amazingly, our Lord Jesus defeated the foes of God and inaugurated the Kingdom, winning the greatest battle of all on the cross, by being killed, not by physically killing others.

In a sense Jesus establishes in his coming the prototype and standard of all legitimate spiritual warfare. We defeat the enemy not by destroying others' lives, but by sacrificing our lives for them; we win the battle against the enemies of God not by killing human beings, but by living as living sacrifices, acceptable to God (Rom. 12.2; John 12.25). We win not by the power of the gun, the knife, and the missile, but by the Word of God and the shield of faith (Eph. 6.10-18). Jesus' defeat of the enemy proves that a significant portion of the fight deals with our own internal struggles against evil remaining within (Rom. 7.7–25; 2 Cor. 10.1–6).

11
Page 52
Outline Point I-D

This idea, that in the coming of Jesus Christ the Kingdom was made visible in the world, is a significant revelation in the fulfillment of God's covenantal promise to restore his reign in the earth. With Jesus we experience the coming of the Messianic age in reality, not merely as an idea or hope or longing, but in actual fact.

G. E. Ladd makes this point explicitly when he suggests:

> *Jesus proclaimed that this Promise [the Promise of the coming of the Kingdom] was actually being fulfilled. This is no apocalyptic Kingdom but a present*

salvation. Jesus did not promise his hearers a better future or assure that they would soon enter the Kingdom. Rather he boldly announced that the Kingdom (Herrschaft) *of God had come to them. The presence of the Kingdom was "a happening, an event, the gracious action of God." The promise was fulfilled in the action of Jesus: in his proclamation of good news to the poor, release to the captives, restoring sight to the blind, freeing those who were oppressed. This was no new theology or new idea or new promise; it was a new event in history. "The wretched hear the good news, the prison doors are open, the oppressed breathe the air of freedom, blind pilgrims see the light, the day of salvation is here."*

~ G. E. Ladd. **The Presence of the Future.**
Grand Rapids: Eerdmans Publishing, 1974. pp. 111-112.

📖 **12**
Page 59
Conclusion

In light of all that Jesus of Nazareth accomplished through his death, resurrection, and ascension, his work as Divine Warrior in ushering in the Kingdom of God is not yet completed. A simple reading of the book of Revelation and the other apocalyptic portions of the New Testament reveal that he will fulfill the ministry that he inaugurated in his life, death, resurrection and ascension. Jesus himself spoke of the mighty day when he as the Son of Man would come on the clouds of heaven with the holy angels, to defeat finally and exhaustively all the powers that would resist his will (Mark 13.26). This vision and language mirrors the great vision of the prophet Daniel, who refers to a similar personage in Daniel 7.13. The Kingdom of God comes with violence, just as John the Baptist predicted it would come. Our Lord, who came the first time to execute God's secret weapon of the cross on his enemies, will in fact return again, this time as the true Divine Warrior whose work is public, exhaustive, and devastating for his enemies. Revelation 19.11-16 describes the coming of our Lord Jesus Christ in classic Divine Warrior imagery; he comes on a white horse, draped with a cape dipped in blood, with a two-edged sword coming from his mouth. Behind him are the veritable armies of heaven as he "judges and makes war" (v. 11).

The final vision of the Bible regarding Jesus as God's Divine Warrior wraps up the revelation with a remarkable picture of the last battle, which, at the very least, must

be a rich and potent symbol of the final judgment to come, and of the vengeance and wrath God dispenses on those who have resisted his rule without repentance. In a real sense, Jesus of Nazareth is the Anointed One, the one chosen by God to end the conflict which began with the rebellion of the serpent and the disobedience of the first human pair. It is he who will crush to pieces the one *kakos*, the one who through his lies and deceptions inflicted misery and suffering upon the earth (Rom. 16.20; Rev. 12.9), and who represents the worst form of stubborn resistance to the rule of God. The promise of Genesis 3.15 has now finally come to pass in the person of the gentle Nazarene, who does the warfare of God, not by killing but by dying and rising again on behalf of those he came to save.

13
Page 59
Student Questions and Response

The goal of these segue questions is not that you feel the need to go through each one of them. Not only would this be laborious and tiresome, it might also deflect you from focusing on many of the tough issues and central concerns of your students. While the segue questions are meant to help you ensure that the students understand the concepts covered in the video, you will have to balance that objective with the obvious goal of dealing with their questions and interests as they respond to the Scriptures and other materials.

14
Page 62
Case Studies

One of the goals in covering the case studies in this lesson is making specific and critical interconnections with what is arguably very difficult eschatology and the practical outworking of ministry in the city. One of the most challenging things for students to do is to see the correlation between the scriptural teachings on the Kingdom and their own lives and ministries. Whether or not you use the case studies below or choose to invent your own scenarios to discuss, you must seek to make the intersection plain between what the students have heard, learned, and discussed, and what they are confronted with in their ministries.

In light of this, the case studies below try to take seriously what would occur if there might be inappropriate or exaggerated emphases on the Kingdom as already present, or if it were conceived as being entirely future. Believe it or not, the way in which an

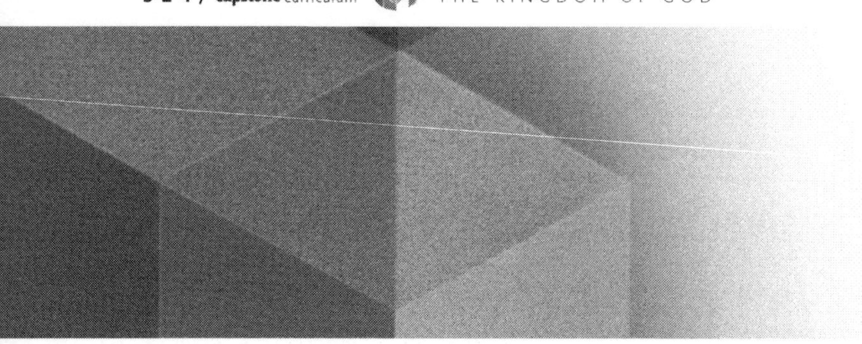

urban minister views this theology will have a profound impact on how they approach ministry and proceed in their own work for the Lord.

15
Page 64
Counseling and Prayer

Do not consider it an overly familiar or unnecessary thing to ask the students if they need prayer for someone or something connected to the ideas and truths presented in the lesson. Prayer is a wonderfully practical and helpful way to apply truth; by taking specific needs to God in light of a truth, the students can solidify those ideas in their soul, and receive back from the Lord the answers they need in order to be sustained in the midst of their ministries. Of course, everything is somehow dependent on the amount of time you have in your session, and how you have organized it. Still, prayer is a forceful and potent part of any spiritual encounter and teaching, and if you can, it should always have its place, even if it is a short summary prayer of what God has taught us, and a determination to live out its implications as the Holy Spirit teaches us.

God's Reign Invading

1
Page 69
Lesson Introduction

Welcome to the Mentor's Guide for Lesson 3, *God's Reign Invading*. The overall focus of the *Kingdom of God* module is to enable your students to grasp the power, wonder, and appeal of the Kingdom of God, and its meaning both for their lives and ministries in the churches they attend and serve. The role of the Church, both universal and local, comes to the fore in this discussion, since the Church is seen as the central venue and vehicle through which the message and power of the Kingdom is demonstrated in this age. This lesson is designed to show the students how God, through Jesus Christ, has made the Church of Jesus Christ the place in which the kingdom splendor and power is displayed for the world to see. Similarly, the Church is the agent, the deputy of God to represent his authority and rule in the world, and give faithful witness and display of its power.

What you want to do with the students in this lesson is to encourage them in the sheer mystery of God's grace to give to the Church such importance and rank, and reiterate the wonderful privilege they have as urban Christians and ministers to love and serve the urban church. Notice in the objectives that these aims are clearly stated, and you ought to emphasize them throughout the lesson, during your discussions and interaction with the students. In every case the focus is upon the Church's ability to give display and witness to the reality of the Kingdom. What is significant here is that this is not merely the result of the Church's resolve and commitment. Through the power of the Holy Spirit, the Church can now be that company through which the rule of God is made known to those who know nothing of God's great kingdom victory in Christ. In a real sense, they will never know of that kingdom victory without the faithful ministry of the Church to display the excellencies of the Lord in such a way as to compel them to consider God's work in Christ (1 Pet. 2.9-10). The more you can highlight the objectives throughout the class period, the better the chances are that they will understand and grasp the magnitude of these objectives.

2
Page 69
Devotion

This devotional ties and links the ministry of Jesus as Divine Warrior and the ongoing ministry of the Church as the soldier of God in the earth appropriating the victory of Jesus in the world (Eph. 6.10-18). Yahweh, through his covenant faithfulness and the revelation of his glory in his Son, has inaugurated his rule in

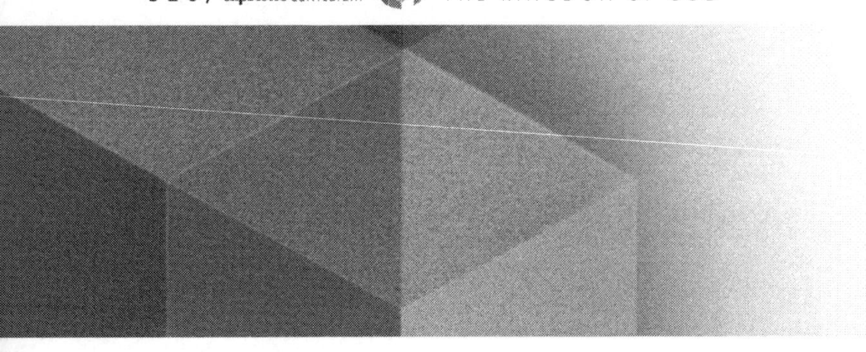

Jesus Christ. As the creator and sovereign God of the universe, now in Jesus of Nazareth he is reasserting openly his rule over all nations (cf. Deut. 7.6). The divine warfare of God in the Old Testament was demonstrated through the Holy war that he initiated through his people against his enemies. As such, spiritual warfare and the "violence" associated with it is definitely a work through which the Divine Warrior executes his will and enforces his high purposes in the universe. Of course, in the current age this is a kind of violence against the principalities and powers which defy his will and animate the affairs of those who do not know him (e.g., Eph. 2.2; Col. 3.5). Nevertheless, the story of the Kingdom is the story of God doing violence against those forces and powers which defy his good will and legitimate right to rule as Lord and King over all.

3
Page 70
Contact

As mentioned before, the heart of this lesson is the formative role that God has given to the Church in giving witness to and evidence of his rule in the earth. The contacts below seek to define precisely the relationship between the Church and commitment to Jesus in the students' minds. It is quite common in our day for people to claim a deep intimacy with Jesus while, at the same time, holding the Church as a kind of appendage of little importance. As a matter of fact, many who profess an intimate walk with Christ attribute that walk to the distance they have to the Church. The Church is viewed, if not as an enemy, at the very least as the key impediment to the growth and depth of Christian discipleship. Ironically, many para-church and other Christian organizations give the sense that they are the nexus of the Kingdom, and that the local church is destined to play second fiddle in the band of God. This lesson is calling this kind of thinking into question. Even more strongly, it is calling such thinking false, and perhaps, depending on its level of mistaken understanding, even heretical.

The aim here is to have the students reflect together on the relationship, in their own personal and corporate frameworks, between their allegiance to the Church as they profess intimacy with and commitment to Christ. The lesson will argue that you cannot have the one without the other. To urbanize the thought of a fine churchman of the fourth century, the Latin Father Cyprian, "If the Church ain't yo mama, then God ain't yo daddy!"

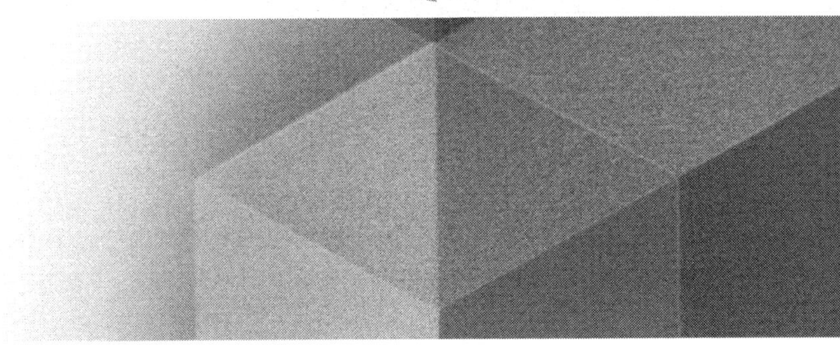

4
Page 72
Summary of
Segment 1

The primary aim in this segment and the one to come is to help our students come to grips with the Church's association to the Kingdom as God's rule in the world. The term "church" is probably derived from the Greek word *kuriakon* meaning "the Lord's house." In the New Testament the term rendered "church" most frequently is the translation of the Greek word *ekklesia*, "assembly" or "called out ones" (probably synonymous with the Hebrew *qahal* of the Old Testament). Both *ekklesia* and *qahal* were used to designate, in simple usage, an assembly, or gathering. The term as used in the New Testament was not identified with a place of meeting or a building ("the church on the corner"), nor in the common way the term is associated with denominations ("The Evangelical Free Church") or with people of a country committed to the same profession ("Church of Scotland"). Rather, the term was used for: 1) a gathering or assembly [Acts 19.32, 39, 41]; 2) for the entire body of all believers who have come to God in Christ by repentance and faith [e.g. Eph. 5.23-29; Heb. 12.23]; 3) as a small gathering of disciples meeting together for fellowship and mission [Rom. 16.5; Col. 4.15]; 4) for the believers in a particular city and locale, as the "Church of God at Corinth" [1 Cor. 1.2, the "Church at Jerusalem," Acts 18.1, or the "Church of Ephesus," Rev. 2.1]; 5) the entire body of living and professing Christians holding to Christ in the world today [1 Cor. 15.9; Gal. 1.13; Matt. 16.18]. This refers to the "Church visible," that is, those believers who publicly hold to the person and hope of Jesus Christ in the world today.

What is critical for you as Mentor is to try to emphasize in the student discussions and interaction that the Church is integral to God's kingdom purposes, that while the Kingdom is not the Church *per se*, it is, in fact the locus and context of the Kingdom; the place where the rule of God is enjoyed, displayed, and given witness to in life, word, worship and service. The goal is to banish all thoughts that the Kingdom can be authentically understood divorced from a critical and biblical comprehension of the Church of Jesus Christ in the world today.

5
Page 72
Outline Point I

One of the wonderful realities about the Word of God in connection to the Church is the remarkable multiplicity of images, metaphors, ideas, and concepts associated with the nature of the Church of Jesus Christ. In Paul Minear's remarkable little book on the Church, *Images of the Church in the New Testament*, its appendix lists some ninety-six images he found on the Church, giving them the various classifications of minor images, the people of God, the new creation, the fellowship in faith, and the body of Christ. What one receives in looking at the revelation in the New Testament about the Church is the profound richness of the apostolic imagination in conceiving and classifying the Church. Among those listed by Minear are the salt of the earth, fighters against Satan, the sanctified slaves, friends, sons of God, household of God, a letter from Christ, branches of the Vine, the elect lady, the bride of Christ, exiles, ambassadors, a chosen race, the holy temple, priesthood, the new creation, members of Christ, and spiritual body. Such a rich enumeration of images demonstrate that the Apostles did not feel any need to restrict the Church's definition according to a few images, or ratchet the Church's meaning in a creedal box of meaning. The role that the Church plays in the world is as full and varied as the images which Jesus and the Apostles gave in regards to it. As a matter of fact, a dramatic amount of diverse understandings of the Church can come from a deliberate study of these images and their relationship to one another.

We have found it helpful at the Institute, however, to embrace a fidelity and commitment to the creedal theology coming out of the Nicene Statement. This commitment, has made it useful for us to describe the role and nature of the Church through the classic categories given in the Nicene Creed, i.e., that the Church is one, holy, catholic, and apostolic. Arising from the Council of Constantinople in 381 and reaffirmed at Ephesus (431) and Chalcedon (451), the Church has affirmed itself to be "one, holy, catholic, and apostolic." While we do not rigidly suggest that these are the only way to understand the nature of the Church, we do suggest that Christians throughout history have found these categories helpful and intriguing in gathering together the diverse and rich material in the New Testament on the Church.

6
Page 74
Outline Point I-C

The image of the body is one of the most significant metaphors of the Church, offering rich understandings of the relationships of the various members of the body to one another, as well as differing groups and associations of the body to each other. The New Testament unequivocally asserts that Christians are one body in Christ containing many members who hold to different offices, gifts, and functions

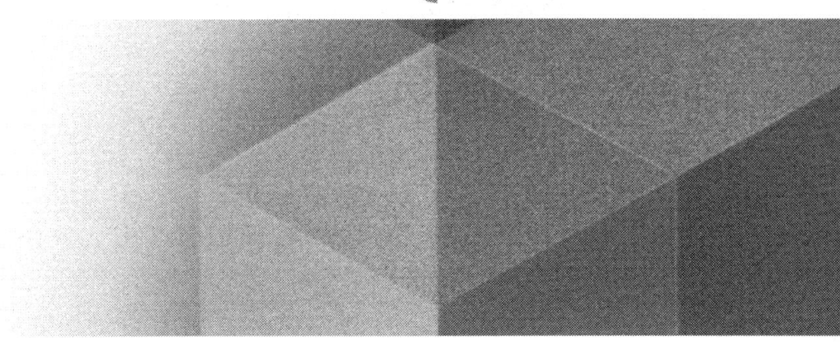

for its common good (Rom. 12.4-5; 1 Cor. 12.27). The Church is designated to be the true and one body of Christ in the world (Eph. 1.22-23; 4.12), with Jesus himself being the Head (authority and source) of the body (Eph. 5.23; Col. 1.18). As the body is utterly dependent upon the head for all of its life, growth, direction, and care (Col. 2.19), so is the Church of Jesus Christ organically connected and dependent upon him. The analogy of the body reveals clearly how the Church is more than a simple gathering, but the very place where those who share Christ's DNA gather, relate, and grow. The Church is the very place where Jesus can be seen in the world; as his body, the Church is literally of the same bone and flesh as the Divine Warrior himself (a truth which is reaffirmed in the metaphor of the Bride in Ephesians 5.22-33). In the biblical understanding of matrimony, the husband and wife are said to be one flesh, and this is the same regarding Christ and the Church (Eph. 5.31-32). Both analogies speak powerfully and directly of the organic unity that Jesus of Nazareth has with his people.

The logic of this cannot be overcome. If Jesus is the Sole Warrior who inaugurates and ushers in the reign of God with power, and if the Church is organically united to him by faith, then there also must be a direct relationship between the living presence of the Church and the actual life and power of the Kingdom. Wherever the true Church exists, there also must be evidence and sign of the Kingdom's presence, life, and power.

7
Page 74
Outline Point II

Perhaps the greatest sign that the Church is the locus and agent of the Kingdom in the current era is the fact that the Holy Spirit indwells the people of God. No other single evidence of the Kingdom's presence is as weighty or conclusive as this, as stated in Peter's own testimony at Pentecost recorded in Acts 2. In Acts 2.14ff. Peter explains the powerful tongues phenomena on the day of Pentecost as a sign of the fulfillment of the prophecy in the book of Joel regarding the coming outpouring of the Holy Spirit upon all flesh in the final Messianic period (cf. Joel 2.28ff.). As a sign of the Kingdom's presence in the Messianic age, this outpouring of the Spirit in the Church was a token of the grace of God bestowed upon Jew and Gentile alike (Acts 10.45; 11.15ff.). This gift of the Spirit, associated with the coming of the *Shalom* of God at the very end of time, can now be received through simple repentance and faith in the saving work of Jesus of Nazareth (Acts 2.38). The gift of salvation associated with the entrance of the Kingdom, the outpouring of the Holy Spirit, is now available to any person, whether Gentile or Jew, upon baptism into the name of Jesus Christ, a promise which is not only for the Jews but, according to Peter, to any and all whom the Lord God may call (Acts 2.39; Joel 2.32). The Church was animated from the beginning by the Holy Spirit's ministry, who selected their leaders (Acts 13.1-3; Acts 20), energized the ministries of its leaders (Acts 4.31; 6.5; 7.54; etc.), and directed the ongoing outreaches and activities of its mission in the world (Acts 9.31; 13.2; 15.28; 16.6-7). Because of the Holy Spirit's presence in the Church, the identical acts of kingdom manifestation (conversion, healing, exorcism, miracles, etc.) were routinely carried out in the midst of the people of God. The Holy Spirit routinely provided revelational visions and prophecies to the members of the Church (Acts 9.10; 10.3; 10.ff.; 11.27-28; 13.1; 15.32) as was clearly foretold in the Joel 2 prophecy. By all signs of the Church's life and mission, it confirmed in its daily experience that the Kingdom of God, the manifestation of God's Messianic age, had indeed come on the day of Pentecost. This kingdom power and presence will be with the Church unto the very end of the age (Matt. 28.20).

8
Page 78
Student Questions and Response

In these questions, you will find the focus is upon mastering the data and the facts associated with the claims made in the first video segment. While many points can be highlighted in this section, perhaps the central fact to be reviewed is how the Church of Jesus Christ is organically connected to Christ through the Holy Spirit. Again, the Holy Spirit in the midst of the Church is undeniable evidence that the Apostles understood the Church to be experiencing the gifts and blessings of the Messianic age right now, today. This is why a full and nuanced, that is, biblically and theologically mature view of the Church is so critical to any factual understanding of the Kingdom. Highlight the biblical truth that Peter made at Pentecost, that the Holy Spirit in the midst of the Church is the fulfillment of the Old Testament's promises regarding the Messianic age come among humankind, in our time and in our day. Concentrate on ensuring that the students understand the answers in light of the lesson aims of the first segment, especially the Church as the locus of God's revelation, Spirit, and life.

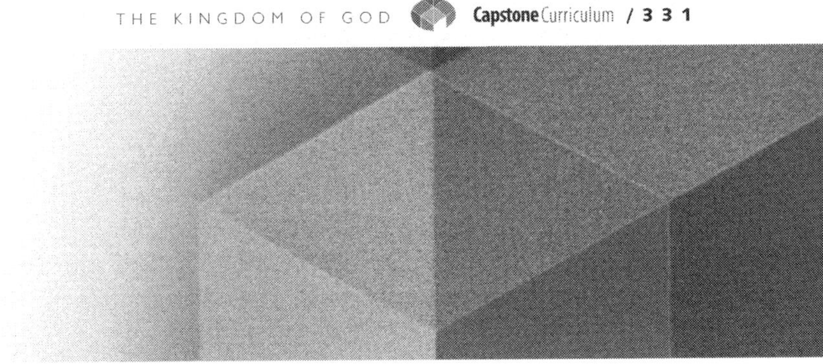

9
Page 79
Summary of Segment 2

The view of the Church as locus is directly related to its role as the agent of the Kingdom. As locus, the Church is the place where the kingdom gifts and blessings are experienced through God's Spirit and presence; as agent, the Church is the vessel through which God's kingdom message and power are displayed and announced in the world. On the one hand, the Church is the recipient of the blessings of the Messianic age, and on the other hand, it is the instrument through which the kingdom blessings are made available in the midst of the world, which now, through God's grace, the offer of forgiveness and reconciliation, is being given. To speak of the Church as the locus alone is to make the Church an isolated community, and makes it appear as if God's kingdom blessing is given with partiality. To emphasize the agency of the Church over its place is to confuse the work of the Church with the actual bringing in of the Kingdom. The Church is neither the Kingdom, nor does she of her own power usher in its power and glory. Rather, through faith and obedience to Jesus Christ, the Church becomes the means by which God literally invades this present sphere with his kingdom power and love.

Your focus here should be to assert that the Church is BOTH the locus and agent of the Kingdom. In other words, the vision of the Church as locus should always be kept in sync and spoken with the Church as the agent of the Kingdom. This is key for the student's proper understanding of the Church's role and responsibility in the world.

10
Page 80
Outline Point I

The Church's responsibility to worship God is its most significant work. In its identity as a royal priesthood, the Church's duty is to declare the excellencies of him who called her to his own splendor and glory (cf. 1 Pet. 2.9-10). The Church was born again to praise, to ascribe to the triune God the worth for which he alone is worthy. The kingdom initiative, from the beginning, was the work of the triune God as Divine Warrior, covenanting and working within human history to restore to this fallen world his own rule and reign. In the person of Jesus Christ, Yahweh has fought the battle and won for his own right hand the glorious victory, and now, throughout the earth, his kingdom offer of reconciliation is going forth. The Church of Jesus Christ, as his agent and steward of this great tale and story, is birthed from the beginning with praises on the day of Pentecost, who declared the great works of God in their languages (cf. Acts 2.13ff). By definition, the Church of Jesus Christ is a worshiping community called into being by God to be the spiritual house spoken of by the Apostle Peter, that holy priesthood which offers spiritual sacrifices acceptable to God through Jesus Christ (1 Pet. 2.5). From the very beginning, the Church has gathered regularly to give God glory for his mighty acts in Christ. Borrowing freely from synagogue worship, the early Church read and expounded the Scriptures, gave prayers, sung psalms, hymns, and spiritual songs, and together observed the ordinances (sacraments) given to it by Christ. Kingdom testimony for the Church has from the beginning and will always be demonstrated in its corporate worship and praise of Almighty God. Much attention, effort, and energy should be given to every generation of believers to finding new and innovative ways to glorify God, without getting rid of the former ways.

11
Page 81
Outline Point II

The apostolicity of the Church is a critical element in its agency of the Kingdom of God. "Apostolicity" (meaning "derived from or of the apostles") is as the Nicene Creed says, one of the central marks of the Church. As an apostolic community, the Church of Jesus Christ, as Ephesians 2.20 states, is itself being built on the foundation of the apostles and prophets, with Jesus Christ himself being the chief cornerstone or capstone. The Apostles were those whom Christ chose personally to become the eyewitnesses of his majesty and ministry. The role of these eyewitnesses differs from the role of any other leaders in the history of the body, because theirs is unique and singular in their unique experience of being firsthand eyewitnesses of Jesus' works in the world, and most importantly, his resurrection from the dead. (Please note the criteria established by the Apostles when they decided to replace Judas Iscariot's position among the twelve, cf. Acts 1.11ff.)

One can see the fundamental role that the Apostles have played in the ongoing life of the Church in the example of the canon, i.e. those books chosen to be a part of our current New Testament. Earlier generations of Christian churches assumed and argued that our New Testament manuscripts were penned either by the Apostles or some trusted person closely connected and authorized with them. Since the 19th century, many in higher critical scholarship have seriously questioned the apostolic

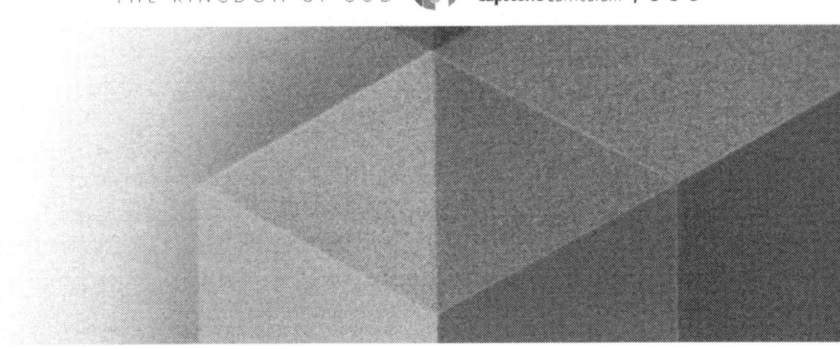

authorship for much of the New Testament, including the four Gospels, Acts, James, 1 and 2 Peter, Jude, and Revelation. Serious questions remain among biblical scholars regarding the Pauline authorship of Ephesians, Colossians, 1 and 2 Timothy, Titus and Hebrews. Yet, in spite of what academic study of religion or so-called biblical scholars believe and assert, and also regardless of who the exact authors are in regards to the Gospels and letters in the New Testament, the confessing Church canonized our current books as apostolic, granting them the weight and authority of the Apostles, and because of that, they are worthy of our complete trust and confidence.

What this example demonstrates is that the Church, regardless of science and/or scholarship, has through the centuries anchored their commitment and faith on what they discovered to have originated from or was authorized by the Apostles. The Church, therefore, has both defended the doctrine that the Apostles argued, and has historically allied itself only with those documents, doctrines, teachings, and practices which can be shown to have originated with the Apostles' teaching and practice. To defend our faith is to understand that the message and the mission of the Apostles is the final authority for the faith and practice of the Church.

12
Page 84
Outline Point IV

As mentioned before, the signal evidence of the Church being a locus of the Messianic age and power of the Kingdom is the Holy Spirit in the midst of the Church. As the very temple of the Living God, believers are today being built together into a dwelling place fit for our God to dwell, as a dwelling place of God in the Spirit (Eph. 4.22). Through the spoils of Jesus over the enemies, he has endowed every believer with grace according to Christ's own determination and measure (Eph. 4.7; cf. Rom. 12.3). Furthermore, Paul suggests that God has proffered gifted persons upon the body of Christ; apostles, prophets, evangelists, pastors, and teachers (Eph. 4.11) in order to equip the saints for the work of the ministry in order that the body might grow, both in number and spiritual vitality. In sync with this purpose, the Holy Spirit has given diverse gifts of spiritual ability to various members of the body for varied callings and kinds of service, for the good of the body corporate (1 Cor. 12.4-11). These manifestations of grace, power, and blessing are associated with God's kingdom rule now being demonstrated through the new covenant (Jer. 31.31ff.; Ezek. 36.14ff.; 26). Through the broken body and shed blood of Jesus, believers now partake of God's Spirit (2 Cor. 3.6ff.), who is the pledge or down payment of our inheritance (2 Cor. 1.22; 5.5; Eph. 1.14), the "firstfruits" and the seal of God (2 Cor. 1.22; Eph. 1.13; 4.30).

Because of these lofty and gratitude-producing truths, we can now expect the Holy Spirit to demonstrate in the midst of the Church acts of power, miracle, blessing, transformation, and healing which correspond to the fact that the new age has already dawned in Jesus Christ. The Spirit of the Messianic age has been poured out, and the enemies of God are being defeated through the active warfare of the Church of God. Jesus will confirm his divine Word in the midst of his people with signs following, both that his own people might know of the truth of the Gospel, as well as be given tangible, objective evidence that Jesus Christ is Lord of all.

13
Page 86
Student Questions and Response

In leading the students through the remainder of this lesson, it will be important for you to remain clear as to the objective of it in the overall sense of the Kingdom module itself. Given the low view of the Church by many in ministry, it is necessary for us to rebuild a better, more biblical view of the Church. For the purposes of our kingdom study, we are looking at the dual role of the Church both as locus and as agent of the Kingdom of God in the world today. As mentioned before, the role of the Church as locus is intimately connected to its role as agent. In these segue questions, strive to enable your students to discover new connections between the two. Do not hesitate to explore their questions over specific items related to the teaching, but if at all possible, underscore this fundamental relationship of the Church in its role as the Kingdom's life and witness. As the locus, the Church experiences firsthand the wonders of the Kingdom it testifies to, and as agent the Church actively demonstrates in its witness, compassion, works of miracles and healings, and its testimony and love the truth that the Messianic age has come in Jesus. Highlight these truths as you review the material from the last segment.

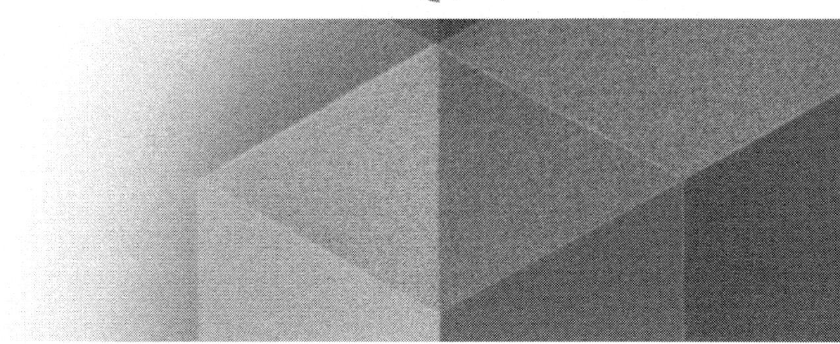

14
Page 90
Case Studies

These case studies seek to draw attention to specific ways in which the Church may struggle in its aspiration to fulfill its roles as both locus and agent of the Kingdom. One of the central issues connected to this is the question of integrity: when, in fact, are we demonstrating through our acts, our worship, and our relationships that we are being an authentic locus of the Kingdom? When does the witness, good works, and wonders we reveal to our neighbors give authentic evidence that we as a Church are revealing ourselves as an agent of the Kingdom? One of the most important things about spirituality is its ability to be counterfeited. Even the pole of Moses was imitated by the shaman and magicians of Egypt. Our role as ministers of the Gospel and the Church is to pray that God would use us to be authentic witnesses of the reality of the Kingdom in our locality. In other words, our responsibility and desire must be that God would use the life and witness of our congregation to shed light on what his rule is like on earth, as it is in heaven. With the Messianic age having come in Christ, we must give witness of the reality of the Kingdom, or risk becoming a dull reflection of the general society.

What is critical to emphasize and highlight in your discussion is how a congregation can know it is fulfilling its calling as the locus and agent of the Church. The following examples are meant to highlight this issue, and make room for your own discoveries together.

15
Page 92
Assignments

By the end of the second class session, you ought to emphasize with the students the need for them to have done the spade work and thought out precisely how they intend on carrying out their Ministry Project. Also, by this time, you should have emphasized their selection of the passage they will study for their Exegetical Project. Both will be done with far better thought and excellence the earlier the students begin to think through them and decide what they want to do. Do not fail to emphasize this, for, as in all study, at the end of the course many things become due, and the students will begin to feel the pressure of getting a number of assignments in at the same time. Any way that you can remind them of the need for advanced planning will be wonderfully helpful for them, whether they realize it immediately or not.

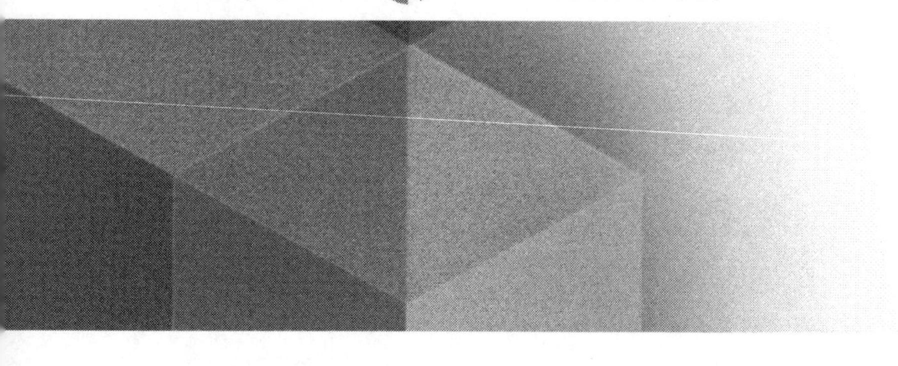

Because of this, we do advocate that you consider docking a modest amount of points for late papers, exams, and projects. While the amount may be nominal, your enforcement of your rules will help them to learn to be efficient and on time as they continue in their studies.

God's Reign Consummated

1
Page 97
Lesson Introduction

Welcome to the Mentor's Guide for Lesson 4, *God's Reign Consummated*. This is perhaps the longest and most difficult lesson to master of them all. The amount of material covered in this lesson is nearly obscene; you ought not assume that you will be able to deal with all the complexity of the issues simply or easily. Frankly, the Church of Jesus Christ, and its godliest, most sincere, and most capable biblical scholars and theologians have disagreed on the specifics of the claims on the issues of death, the intermediate state, the structure of the resurrections, the Rapture, and the tribulation, let alone heaven. Your class and students will probably not be any different. Expect a goodly amount of disagreement on the various details associated with the Second Coming and the events connected to it. The level to which you all disagree will undoubtedly be dependent upon the denominational background of the students, their own doctrinal orientation, the level of study they've done on these issues, and their ability to weigh carefully opposing and complex theological views on controversial matters.

What is significant in this lesson are the essential truths associated with the end times and eschatological themes. It will be important for you, as a kind of coach and referee, to mediate the various opinions shared by your students with the basic creedal theological claims made about the Second Coming. In other words, it will be important for you to stay on the main road of the Kingdom's consummation at the Second Coming of Jesus Christ, and deliberately downplay the wide range of possible alternative renderings on the details. The "Big Picture" must become your theological and pedagogical purpose, for if you become distracted, given the amount of material you have to cover, your teaching session will undoubtedly suffer. There simply is not enough time to deal with all the questions that will come up, so you will have to use your discretion as you go along.

The goal of this *Kingdom of God* module is to provide your students with a biblical framework to understand what God is doing in human history, and prepare them to be able witnesses of Christ and his Kingdom. This final lesson concentrates on a number of big ideas which are critical for bringing our Kingdom module studies to a close. This lesson deals with all the classic themes covered in eschatology in systematic theology volumes, in other words, the study of the last things. In it you will find summary teachings on all of the major ideas associated with it–the reasons why studying eschatology is important, the theme of death, resurrection, and the Intermediate state. Also the subjects of the Second Coming, the final judgment, and the recreated heavens and earth are covered. What you will want to do is to see all of the specific themes against the backdrop of the Story of God itself. The great reason why many Christians fail to attend the prophecies regarding the things to come is that they get bogged down in the details and lose sight of the broad vision–God Almighty, in a time and manner known only to himself, has determined to consummate all things through the Coming of his Son to earth, who will eradicate all vestiges of sin and establish a new heaven and earth where God rules forever. That is the biggest picture of all, and ought to be the one you seek to highlight as you go through the lesson.

Please notice again in the objectives that these truths are clearly stated. As usual, your responsibility as Mentor is to emphasize these concepts throughout the lesson, especially during the discussions and interaction with the students. The more you can highlight the objectives throughout the class period, the better the chances are that they will understand and grasp the magnitude of these objectives.

2
Page 97
Devotion

This devotional deals with the point made at the beginning of these Mentor's notes, that is, that the focus of the study of eschatology ought to be on the ways we see God consummating his plan in his Son, and less on the minutia that the human mind, through its idleness and curiosity, is prone to wander towards. Said differently, this text reveals that the heart of what God wants to do in bringing his Story to a close is to concentrate on the worthiness and splendor of his Son, who alone has been found worthy by the Father to make an end of all things. This is not merely a devotional idea; rather, it is the deepest theology we can muster. In Jesus of Nazareth we now have come to understand him through whom God will judge the worlds and restore all things to the pre-Fall excellence and glory. He has been given much, but, as Lord of all, he can and will accomplish much. It is here that we come to comprehend Jesus' role as the Father's Anointed One, the one chosen by God to render this world back under his reign, and the one who will in fact rule forever at God's behest.

As the saying goes, "The main thing is to keep the main thing the main thing." This is literally true when studying the issues and themes associated with the end times.

Please notice again in the objectives that these truths are clearly stated. As usual, your responsibility as Mentor is to emphasize these concepts throughout the lesson, especially during the discussions and interaction with the students. The more you can highlight the objectives throughout the class period, the better the chances are that they will understand and grasp the magnitude of these objectives.

3
Page 99
Contact

While much of God's divine revelation in the Bible is preoccupied with discovering the will of God for his creation in the future consummation of all things, one quick glance at the teaching and preaching of the modern Church reveals a patent neglect of prophecy. Our sermons, Bible study curricula, counseling, teaching, and worship services are only sparsely filled with any allusions to the Second Coming of Jesus. In many churches, pastors have gone for months even years without ever referring to the consummation of the Kingdom. One of the key objectives of your time together in this session is your ability to get your students to understand the relative importance that this teaching has on our ethics, our theology, and our ministry. The contacts below are focused on the lack of focus on the Second Coming, and deals with some of the ways that we tend to think about the great issues associated with Christ's return. A broad range of responses exist in churches, with everything from a total neglect of the biblical prophecy to a kind of obsessive focus on the details associated with the end times. The goal is to help your students, most of whom are ministering to others in the city, to understand why God gave us this material, and what practical difference it can make to our lives and ministries when we properly and appropriately attend to it.

4
Page 100
Summary of
Segment 1

It is important to note that in one sense, the consummation of the Kingdom is directly related to Jesus' role as the King himself. In other words, the Father has granted all authority in heaven and in earth to Christ (cf. Matt. 28.18), and as such, Christ as the Conquering Lord has the authority and the mandate to bring to an end all vestiges of rebellion, sin, and unrighteousness, as the Father's appointed and

Anointed Lord. It is God who has highly exalted Christ, and given him a name above all names in this age and the next, who himself will ensure that every knee bow and every tongue confess that Jesus is Lord, to the Father's greater glory (Phil. 2.9-11). As the Lord of lords and the King of kings, Jesus now takes his position as the executor of the Father's will, and calls out of the world a people for himself, who belong exclusively to him and are zealous for good deeds (Isa. 55.5; John 10.16, 27; Titus 2.11-15). As reigning Head of the Church, he walks among them, granting to them his own gifts and leaders, governing them through his direct counsel and power in the Spirit (1 Cor. 5.4-5; 12.28; Eph. 4.11-12; Matt. 28.19-20; 18.17-18; 1 Tim. 5.20; Titus 3.10). As protective Shepherd, he is preserving and supporting his flock in every situation they face, helping them overcome in the midst of all their temptations and sufferings (Heb. 13.20-22; 2 Cor. 12.9-10; Rom. 8.35-39). As the Divine Warrior ascended to a position of glory and honor at the Father's right Hand, our Lord is restraining and overcoming all the enemies of God, and making real in the midst of the Church the blessings of the Messianic age which he personally ushered in (Acts 12.17; 18.9-10; 1 Cor. 15.25). As Mighty God and triumphant Son by the Father's bidding, he superintends the mission of his Church, whom he has ordered to the very ends of the earth to bear witness of the peace and reconciliation that he has won for all humankind through his death on the Cross (Acts 1.8; Mark 16.14ff; Rom. 8.28; 14.11; Col. 1.18; Matt. 28.19-20). Lastly, all judgment has been appointed to him (John 5.22-23); he is the appointed executioner of the Lord's enemies and rewarder of the Lord's saints, the one chosen by God to rule the nations with a rod of iron and take vengeance on those who know not God and who obey not the Gospel (Ps. 2.9; Isa. 9.6-7; Rev. 19.11-21; 2 Thess. 1.8).

All these citations point to one and the same cardinal truth: the consummation of the Kingdom is the manifestation of the person of Jesus as the Son of Man, the one who has been appointed by God to bring the world finally back under God's reign, to right all wrongs, and to end all hurt. Jesus is the one who has been commissioned to represent the Father's interests without limit or bounds. This is the "big picture" of the consummation, and why any serious talk of the consummation of the Kingdom must focus on the person of Jesus, and not devolve into the meaning of the seven heads and ten horns on the dragon in Revelation 12. This is not to say that we

ought not seek the meaning of specific prophecies given to us through the inspiration of the Holy Spirit; it is, rather, to suggest as the angel tells the Apostle John in the Apocalypse that the testimony of Jesus is the spirit of prophecy (Rev. 19.10).

5
Page 100
Outline Point I

The theme of eschatology usually appears in the final volume of systematic theologies, and has traditionally been categorized as study of "last things" (Greek *eschata*). Theologians and scholars usually divide their commentary about the last things into two broad categories, dealing with issues that relate either to individuals (which tend to focus on issues regarding the issues of death, resurrection, judgment, and the afterlife) or to the cosmos (dealing with the state of the entire human race, all beings and creatures, and finally all creation itself). Sometimes you find in theological works that cosmic eschatology is narrowly bounded to the events and issues which relate to the end of the world. This kind of study, however is not as good or as credible as those interpretations which seek to deal with the whole of the universe, for the terms in biblical use, like the Hebrew *be'aharit hayyamim* (in the Septuagint [LXX] written as *en tais eschatais hemerais*, "in the last days") may refer either to the end of the present order or even, more generally, "hereafter."

The biblical view of time actually affects our understanding of eschatology. Of course, the biblical notion of time does not see time as cyclical (meaning that eschatology would only talk about events in the completion of a cycle), nor does it view it as we are prone to think about time, as merely or purely linear (meaning that eschatology would be unable to look at things dynamically). It would be best to say that the Bible's view of time is a kind of a recurring pattern where God's wrath and grace interact together until the pattern of his own sovereign will becomes known. Eschatology, then, should be seen in a dynamic way. It may speak of the consummation of the Kingdom in all different kinds of ways, whether it deals with the world's end, a character's end, or whatever. What is important is that when we discuss issues associated with the end of the world, we ought to know that for the sake of discussion, we freeze frame some subject for the sake of study. In reality, however, when the Kingdom is consummated, many of these various themes and realities will be occurring simultaneously, and this makes it quite difficult to

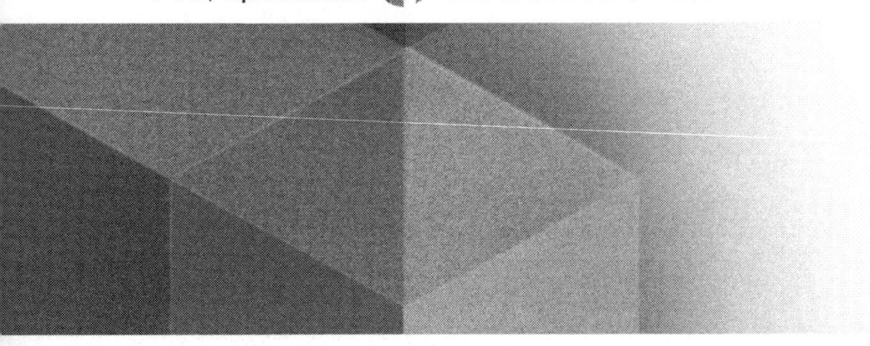

pinpoint the specific times on a line (as it were) regarding the disposition of the end. The best advice, therefore, in dealing with issues of the end times, is to remember the good wisdom of Deuteronomy 29.29: the secret things (of specific time, place, occurrence of the end times) belong to the Lord, but the things revealed (those larger, great issues, e.g. the certainty of Jesus' return) belong to us. These prophecies are not to satisfy our curiosities, but that we might live informed by the truths they represent.

6
Page 102
Outline Point II

The consummation of the Kingdom, in many ways, is the overcoming of this, the final enemy, which is death (1 Cor. 15.54-56). In the Old Testament death is often perceived as merely a natural part of human existence. Death entered into the world through the disobedience of Adam and Eve, and yet, human life through Adam was not seen as immortal, but as a kind of contingent immortality, based on humankind's ability to follow the rule of God. Often, the goal spoken of in the Old Testament vision of life is to live a long, full life with one's loved ones, and to die in honor and peace, not due to shame and corruption. To die early is usually viewed as a great evil (2 Kings 20.1-11), and its reality was taken to indicate some kind of judgment from God due to immorality or sin (Gen. 2-3; Deut. 30.15; Jer. 21.8; Ezek. 18.21-32). Death does, however, carry a sense of being horrific, since to die is to be separated from one's loved ones, from worship, from the people of God, and from God himself (Pss. 73.23-28; 139.8). Because of these and other negative connotations associated with death, suicide was rare among the people of God (1 Sam. 31; 2 Sam. 17.23), and capital punishment (i.e. the death penalty) was determined to be grave and severe.

In the New Testament, with its explicit focus on the Kingdom of God in Jesus Christ, the notion of death is perceived as a theological problem. Life comes from God, who alone possesses in his own self-existent life, the springs of immortality (1 Tim. 6.16). Human beings are subject to death, not merely due to their natural state as fallible, created beings, but on the basis of their own sinfulness as well as being under the curse they share with all others because of their connection to Adam (cf. Rom. 6.23; 5.12ff.). Because of this association with judgment, human beings live in fear of death as associated with the curse (Matt. 4.16; Heb. 2.15).

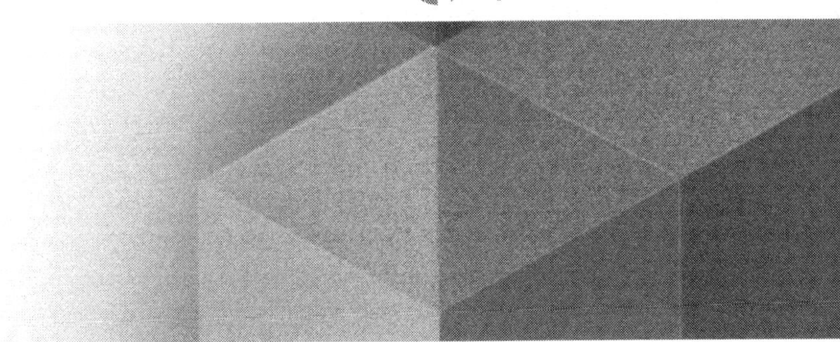

Therefore, since the Lord God is alone the genesis and spring of all life (Rom. 4.17), we die because in some way we are alienated, estranged from the life of God; an alienation which arose from Adam's rebellion to God's rule, and now through him has passed on to all of us (Rom. 5.15, 17-18; 1 Cor. 15.22). We all, as fallen and estranged human beings, participate in our own sin and subsequent judgment upon us (Rom. 3.23; 5.12), and we have brought on ourselves the judgment and result that death represents (Rom. 6.23; Heb. 9.27).

The reality of death, therefore, in both individual and cosmic eschatology, is a power, a force originating from the seminal rebellion of humankind in the world, which touches the life of all persons. Death is not merely the natural result of age and fatigue; rather it is the result of being disconnected from God due to our own rejection of his rule and reign in our lives. It is a separation from God. In some tragic sense, all human life to its very core participates in the effect of Adam's sin in the flesh (Rom. 8.6; 1 John 3.14), and that particular sin orientation remains in us despite our intent to keep God's law (Rom. 7.9; 1 Cor. 15.56; James 1.15). As the father of lies and rebellion, the devil is seen in the New Testament as a kind of lord of death (Heb. 2.14), and in places, death itself may be seen as a demonic power (1 Cor. 15.26-27; Rev. 6.8; 20.13-14).

Death shall be rendered powerless at the Second Coming of Christ, whose death on the cross has broken its power, and given those who trust in him the prospect of living forever through faith in him (John 11.22-23; 1 Cor. 15.54-58).

7
Page 106
Outline Point III

In all of your discussions with the students on the various theories surrounding the Intermediate state, it is important to highlight the central element of hope associated with the kingdom victory of Jesus Christ. In other words, the work of Jesus on the cross was not to give us additional topics of theology to discuss, but to give us definite, clear, and undeniable truth that we can base our lives on, and that can provide encouragement for us and others in the midst of a world where thousands die each day, often with little or no hope and no understanding of what the loving Father God has done for them in his Son. The good news of the Kingdom of God in Christ is that he himself, the one who did not need to die nor was under any obligation to aid our sinful selves in attaining to a new relationship with God, participated fully in human death on our account (Phil. 2.7; 1 Cor. 5.7; 1 Pet. 3.18). The Author of life and creation became a human being and expired; he died "for us" (Mark 10.45; Rom. 5.6; 1 Thess. 5.10; Heb. 2.9). According to the Apostles' word, the Lord through death crushed the devil and conquered death itself, and now possesses the very keys of Hades and death (Heb. 2.14-15; Rev. 1.17-18). He singlehandedly broke the death grip for all who by faith have become organically united to him by being "baptized into Christ" (Rom. 6.3-4). Through this unity we share with the risen Lord, we have died with him to sin and to the world (Rom. 7.6; Gal. 6.14; Col. 2.20).

In the very person of Christ every believer has passed through death's long tunnel; in him we tasted God's wrath against our sin, and in him we have suffered its actual penalty, shame, and total tragedy (2 Cor. 4.10; 5.14-15; Col. 3.3). In other words, the effect of Jesus ministry was to join the status, history, and lives of every human being to his own, and now, those who trust in him by faith, are set free "in Christ." We who, by faith, belong to Jesus have passed from death to life in him (John 5.24). Because of our unity with him, we will never see real death (John 8.51-52). What a contrast this is to the world, which as a world without God and Christ is already dead (Rev. 3.2), and already ticketed for the horrific end of eternal alienation and disconnection from the Father, called by John as mega-death, a second death (Rev. 20.14).

As human beings, disciples of Jesus are still subject to the same effects of the curse on our physical bodies (i.e. we die, we are mortal, we suffer disease, we are the victims of violence, we become disabled, etc.). We will in fact die, if we do not live to experience the transformation spoken of in 1 Corinthians 15. Nevertheless, those believers who do die physically, die "in Christ" (1 Thess. 4.16) or "fall asleep" (Acts 7.60; John 11.11-14; 1 Cor. 7.39; 15.6, 18, 20, 51; 1 Thess. 4.13-15). This is not death in the same tragic sense as those who are disconnected from the life of God. Physical death exists for the Christian, but its cruelty is gone for nothing can separate the Christian from the love of God in Christ Jesus their Lord (Rom. 8.35-39). Remarkably, now, death ends the veil between the Christian and her lord, and to depart this life is to be transported into the very presence of him who tasted death

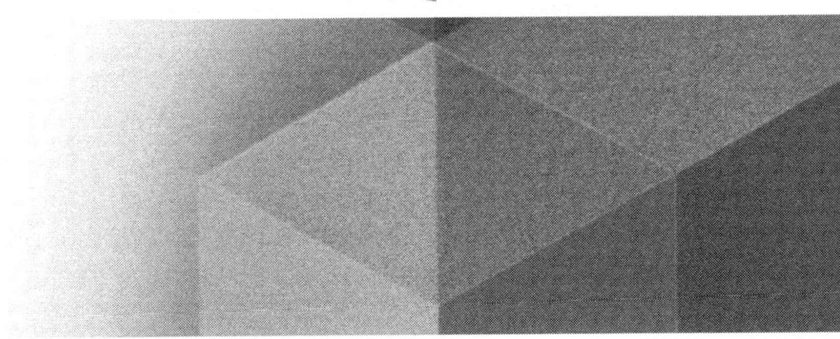

for every person (2 Cor. 5.1-10; Phil. 1.20-21), and who will raise all believers who have died back to life again to enjoy unending peace in a new heaven and earth. This is the meaning of the Kingdom's consummation for us who believe (1 Cor. 15.20; Col. 1.12).

8
Page 111
Student Questions and Response

These questions are designed to highlight the main points associated with the first video segment. Remember the good advice given before, and concentrate on the ways the various questions help us understand the centrality of Christ in the consummation of the Kingdom. In one sense, all issues of the Kingdom's consummation are ultimately issues that relate to the person of Jesus Christ.

Pay attention to the questions your students have regarding this data, but make certain that they understand that the Christocentric focus of the end times represents a master key to understanding all of the fullness of God's revelation on these subjects. The Church of Jesus Christ is organically connected to Christ, whose person, works, and benefits accrue to us now by faith, through the Holy Spirit. Keep this truth in the center as you discuss the details of eschatology now.

9
Page 112
Outline Point I-A

It is important to note the various terms that theologians use when speaking of the comings and/or manifestations of Christ in the world.

Parousia

This is perhaps the most frequently used of Jesus' Second Coming, and literally means "being by." It signifies and means "presence, coming, or arrival." Paul uses the term in 1 Thessalonians 4.15 to designate Jesus' arrival to come and to raise the righteous dead and catch them up (i.e. rapture) to be forever with him. The term is also associated with that phase of his arrival which involves the destruction of the man of lawlessness, the anti-Christ (2 Thess. 2.8). *Parousia* is neither a secret or hidden happening, but a glorious revelation and demonstration. The term is also associated with its corollary ethical meaning; through Paul's instruction, believers are to ready themselves, to ask God for his strengthening grace in order that they

may be without blame in sanctification before God the Father at the *parousia* of the Lord Jesus with all his saints (1 Thess. 3.13).

Apocalypse

This Greek term means "revelation." The Apostle Paul challenges the church of Corinth as it waits for the "the revealing (apocalypse) of our Lord Jesus Christ" (1 Cor. 1.7). The term appears also in 2 Thessalonians 1.6-7 and 1 Peter 4.13, both of which indicate that the apocalypse will be a time of God's great judgment on God's enemies, and great rejoicing for those awaiting his appearing.

Epiphany

In one sense, this meaning nuances everything we know about the Second Coming. This word carries the meaning of "manifestation." When Jesus is revealed or manifested at the end of the great tribulation period, he will manifest his glory in the world, resulting in the judgment of God's enemies, and the reward of those who have placed their complete hope in his appearance, and have patiently waited for the rewards associated with that appearing (1 Tim. 6.14; 2 Tim. 4.8). It is the completion of their salvation (Titus 2.13-14).

10
Page 113
Outline Point I-C

The list of attributes covered here represent the core of essential, evangelical, and historically orthodox claims made in regard to the Second Coming of Jesus Christ. Again, while there are many lesser claims concerning his coming which have been and will continue to be disputed in various theological and academic contexts, the heart of the teaching regarding Jesus' coming deal with his person, and his own actions involved with the coming. This is critical for the sake of grounding new believers in the basic minimum deemed critical for faith in the Creed. Furthermore, even while those who are being trained in the apostolic doctrine might want to do more in terms of historical theology on these issues, they themselves represent a kind of baseline of characteristics that orthodox leaders in the Church of Jesus Christ have historically asserted regarding his Second Coming. In this sense, these items are of critical importance for the developing Christian leader to know, to defend, and to be able to articulate and equip others in.

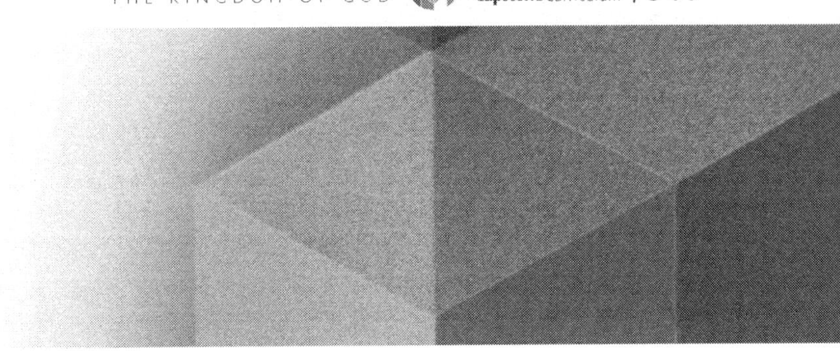

11
Page 116
Outline Point II

In regard to the consummation of the Kingdom, millennialism is critical, since these views tend to speak of the actual effects of Jesus' kingdom rule in the world. The term itself, "millennium," comes from a Latin word meaning thousand (in a similar way, so the word "*chiliasm*," based on a Greek word, is similarly used). Millennialism refers to a particular doctrine of eschatology based on Revelation 20.1-10. In this text, John sees and describes Satan being bound and thrown into a bottomless pit for a thousand years. The dead in Christ are resurrected, who are given a position to reign on earth with Christ during the 1,000 year period, or millennium. Peace and *shalom* are experienced on earth as Yahweh's *shalom* is finally experienced in this prolonged reign of Jesus, devoid of the lying and corrupting influence of the Evil One. One is reminded of the numerous Old Testament prophecies regarding the Son of David ushering in the reign of God on earth among the nations, with the transformation of all life in sync with God's good and holy will (e.g. Isa. 2.1-4; 11.1-9).

The following summaries of millennialism are sufficient for our task in speaking of the consummation of the God's Kingdom. Some study of millennial views are important since they tend to speak to issues which can easily be missed or overlooked in traditional eschatological views. While virtually all Christian traditions in their eschatological treatments deal with the issues contained in this lesson (e.g., death, immortality, the end of the world, the final judgment of humankind, the rewards of the just, and the punishment of the lost, etc.), they may easily deal with issues relating to individual eschatology while ignoring issues of cosmic eschatology, which millennialism seeks to address. To their credit, various millennial discussions concern themselves with the nature and the status of humanity's future life on the earth. A general knowledge of the arguments is sufficient for solid leadership preparation.

12
Page 118
Outline Point II-B

The various tribulational views all are contingent and interact with the biblical teaching regarding "the great tribulation," a term associated with the end times, and especially with the references and teachings of Jesus and the Apostle John. The exact term, "great tribulation" (Matt. 24.21; Rev. 2.22; 7.14, in the Greek *thlipsis megale*), hints at the quality of the tribulation to occur at the end time, and may therefore distinguish it from familiar and ongoing tribulation that disciples of Jesus endure as they live in the world (e.g. John 16.33). The term has come to refer to a kind of theological shorthand, a terse and powerful summary of a coming horrific, global, and uniquely experienced time of worldwide chaos, judgment, and trouble which itself will be the primary historical precursor to the *parousia*, the glorious and mighty revelation of Jesus Christ back to earth in great glory. The great tribulation is referred to in paralleled renderings, which refer to the same event using different terms, such as in Mark 13.19 where the event is rendered "tribulation," in Luke 21.23 which refers to the happenings and occurrences associated with the great tribulation as the "great distress" and in Revelation 3.10 as the "hour of trial" which shall try all of the nations.

The heart of the tribulational discussions hinge on what is the nature of the Church's involvement in this horrific and unrepeatable time of judgment and trouble. Will the Church go through the time, and be rescued afterwards (the posttribulational view), will it be rescued before the terrible judgments begin (the pretribulational view), or will their deliverance take place some time in the midst of the period (midtribulational view). Regardless of the view one ascribes to, we who believe know our God to be a stronghold in the day of trouble (Nah. 1.7), the one who knows the one who trusts in him and knows how to rescue his own from the fire and the flood (Isa. 43.1-2).

The final judgment is an integral part of the consummation of the Kingdom, and is attested to much, in both the Old and New Testaments. In the Old Testament, for instance, the texts seem to focus on the prophetic treatment of the day of Yahweh, when Almighty God will deal with all of the evils which human beings have destroyed his creation with. In that eventful and awesome day, the Lord will bring to an end all the various forms of rebellion which have characterized humankind from the Fall. This includes our pride (Isa. 2.12-17), our worship of false gods and paganistic practices (Isa. 2.18-20; Zeph. 1.8), all forms of human violence and fraud (Zeph. 1.9), spiritual indifference and complacency (Zeph. 1.12), and everything that allows us to be named as transgressors and sinners (Isa. 13.9). The day of the Lord is universal in scope, dealing with the Gentiles and the covenant people (cf.

13
Page 123
Outline Point IV

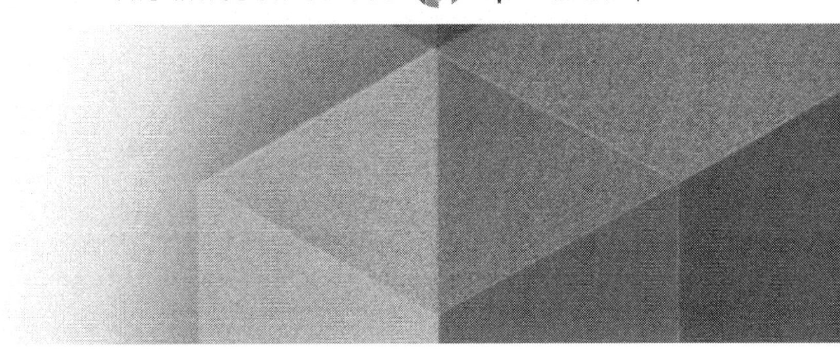

Amos 1.2; 9.1-4; Joel 3.2; Mal. 3.2-5), who all will be cleansed and purified as to rid God's creation of all things that offend his holiness and loving-kindness. The glorious result will be the universal knowledge of God among all peoples and nations, with the knowledge of God touching every clan, people, tribe, and nation (Isa. 11.9).

In the New Testament, the final judgment is perceived in light of the Kingdom of God, and Jesus' role as the final Judge (2 Tim. 4.1), who himself will oversee and superintend the final resolution and state of all human beings (Mark 15.62; Matt. 10.15; 11.22, 24; 12.36, 41-42; 23.33). The judgment is a time of winnowing and separation, of identifying all that offends and separating it from God's new, refreshed earth (Matt. 13.41-43, 47-50). The final judgment has been given to the Son by the Father (5.26-27), and will be followed by the resurrection of the just and the unjust (5.28-29 and 1 Cor. 15.22-25).

Moreover, the final disposition of all things is connected to its qualities: the final judgment under Christ's oversight will be perfectly just (Rom. 2.11), extend to all people everywhere (Rom. 2.6; 14.10; 2 Cor. 5.10), and precisely complete (Rom. 2.16). Though it tarry it will come, for certain (2 Pet. 2.4-10; Jude 5-7). It is important to recognize that the propitiation and justification experienced by believers changes both the end and flavor of the judgment for Christians. Because the sin question has forever been settled at Calvary (Rom. 3.21-26; 8.1, 31-34; Heb. 10.10,14), disciples of Jesus are judged regarding their rewards for service to Christ (Rom. 14.10; 1 Cor. 9.24-27; James 1.12; 2 Cor. 5.10; 1 Cor. 3.13-15).

Undoubtedly the most terrifying tragedy in all of life is the fact that, as a result of the final judgment and disposition of unbelievers, they will be eternally separated from the presence and life of God (1 Thess. 5.3; 2 Thess. 1.9; Phil. 1.28; 3.19; Rom. 6.21); divine judgment is both a present and future reality (Rom. 1.18-32). Offering a kind of general timeline of events, the book of Revelation provides clues into the final resolution of those who resist the reign of God. Through the judgments of the seven trumpets (8-11) and the seven bowls (16), we see the awesome woes and troubles upon humankind before the final judgment appears. In the last chapters of the Apocalypse of John we see the judgment of the blaspheming leaders, who are reckoned to the lake of burning sulphur, itself a powerful image of suffering, misery, and judgment (19.20-21). The devil, who is seized and thrown into the abyss during the 1,000 year period of millennial peace (20.1-3), is released, resulting in renewed deception of the nations. In an awesome scene, heaven and earth flee away from before the throne of God, the books of judgment are opened (a metaphor for careful archiving of all deeds), and all those not found in the Book of Life are cast into the lake burning with sulfur (20.11-15). This awesome, symbolic portrayal of the final judgment reveals the breadth of the cosmic scope of the judgment (20.11; 21.1). The book ends with the descent of the New Jerusalem as the dwelling of God with humankind, a new heaven and new earth being ushered in, and the saints of God living in a new creation where Jesus is the light of the city forever (Rev. 21-22). Then the great prophetic visions of old will become reality: Yahweh will make all things new in his recreated universe (Isa. 11.6-9; 65.17-25 cf. Rom. 8.22-23).

The actual power of the doctrine of the final judgment, in association with the consummation of the Kingdom of God, is its ability to inspire commitment and discipleship. Knowing that the world is soon to endure the critical eye of the Lord of hosts, this idea ought to inspire godly living and innovative ministry, knowing that the very heavens themselves will be burned in the refreshing to come (2 Pet. 3.11-13).

14
Page 126
Outline Point V

The Christian imagination can never plumb the depths of the wondrous things that await those who believe in Jesus the Christ. Everything referring to the change that awaits us gives hints that the new order will transcend all we know; not that we will become a new species, but rather a new humanity. There is both continuity and discontinuity with the world and existence as it is today.

For instance, our bodies will no longer be categorized as flesh and blood bodies (1 Cor. 15.50), but they will have some kind of continuity with our present bodies, perhaps in terms of both form as well as the "new physics" of our new bodies (e.g., Matt. 5.29, 30; 10.28; Rom. 8.11, 23; 1 Cor. 15.53). We will not be disembodied in the new Kingdom of Christ, yet we may not need physical nourishment to sustain us (Rom. 14.17), nor be driven by desires for copulation or sex (Matt. 22.30; Mark 12.25; Luke 20.35). Many analogies regarding the idea of feasting sprinkle through

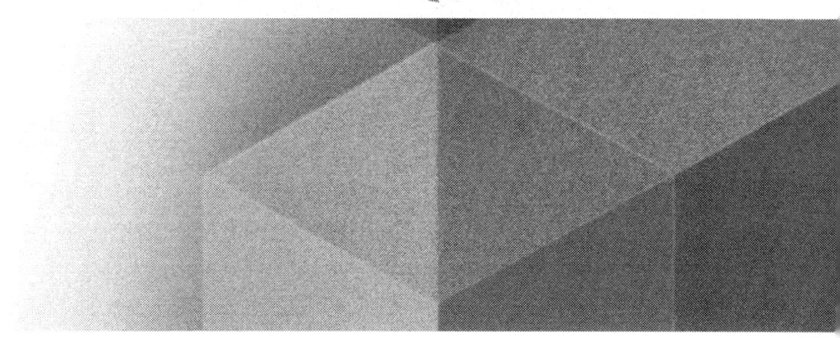

the New Testament imagery of the Kingdom, and Jesus promised he would drink together with his disciples the fruit of the vine in the Kingdom (Matt. 26.29). The images of our existence in God's new order is fabulously delicious: we will forever delight in God's presence as his servants, living in his city, ruling the nations as he directs (Luke 19.17; Matt. 25.20-21). There we will serve him in the city designed by his imagination alone, and we will understand as we are understood (1 Cor. 13.12). We will be conformed to the image of Jesus, in all his glory and splendor, and will see him as he is (1 John 3.2). In some remarkable way, we will be transformed to relate intimately, as our Lord does, to the Lord of hosts (Isa. 6.3; Rev. 4.8). Yes, we will dwell in his dwellings forever (John 14.2), the city of the Living God, the heavenly Jerusalem (Heb. 12.22), experiencing his love and purpose, being his people, and he being our God (Rev. 21.3).

15
Page 128
Student Questions and Response

Again, concentrate on the ways that Jesus' work is seen in the consummation of the Kingdom of God. While good and open consideration of the various questions of the students is appropriate, you want to make clear the Christ-centered focus of this material.

In particular pay attention to the way in which the resolution of the original questions of the course come into play here. In other words, seek to connect the answers given to the entire course, and see how God, in the consummation of the Kingdom, resolves the various issues, problems, and concerns which the Fall originated.

16
Page 132
Case Studies

These case studies seek to wrestle with the relative importance of these truths for the life of the Church in the examples given. There appears to be a kind of intrinsic close-mindedness to prophecy in many evangelical settings. Having been largely turned off by the conferences and other doctrinal emphases on prophecy which seek to align various contemporary events with biblical prophecies, many seem disillusioned at the ability of the truth regarding the consummation of the Kingdom to affect their lives in positive ways.

We must strive to help urban Christian workers, pastors, and ministers recover the hope of the Kingdom through these texts and scriptural teachings. Therefore, as we explore the implications of this teaching, try to focus on ways that this teaching can be credibly reintroduced in settings which, for the most part, have place the apocalyptic teaching of the Church in exile. Of course, this section of the lesson ought to be driven by the questions and concerns of the students. Still, this need to enable congregations to awaken to a theology of hope, of the Kingdom's consummation is of critical importance.

17
Page 134
Assignments

Your work as an instructor and grader begins in earnest now. Make sure that you have commitments for the ministry projects, exegetical projects, and other data together as this will be important for you to determine the student's overall grade. Again, your discretion regarding late work can easily determine whether you dock students of points, resulting in letter grade changes, or give students an "Incomplete" until the work is finished. However you adopt your standard regarding their work, remember that our courses are not primarily about the grades that students receive, but the spiritual nourishment and training these courses provide. Also, however, remember that helping our students strive for excellence is an integral part of our instruction.

18
Page 135
The Last Word about this Module

Congratulations, you have finished the Capstone module on the Kingdom of God. We celebrate with you, as co-laborers in the Gospel of our Lord Jesus Christ! You have led your students through some difficult concepts, and encouraged them through what is arguably one of the most important teachings in all of God's Word - the Kingdom of God and Christ. Our sincere prayer is that the investment that you have made in the hearts and minds of your students will not return unto the Lord void, but that much abundant and lasting fruit will be borne for Jesus Christ through your efforts, prayers, and work. May God richly bless you as you continue to equip leaders for the urban church!

Made in the USA
San Bernardino, CA
20 January 2017